T0305595

Internet of Behavior (IoB)

This book is intended to survey the Internet of Behavior (IoB). The book begins with the benefits and potential pitfalls of IoB. Today, IoB has huge potential in every sector of the world. There are numerous applications for IoB which benefit users as well as the business market in order to enhance the user experience. In this book, the benefits of IoB and its negative constraints are discussed in detail. It is a high time that IoB is to take its crown and ruled the world. The work of IoB is critical in keeping our data secure because it can currently identify all humans who attempt to steal someone's data. Moreover, the business uses of IoB are in high demand. By leveraging promising technical improvements and advances in machine learning algorithms, IoB enables capture, analysis, comprehension, and response for all types of human behavior in a technique that enables the tracking and interpretation of the behavior. IoB can be very useful wherever the behavior, preferences, interests, and location of people need to be examined. On the other hand, an analytical study on consumers' social and behavioral psychology and their influence on online purchasing is much needed. With the help of visualization tools such as Tableau and detailed reporting on selection patterns, the impact of social media on decision making and the relationship between personality and purchasing power in various age groups is found. The presented study lists major decision-making psychometric factors and highlights critical factors affecting online purchases. The role of IoB is to shape customer service through the use of artificial intelligence, cloud computing, data, smart analytics, machine learning, and other volatile technologies.

The attractive components of this book are discussions of dynamic routing mechanisms to reduce energy consumption in software-defined networks; deep insight into Internet of Things (IoT) and IoB security and privacy concerns – applications and future challenges; sentiment analysis and feature reduction using an arboreal monkey compression algorithm with a deep modified neural network classifier; cybersecurity concerns for IoB; and identification of nutrients and microbial contamination in fruits and vegetables using a technology using the Internet of Behavior. There is no doubt that this book covers numerous interesting themes and details on the Internet of Behavior.

ABOUT THE EDITORS

Dr. R. Dhaya is presently working in the Department of Computer Science at King Khalid University, Abha, Kingdom of Saudi Arabia. She has teaching and research experience of over 16 years. Her research areas include wireless communication, advanced embedded systems, AI, ML, grid and cloud data communication, image classification, big data, and computing techniques. She has published more than 100 research articles in reputed journals and international conferences, which include SCI, Scopus, and IEEE/Springer/ Elsevier/ESI conferences. She received the Institute of Engineers, Kolkata's Outstanding Young Women Engineer award as well as the Young Women Scientist award.

Dr. R. Kanthavel is presently working in the Department of Computer Engineering at King Khalid University, Abha, Kingdom of Saudi Arabia. He has 23 years of teaching and research experience. He has been doing continuous research works in the field such as wireless communication, AI, machine learning, cooperative communication, image classification, and computing techniques. He published more than 150 research articles in refereed journals and peer reviewed international conferences.

Internet of Behavior (IoB)

Edited By
Dr. R. Dhaya and Dr. R. Kanthavel

CRC Press
Taylor & Francis Group
Boca Raton London New York

CRC Press is an imprint of the
Taylor & Francis Group, an **informa** business

Cover Image: Pixabay

First edition published 2023
by CRC Press
6000 Broken Sound Parkway NW, Suite 300, Boca Raton, FL 33487–2742

and by CRC Press
4 Park Square, Milton Park, Abingdon, Oxon, OX14 4RN

CRC Press is an imprint of Taylor & Francis Group, LLC

Library of Congress Cataloging-in-Publication Data
Names: Dhaya, R., 1983– editor. | Kanthavel, R., 1974– editor.
Title: Internet of behaviours (IoB) / [edited by] Dr. R. Dhaya, King Khalid University Abha, Saudi Arabia, Dr. R. Kanthavel, King Khalid University Abha, Saudi Arabia.
Description: First edition. | Boca Raton : CRC Press, 2023. | Includes bibliographical references and index.
Identifiers: LCCN 2022055185 (print) | LCCN 2022055186 (ebook) | ISBN 9781032304533 (hardback) | ISBN 9781032304540 (paperback) | ISBN 9781003305170 (ebook)
Subjects: LCSH: Internet of things—Psychological aspects. | Human-computer interaction—Psychological aspects. | Internet users—Psychology. | Consumer behavior. | Computer security—Psychological aspects.
Classification: LCC TK5105.8857 .I544 2023 (print) | LCC TK5105.8857 (ebook) | DDC 004.67/8—dc23/eng/20230222
LC record available at https://lccn.loc.gov/2022055185
LC ebook record available at https://lccn.loc.gov/2022055186

ISBN: 978-1-032-30453-3 (hbk)
ISBN: 978-1-032-30454-0 (pbk)
ISBN: 978-1-003-30517-0 (ebk)

DOI: 10.1201/9781003305170

Typeset in Sabon
by Apex CoVantage, LLC

Contents

Contributors

Bobin Chandra B
Vel Tech Rangarajan
Dr. Sagunthala R&D Institute
    of Science and Technology
Tamil Nadu, India

Hina Bansal
Amity University
Uttar Pradesh, India

Rajesh Bansode
Thakur College of Engineering
    and Technology
Mumbai, India

J. Banumathi
University College
    of Engineering
Nagercoil, Tamil Nadu, India

N.P.G. Bhavani
Saveetha School
    of Engineering
SIMATS
Chennai, Tamil Nadu, India

P. Devisivasankari
CMRIT
Bangalore, India

Niaz M. Doostyar
Osmania University
Telangana, India

Viji Florance G
New Horizon College
    of Engineering
Bangalore, India

Aditya Gaisamudre
Aditya Gaisamudre MIT World
    Peace University
Pune, Maharashtra, India

G. Victo Sudha George
MGR Educational and Research
    Institute
Chennai, India

Aayush Gupta
MIT World Peace University
Pune, India

Rajalaxmi Hegde
NMAM Institute of Technology
Karnataka, India

Sandeep Kumar Hegde
NMAM Institute of Technology
Karnataka, India

Pratyush Jha
Dr. Vishwanath Karad's MIT World
   Peace University
Pune, Maharashtra, India

Jaspreet Kaur
Hans Raj Mahila Maha Vidyalaya
Jalandhar, India

D. Kirubakaran
St. Joseph's Institute
   of Technology
Chennai, India

Veronica Kumar
Amity University
Uttar Pradesh, India

M. Mahalakshmi
CMR College of Engineering &
   Technology
Telangana, India

MSR Mariyappan
Vel Tech Rangarajan
   Dr. Sagunthala R&D Institute
   of Science and Technology
Tamil Nadu, India

Rishikesh Mate
Rishikesh Mate MIT World Peace
   University
Pune, Maharashtra, India

Viren Modi
MIT World Peace University
Pune, Maharashtra, India

Monica R. Mundada
M S Ramaiah Institute of
   Technology
Karnataka, India

Sainath Patil
Vidyavardhini's College
   of Engineering & Technology
Mumbai, India

Shravani M. Phatak
Amity University
Uttar Pradesh, India

Vusala Sri Sai Pravallika
Amity University
Uttar Pradesh, India

Parth Rainchwar
Dr. Vishwanath Karad's MIT World
   Peace University
Pune, Maharashtra, India

A. Rahul Raj
CMR College of Engineering &
   Technology
Telangana, India

B. Venkateshwar Rao
CMR College of Engineering &
   Technology
Telangana, India

Seema S
M S Ramaiah Institute
   of Technology
Karnataka, India

Aiswarya Sanal
Systems Engineer
Infosys Private Limited
Kerala, India

S.K.B. Sangeetha
SRM Institute of Science
   and Technology
Chennai, India

Karan Ajit Shah
MIT World Peace University
Pune, Maharashtra, India

Spriha Shekhar
MIT World Peace University
Pune, Maharashtra, India

Harpreet Singh
Hans Raj Mahila Maha
    Vidyalaya
Jalandhar, India

Shilpa Sonawani
MIT World Peace
    University
Pune, Maharashtra, India

V. Srividhya
Meenakshi College
    of Engineering
Tamil Nadu, India

B. Sujatha
Osmania University
Telangana, India

K. Sujatha
MGR Educational and Research
    Institute
Chennai, India

M. Sujitha
MGR Educational and Research
    Institute
Chennai, India

Vijayalakshmi V
CMRIT
Bangalore, India

Ashish Vanmali
Vidyavardhini's College of Engi-
    neering & Technology
Mumbai, India

Anusha Vasamsetti
CMR College of Engineering &
    Technology
Telangana, India

Manisha Verma
ITM University, Gwalior
Madhya Pradesh, India

R. Vijayakumar
Jain University
Bangalore, India

Soham Wattamwar
Dr. Vishwanath Karad's MIT
    World Peace University
Pune, Maharashtra, India

Chapter 1

Benefits and Pitfalls of Internet of Behavior

*Bobin Chandra B, MSR Mariyappan,
and Aiswarya Sanal*

CONTENTS

1.1 INTRODUCTION

The Internet of Behavior (IoB) cannot be discussed without mentioning the Internet of Things (IoT). The IoT can be defined as the interconnected network of devices which collects data and further shares it online. Technological advancements are happening day by day. Moreover, this is reflected in the IoT. Today, the IoT involves more complexities than before. It has evolved to a level where calculations can be performed on its own. The IoT comprises network-enabled devices which gather, transfer and process the data captured with the help of embedded systems. They provide sensor data collected via connecting IoT gateways. Furthermore, the data is passed to the cloud server for detailed analysis or analyzed locally. These devices have the proper communication abilities to share valuable information. These devices work without human aid. However, humans can have interaction with these devices for device setup and to assign tasks and access data. The IoT helps upgrade the lifestyle of people with smarter work and gadgets. It helps people have control over their lives. Besides producing smart devices for the automation of houses, IoT devices are inevitable in the business sector. They provide real-time insights into ventures inclusive of supply chain, logistics and machine performance. This helps in the reduction of labor costs and other expenses. Moreover, it enhances service delivery and initiates transparent transactions.

DOI: 10.1201/9781003305170-1

1

It also aids in cost cutting of manufacturing and goods delivery. IoT can be considered the most prominent technology in our daily life in order to ease our daily tasks and make our life smarter. It is gradually improving as more companies recognize the potential applications of devices [1–3].

IoB is the process of analyzing user-regulated data from a behavioral and psychological point of view, using the results of this analysis to inform analysts about new perspectives to design user experience and sell end products and services offered by the venture. Therefore, implementing IoB in an organization is technically simple but psychologically complex. For ethical and legal reasons, we need to conduct statistical surveys that map daily habits and behaviors without fully disclosing consumer information [4]. IoB aims to understand and analyze every human behavior, further utilizing data in the enhancement of digital experience and other technological advancements. People's behaviors are monitored and incentives or disincentives are carried out to persuade them to act in the direction of a favored set of operational parameters. IoB is not descriptive but proactive. IoB impacts purchaser choice; however, it additionally redesigns the fee chain. While a few customers are cautious about supplying their data, many others are willing to do so as long as it provides a fee – a data-pushed fee. For companies, this indicates being capable of extending their image or marketplace merchandise to their clients or enhancing the customer experience (CX) of a product or service. Hypothetically, statistics may be accumulated for all aspects of a user's life, with the final aim of enhancing performance and quality [5].

The IoB aims to discuss how data can be better understood and used to build and promote new products from the perspective of human psychology. IoB can be used in different ways by public or private institutions. This technology is becoming an attractive new marketing and sales platform for businesses and organizations around the world. The IoB platform enables the development of a comprehensive customer understanding that every company needs. For example, IoB can connect all the phones in an app, check for mistakes and get visual recommendations for enhancing swings and shots. Device networking creates many new data points, including from the Internet of Things. Ventures collect information from their customers by data sharing between connected devices [6]. These devices are actually monitored by a single computer. Aggregating usage and information from IoB devices provides useful insights into consumer behavior, desires, and preferences, which can be simply referred as computer network. This includes devices ranging from phones to vehicles, training replenishments, and credit cards, to those that are literally connected to the Internet. Therefore, the goal of IoB is to record, analyze, understand and respond to all forms of human behavior so that people can be tracked and understood by advances in technology and machine learning algorithms.

Studies show that IoB tends to be an advancing technology which has huge potential in the future. However, it has several risk factors which may or may not affect humans directly. IoB will take its crown in the near future, providing smarter solutions to the world. Both customers and organizations will benefit from IoB. This chapter discusses the benefits and challenges of IoB with the help of online surveys and analysis of various research papers.

1.2 METHOD OF STUDY

IoB is an advancing technology which has huge future potential. Many studies have been performed for the applications and future scope of IoB. Furthermore, researchers have shed light on various sectors where IoB plays a major role. Our chapter mainly focuses on the benefits and challenges of IoB in various scenarios [7, 8].

IoB is considered an expansion of the IoT since it has the capability to reproduce various patterns in order to have an influence on human behavior. Consequently, IoB can be referred to as a mixture of technology, data analytics and behavioral psychology. Studies have already proved the potential of IoT in various scenarios. Therefore, one can imagine how powerful the combination of IoB and IoT could be. IoB can easily tackle consumer behavior and gather relevant data for the improvement of the consumer experience. Subsequently, the area of digital marketing is also affected as consumer interests become available via IoB. Digital marketing becomes easier with personalized content interests. The IoB can very well be associated with social media platforms and the most-used search engine, Google [9, 10]. The advertisements shown between surfing the Internet and scrolling social media would be the ones the user was looking for. This happens with periodic tracking of customer behavior and interests. However, IoT devices fail to gather data easily. The data processing in the IoT is bit complex, and hence many companies do not have access to the data from it, whereas IoB is customer centric, and it is easier to track human behavior and share data with the relevant companies. More often companies may prefer IoB because of its customer-centric behavior. It has the potential to trigger customers in favor of a product purchase. Through such approaches, companies get an insight into product enhancement according to consumer interests. Thus, sales can be increased. Similarly, various sectors have advantages through IoB with relevant applications. Besides these benefits of IoB, the design of the most efficient approaches to capturing human psychology is increasingly important and needs to be focused on [11–13].

We have gathered information through the review of various studies performed on IoB. The studies mainly focused on consumer experience and product development. An online survey was conducted for the collection of customer experience regarding the appearance of advertisements and data sharing in various applications. This helped us calculate a periodic tracking system of IoB [14, 15]. Service quality and the value chain can be improved with the aid of such data gathered. The analysis of this data helped to elucidate the benefits and risk factors or drawbacks of IoB in various sectors.

1.3 RESULTS AND ANALYSIS

IoB is applicable in various sectors. This section deals with the benefits and pitfalls of IoB in various sectors. With the ability to decipher customer intent as described in natural language statements, search engine optimization focuses heavily on intent, as well as words and keywords that describe the function and benefit of the product. Therefore, it is possible to take advantage of much better insight into user psychology and a product outlook with an understanding of the possible ways of choosing a product and services. Being alert about the time and place of customer shopping can affect your business positively, as notifications can be pushed regarding offers and discounts. In addition, IoB allows personalization, which helps in the enhancement of service quality and efficiency [16, 17]. With the help of IoB, you have the opportunity to improve the quality of the data collected and combine data from different sources to gain your own insights from this information. Companies need to be very cautious regarding privacy concerns and cyber security of the customer data. If any kind of violation occurs, it may directly affect the company's reputation and service. As we know in the advanced technological era, hackers and cyber criminals could misuse sensitive data. Therefore, it is highly important to adopt measures against these concerns in order to implement IoB in any application.

1.3.1 Benefits of IoB

Sales Industry: The sales industry greatly benefits from IoB. Products and services can be offered to customers with knowledge on the personal interests of the customers. This provides a very good customer flow for demanding products and services. Since the dawn of advertising, marketing and psychology have been intertwined. Therefore, behavioral analytics and psychology could provide new insights into the data generated by the Internet of Things. For businesses and organizations around the world, IoB has the potential to become a powerful new marketing and sales tool [18–20]. Organizations can use the concept of IoB to look at past performance and predict the future. Enterprises organize their development, marketing and sales activities based on the data received via the IoT. Several companies and organizations have created health apps for cell phones that track food, sleep habits, heart rate and blood sugar levels in the medical field. The software finds the issue with the health of the user and suggests behavioral changes for the best outcome. To cite an example, let us consider the over-the-top platform Netflix. Netflix gets user data to predict the likes and dislikes of the viewers. It recommends movies and shows based on personal interests and ratings. Another example: Uber and other taxi aggregators use the IoT to track drivers and passengers. They provide a survey after each trip to review the guest's experience. However, you can observe driver behavior, understand passenger reactions and automatically construct those inputs via IoB, so you can collect historical data and avoid investigations. The behavioral insights obtained can be used to transform a major prospect to sales. With the help of behavioral psychology, IoB identifies and interprets human behavior by analyzing how human humans react in each situation via various technologies. Some companies utilize facial recognition to examine behavior patterns at a specific time. This helps in the improvement of sales team efficiency by examining their behavior. IoB aids in alteration of sales engagement with consumers in real time.

Marketing Sector: IoB plays a major role in the marketing sector and has huge potential to trigger marketing, which further affects sales and services. The behavioral data gathered with the help of IoB aids in effective campaigning. It helps in the optimization of marketing campaigns and marketing to consumers efficiently. IoB data can be collected from various platforms in order to analyze customer buying habits. This includes the place and time of shopping, which aids in the personalization of advertisements on various platforms. Besides these, IoB initiates marketing notifications on the latest offers and discounts depending on behavioral data. Furthermore, IoB data helps in analyzing the needs of customers, and companies can provide the required User Interface (UI) [21].

Marketing, or rather digital marketing services, will be one of the biggest winners of IoB technology, as Internet connectivity is a prerequisite for IoB. Digital marketing is an area where data is used primarily to sell products and services to people around the world. With access to behavioral analytics and interpretation tools, we are in a stronger position to provide better reach to those at the end of the purchasing process. Digital marketing services are booming all over the world. Digital marketing is being used more prominently by brand promotion, lead generation, sales generation and people. If you also need digital marketing help or advice, hire a true wireless stereo digital marketing expert to meet your needs.

Customer Experience: The Internet of Behavior helps agencies learn everything about consumer behavior so they can deliver exactly what their clients want. If a customer encounters positive issues during the adventure, the agency can deal with them and enhance overall customer happiness. This allows them to stabilize (and study) consumer loyalty over time [22].

Companies use the Internet to collect various facts about consumer behavior. The Internet of Behavior transforms these personal facts into valuable records. This helps companies improve their business performance by knowing everything about their customers. In addition, the Internet of Action makes it possible to collect facts about some contacts. Therefore, the agency can oversee the entire consumer adventure from the beginning to the end. This is how the Internet of Behavior helps businesses follow in the footsteps of their customers. IoB helps to tailor every need of the customer based on their likes and dislikes. This helps both the company and the customer in saving time and effort to choose the best product and best customer experience.

Research and Manufacturing Industry: IoB can benefit not only customer experience and sales but also can be utilized in the collection of data for research purposes. Research includes the testing and analyzing of various applications with the gathered human behavioral data. The research industry is supported by customer research, product research, observational research, experimental research and simulation data, bringing innovative technology to the market. The research industry will better understand market needs to derive profound solutions.

Manufacturing is the largest area strongly influenced by digital transformation technology. The Internet of Things is slowly playing a role in the misleading debate surrounding IoT development, artificial intelligence and robotics used in the manufacturing industry. The Internet of Behavior is used in the manufacturing industry to monitor employee and worker behavior. It increases productivity, reduces idle time, reduces unnecessary activity and is monitored to work on time.

Miscellaneous: All new technologies affect some areas of the business world. What is the real reason behind all these possibilities for the internet downpour of standing (IoB) behavior IoB in the home? To answer this, there are many behavioral Internet offerings for the general household. Individuals gain safety, comfort and efficiency in their daily lives. With the help of IoB, you will be able to make better decisions. To cite an example of Internet behavior, IoB was used during Covid-19 to determine if a person wore a face mask and washed their hands. People have always been reminded to follow guidelines to protect themselves. Shopping giants such as Wal-Mart, Amazon, Costco, Kroger, and Home Depot use the Internet of Behavior prominently to monitor store activities. All places where large numbers of people gather, not just shopping places, are monitored by IoB to promote specific etiquette. By 2025, physical checkout process staff will be mostly eliminated, and automatic checkout systems will be installed in most shopping locations. All this is made possible by the Internet of Action. Big data is used to improve people's lives. The Internet of Behavior is a revenue-generating tool for most people, businesses and organizations. IoB certainly brings technical know-how to all sectors of the population. IoB provides enough data for market research. IoB can also be used to improve the security of public places with facial recognition. IoB advocates a personalized approach to all users. It will bring more business opportunities to people. This reduces industry monitoring costs and delivers a better customer experience through personalized targeting of products and services. IoB will usher in a new era of being in the digital world. Behavioral data can by analyzed to determine product demand and adjust production accordingly; collect previously unavailable data about how prospects and customers interact with a business, products and services; analyze staff behavior to improve the quality and efficiency of production and service departments; monitor customer and employee behavior to improve public health and safety; convert IoT data to IoB insights; and test the effectiveness of commercial and non-profit campaigns. Governments can adapt support programs and content to new legislation. In the healthcare field, healthcare providers can assess a patient's condition and treatment efforts and obtain more lifestyle data.

1.3.2 Pitfalls of IoB

Internet of Behavior protection is an important concern to be addressed. No technology can be considered fully secure, as it may have risks in the long run. There are enormous probabilities of data robbery and leakage of sensitive data that could adversely affect each individual or user. The abundance of information and perception can be a big undertaking to control and secure. There can be an extra desire for cyber security to prevent crimes. The Internet of Behavior continues to be in its early days and therefore numerous drawbacks may also pop out along with it. The blessings of Internet of Behavior structures are plausible for agencies that overcome the demanding situations inherent to deploying and keeping an IoB system. The toughest roadblock to achievement will be the gathering of highly secure information from clients and workers. People are already conversant with surrendering some non-public information for comfort and different benefits. The IoB calls for even more non-public information, together with intimate bodily information that measures outward appearances and inner functions. Convincing humans to give up non-public information on incredibly sensitive data won't be easy. Companies will have to deal with customers' privacy concern with contractual or monetary agreements. Subsequently, data will become more secure, preventing leakage and misuse.

The Internet of Behavior is user-identifiable information using the Internet of Things and wearable technologies such as smart watches. It is a concept that collects and identifies user behavior. Through IoB, this data is combined and processed to generate information that can create new approaches to user experience development, search experience optimization and enterprise product and service promotion. The more data you get from the IoT, the deeper your data insights will be. In general, the data collected by IoT comes from a variety of sources, including customer data, social media, public data, face recognition, location tracking and civilian data processed by government agencies. Inevitably, as the life of the IoT became easier, people were unaware that they were able to disclose their personal information and allow certain organizations and businesses to share data without asking for permission. This led to Io's ethical issues, as there was no clear line between maximizing user needs and tampering.

Cyber Security: The primary issue with the Internet of Behavior is the way information is amassed and stored. The Internet of Behavior is a huge database for cybercriminals to benefit from. Exclusive information from customers also can be compromised if it falls into the hands of unethical users. The integration of behavioral data with the IoT gives cybercriminals access to sensitive data that reveals user behavioral patterns. Leaked information makes users more vulnerable to cybercriminal activities such as ransomware, fraud, money laundering and theft of personal information. However, many companies and groups have all begun to deal with this issue. New cyber security protocols may come into existence that makes the use of the Internet of Behavior safer. Nonetheless, the Internet of Behavior is a modern concept predicted to affect marketing and advertising to an awesome extent.

In summary, IoB risk is an issue whenever organizations that use sensitive data are unaware of their responsibility to protect their personal privacy. Therefore, organizations that decide to adopt the IoB approach must ensure that they implement a robust cyber security strategy to protect all sensitive data.

Data Privacy: When an agency collects a vast amount of information about a customer's mood, behavior and likes and dislikes, the customer has the opportunity to claim their right to privacy. A lot of information is collected through various sources. This is good in the first place, as people benefit from the facility. However, the biggest concern is the collection, navigation and usage of information, especially on a large scale. Behavioral data may provide cybercriminals with access to sensitive data that reveals consumer behavioral patterns. Cybercriminals may collect hacked property access codes, shipping routes and even bank access codes and sell them to other criminals. The possibilities are endless. However, impersonating an individual for fraudulent or other purposes is likely to take phishing to a new level. The rapid expansion of networks of IoT devices means that new cybersecurity protocols are being developed and enterprises need to be more vigilant and proactive than ever before.

IoT gathers information from various companies. For instance, bike insurance may check your history for ensuring you are a good rider. As a society, we have decided that this is fair. However, insurance companies can also look at your social media profiles and interactions to predict if you are a safe rider. This is a suspicious and illegal move. It's not difficult for businesses to link their smart phones to laptops, home voice assistants, home and car cameras and perhaps cell phone records. And it's not just the device itself. Behind the scenes, many companies exchange data between corporate lines or with other affiliates. Google, Facebook and Amazon continue to acquire software that has the potential to bring users of a single app into the entire online ecosystem. In many cases, they do not have permission. This poses significant safety and legal risks, and there is little legal protection against these concerns. The outlook for IoB is still in its infancy, but as more and more new data and analytics become available, companies need to make sure they are aware of consumer behavior and trends. Adopting a strong data security regime followed by data stewardship best practices, cyber security training and awareness programs helps organizations stay ahead of the curve. In fact, IoB is expected to become widespread soon, and by the end of 2025, more than half of the world's population will be covered by at least one IoB program, whether commercial or governmental. Data privacy is the basic need for each customer and has to be valued and respected by companies. It should not be misused for monetary purposes.

Data abundance and visibility are difficult to manage and protect, leading to major cybercrime. After all, IoB is currently in the growth stage and can be life-changing for people. IoB will bring a lot of excitement to achieve innovation and a lot of change to the world of technology. As a pyramid, the IoT transforms data into information, while IoB transforms knowledge into true wisdom. Therefore, while IoB provides contributions, especially in business and health care, its risks should not be ignored. Also, IoB is a personalized one-on-one marketing holy grail. It can combine online and offline data with behavioral science and use detailed data profiles to influence behavior. For example, coffee chains use facial recognition software associated with surveillance cameras to track customers across locations and match faces to transactions and use data to geofence relevant marketing offers. Organizations can force employees to comply with standards, for instance, to wear a mask, by using facial recognition to identify nonconformities. Governments can use this data to track citizens and monitor IoB data for signs of unwanted behavior such as terrorism or the organization of political protests. The IoT itself is not a problem in nature. Many people prefer to synchronize their devices to benefit from this setting. IoB raises issues regarding data ownership, privacy and data security. These datasets can be combined between intermediaries, and third parties buy and sell aggregated data to provide businesses with more detailed insights into individual consumers. There are also ethical concerns associated with tracking individuals and aggregating their data into a viable format to influence their behavior.

Miscellaneous: Privacy has turned out to be a political concern in many jurisdictions, especially after massive data breaches by platforms that rely on personal data such as Facebook, Yahoo and LinkedIn. Ventures need to develop IoB devices and systems that comply with the regulations of multiple jurisdictions. On IoB systems, it may be necessary to disable some features of the area that limits data collection. People want better products and services, better customer experiences and improved lifestyles in exchange for sharing personal information. The value provided to consumers must be commensurate with the risk, as IoB data can contain highly sensitive information. Like IoT devices, IoB technology is another potential attack vector for criminals. IoB data can contain highly sensitive information, which can increase the severity of the attack. Behavioral data can provide cybercriminals with access to information and leave people vulnerable to digital and physical attacks. Personalization aids in the enhancement of products and services affect our values. It can go to extremes to make products customers love. Some studies show that when too many products were identified, it resulted in pregnancy prediction. It was followed by customer complaints, as they were not aware of it and their personal data was not safe [9–21]. Organizations should ensure that privacy laws are followed before implementing any solution. In addition to complying with the law, we need to ensure that the collection and utilization of data is ethical and follows moral standards from the perspective of public and consumers. An organization may use IoB data by in violating existing local privacy laws. These violations can result in penalties and police cases and therefore loss of reputation. In such cases, businesses will be at risk of being sued by an individual and facing government fines. Organizations must agree with local data protection laws, which can vary widely from region to region. They need to perform rigorous data attribution to evaluate which data is stored for which client, client or user, and they need to comply with the law regarding where and how that data is stored. Only then can data be deleted at the request of the user and no fines for violations imposed. The company may agree to the laws but continue to behave unethically in front of both internal and external stakeholders. The use of IoB data to monitor the staff in an organization may improve the efficiency of work. But it can badly affect the relationship between the employees and their trust of the management of the organization, as their privacy is not considered.

According to McKinsey, there are more connected devices today than people. From smart phones to smart watches, speakers, voice assistants and surveillance cameras, more than 30 billion connected devices have been added worldwide. With sensors and auto-launch capabilities, these devices permeate every area and constantly send large amounts of sensitive data to businesses for data analytics. After a few years, around 40% of the world's population will be digitally monitored for minute actions [22–24]. It will hardly be possible to evade the tracking systems of devices. All our actions are being monitored. In the present scenario, where we are being tracked by almost all devices and artificial intelligence provides faster and more accurate data, IoB will have a huge impact on philosophical, ethical and legislative business and society in general. As Daryl Plummer, chief research officer and Gartner Fellow, points out, the very existence of these devices and how governments and businesses use the data need to be rethought in existing frameworks. Therefore, in the long run, almost everyone in the society will be influenced by the impacts of IoB [25, 26].

1.4 CONCLUSION

Internet of Behavior is a technology that uses the Internet of Things in order to gather behavioral patterns of humans for the enhancement of digital experiences, sales, marketing and many more sectors. This chapter focused on the benefits and pitfalls of Internet of Behavior. Each sector was studied in detail, and the benefits of IoB in those sectors were analyzed. IoB applications range from the sales and marketing sector to consumer experience. IoB works based on behavioral psychology. Human behaviors are analyzed and recorded for the enhancement of various platforms and applications in order to improve production and services. For companies, it becomes easier with IoB to attain a huge turnaround annually. Even marketing becomes easier, as advertisements and campaigns can be personalized based on consumer interests and dislikes. From the research, it is clear that IoB has a huge potential in the future. IoB can revolutionize the technological area in no time. Further research is needed to learn about the applications of IoB in sensitive sectors. IoB aids in providing business solutions to achieve more sales and keep clients highly satisfied. IoB can replace multiple customer surveys, which are a complex task and time consuming for clients as well as the companies. It helps gather sensitive information on customer interaction with the provided products and services. Companies can get a good understanding about the shopping habits of consumers. Companies can also track the period of time in which a customer is purchasing or browsing for products. It can help in initiating notification alerts at that particular time. This will provide more efficiency in offering products and services.

As we are aware that IoB is in early stages, there are lot of challenges to be tackled. The chapter also analyzed various risk factors and challenges of IoB which can arise besides the huge benefits. The major factor to be considered is the protection of data, or data privacy. As far as political laws regarding cyber security and data privacy are exist, IoB faces challenges, especially when gathering sensitive customer data. Data shared using IoB can be misused by hackers and cyber criminals for monetary purposes. If this occurs, companies might be at risk, which may affect their reputation and services. IoB can negatively impact people, as it may gather sensitive information on people, which is against privacy protection laws. It can even trigger unnecessary conflicts in political bodies. Therefore, IoB should be implemented with utmost awareness regarding the laws and concerns of the public. Companies must ensure data privacy protection of users. IoB can revolutionize the tech era with smarter solutions and smarter implementations using human behavior analysis. IoB can be a life saver if properly implemented and utilized. This chapter covered major areas where IoB is beneficial and the risk factors it entails. Therefore, one can easily study the potential risks associated with IoB along with the enormous possibilities offered by IoB.

REFERENCES

1. Javaid, M., Haleem, A., Singh, R., Rab, S., Suman, R. Internet of Behaviours (IoB) and its role in customer services, *Sensors Int.* (2021). https://doi.org/10.1016/j.sintl.2021.100122.
2. Stary, C. The Internet-of-Behavior as organizational transformation space with choreographic Intelligence. *International Conference on Subject-Oriented Business Process Management. The Digital Workplace – Nucleus of Transformation. S-BPM ONE 2020. Communications in Computer and Information Science*, vol. 1278. Springer, Cham (2020). https://doi.org/10.1007/978-3-030-64351-5_8.
3. Holland, J. H. Complex adaptive systems, *Daedalus.* 121 (17–30) (1992).
4. Goto, S., Yoshie, O., Fujimura, S., Tamaki, K. Preliminary study on workshop facilitation for IoT innovation as industry-university collaboration PLM program for small and medium sized enterprises. In: Ríos, J., Bernard, A., Bouras, A., Foufou, S. (eds.) *PLM 2017. IAICT*, vol. 517, pp. 285–296. Springer, Cham (2017).
5. Gilchrist, A. *Industry 4.0: The Industrial Internet of Things.* Apress, New York (2016).
6. He, J. S., Lo, D. C., Xie, Y., Lartigue, J. W. (2016). Integrating Internet of Things (IoT) into STEM undergraduate education: Case study of a modern technology infused courseware for embedded system course. *2016 IEEE Frontiers in Education Conference (FIE)*, Erie, PA, USA, pp. 1–9.
7. Fleischmann, A., Schmidt, W., Stary, C., Obermeier, S., Börger, E. *Subject-Oriented Business Process Management*, ISBN 978-3-642-32392-8. Springer, Heidelberg, https://doi.org/10.1007/978-3-642-32392-8.
8. Guo, B., Zhang, D., Wang, Z. Living with Internet of Things: The emergence of embedded intelligence. *2011 International Conference on Internet of Things and 4th International Conference on Cyber, Physical and Social Computing*, pp. 297–304. (2011).
9. Fleischmann, A., Schmidt, W., Stary, C. (eds.). *S-BPM in the Wild: Practical Value Creation.* Springer, Cham (2015).
10. Lingling Gao Xuesong Bai. A unified perspective on the factors influencing consumer acceptance of Internet of Things technology, *Asia Pac. J. Mark. Logist.* 26 (2) (2014) 211–231.

11. Hevner, A. R. A three cycle view of design science research, *Scand. J. Inf. Syst.* 19 (2) (2007) 4.

12. Li, S., Chung, T. Internet function and Internet addictive behavior, *Comput. Hum. Behav.* 22 (2006) 1067–1071.

13. Gross, T., Stary, C., Totter, A. User-centered awareness in computer-supported cooperative work-systems: Structured embedding of findings from social sciences, *Int. J. Hum. Comput. Interact.* 18 (2005) 323–360.

14. Shih, H. Extended technology acceptance model of Internet utilization behavior, *Inf. Manag.* 41 (2004) 719–729.

15. Smith, Donnavieve N., Sivakumar, K. Flow and Internet shopping behavior: A conceptual model and research propositions, *J. Bus. Res.* 57 (10) (2004, Oct) 1199–1208.

16. Patrick, Y., Chau, K., Hu, Paul J. Examining a model of information technology acceptance by individual professionals: An exploratory study, *J. Manag. Inf. Syst.* 18 (4) (2002) 191–229. https://doi.org/10.1080/07421222.2002. 11045699.

17. Chau, P. Y., Hu, P. J. Investigating healthcare professionals' decisions to accept telemedicine technology: an empirical test of competing theories, *Inf. Manag.* 39 (2002) 297–311.

18. Chang, M. K., Cheung, W. Determinants of the intention to use Internet/WWW at work: a confirmatory study, *Inf. Manag.* 39 (2001) 1–14.

19. Adams, D. A., Nelson, R. R., Todd, P. A. Perceived usefulness, ease of use, and usage of information technology: A replication, *MIS Q.* 16 (1992) 227–247.

20. Ajzen, I. The theory of planned behavior, *Organ. Behav. Hum. Dec. Proc.* 50 (1991) 179–211.

21. Tsitsika, A., Janikian, M., Schoenmakers, T. M., Tzavela, E. C., Olafsson, K., Wojcik, S., Macarie, G. F., Tzavara, C., EU NET ADB Consortium, Richardson, C. Internet addictive behavior in adolescence: A cross-sectional study in seven European countries, *Cyberpsychol. Behav. Soc. Netw.* 17 (8) (2014 Aug 1) 528–535.

22. Fleischmann, A., Schmidt, W., Stary, C., Strecker, F. Nondeterministic events in business processes. In: La Rosa, M., Soffer, P. (eds.) *BPM 2012. LNBIP*, vol. 132, pp. 364–377. Springer, Heidelberg (2013).

23. Guo, B., Zhang, D., Wang, Z., Yu, Z., Zhou, X. Opportunistic IoT: Exploring the harmonious interaction between human and the Internet of Things, *J. Netw. Comput. Appl.* 36 (6) (2013) 1531–1539.

24. Andrews, L., Bianchi, C. Consumer Internet purchasing behavior in Chile, *J. Bus. Res.* 66 (10) (2013 Oct 1) 1791–1799.

25. Crespo, A. H., Del Bosque, I. R., de los Salmones Sanchez, M. G. The influence of perceived risk on Internet shopping behavior: A multidimensional perspective, *J. Risk Res.* 12 (2) (2009 Mar 1) 259–277.

26. Buente, W., Robbin, A. Trends in Internet information behavior, 2000–2004, *J. Am. Soc. Inf. Sci. Technol.* 59 (11) (2008 Sep) 1743–1760.

27. Kidd, C. *What Is the Internet-of-Behavior.* IoB Explained, The Business of IT Blog, BMC (2019).

Chapter 2

Working of IoB

Manisha Verma

CONTENTS

2.1 INTRODUCTION

In the last few years, the use of Internet of Things (IoT) devices has more than doubled. All the small appliances being used around us, whether it is smart watch or washing machine, the modernity of these machines has given only the feeling of interacting with the world. Data and data collection by these modern machines provide important information about the behavior and interests of the user, and thus a new process of Internet of Behavior is born. It is one step ahead of the IoT [1]. We can say that where the work of IoT ends, that is where IoB starts. The IoB pioneers the Internet of Things system. With the help of which we analyze the collected data completely. In today's modern world, we are all surrounded by different types of devices that are fully connected to the Internet, such as mobile phones, smart watches, and smart TVs. Today our daily life has become dependent on many such devices, whether it is online shopping or ordering food. Internet of Behavior is a part of the IoT. The Internet of Things connects all types of devices to a network and collects all kinds of different information. From there the work of Internet of Behavior starts. Internet of Behavior analyses the collected data and better facilitates the user experience. The Internet of Behavior is able to interpret the future reaction of any person according to the data used. The great researcher Gartner has also said that in the year 2023, the use of Internet of Behavior will be at its peak level. Any big company can see from the experiences of their customers what they like and what they do not.

Earlier, a study would be used to examine consumer behavior and response to a product or service. Customer feedback and background may be a response to a product or service. Initially sample analysis is completed; then trust in the product or its service within the firm is discovered. IoB platforms are designed to gather, combine, and analyze data generated from a large number of sources, as well as digital devices, wearable computers, and online human activity. The information is then analyzed in terms of activity science to uncover patterns that may be employed by promotion and sales groups to influence future shopper behavior.

Today the Internet of Behavior is being used in all kinds of small and big companies. Wolfram Alpha is a type of computational knowledge engine that was developed by Stephen Wolfram. It can provide information based on the activities of any person on Facebook and is also able to discover their thoughts and interests. The Internet of Behavior creates other opportunities for companies to collect and analyze data, the purpose of which is to provide better facilities to employees and customers.

2.2 MATERIALS AND METHODS OF IOB

We are surrounded by the Internet of Behavior; today the trends of devices and technology are happening all around us. One of these is the Internet of Behavior, so this section examines how its use affects our lives and in which areas it is useful.

In the Field of Business

- Today, business is dominant, and people are trying to connect with customers through online advertising through various businesses, providing all they want to any customer according to their own interests [1, 2]. Google and Facebook both use the Internet of Behavior the most to show ads on their sites. These companies interact with their customers and observe their experiences through their own advertising through the medium of ClearDro.
- In the same area, YouTube also knows the experiences of its users, which allows it to show only those videos and topics in which the user is interested.

During the COVID–19 Pandemic

- At the time of the pandemic, when the world was going through a big crisis, the use of Internet of Behavior increased. Employers can use sensors or tags to see if there are any discrepancies in compliance with security standards. For example, if we talk about any food delivery application, they also use protocol information to guide their decisions [3–5].

- Take, for example, Zomato and Swiggy, both of which demonstrated and promoted restaurant safety practices. They recorded and transmitted delivery person's temperature to assure the consumer that they were safe.

For the Insurance Industry

- IoB has become very beneficial for the insurance industry. Driving tracking tools are increasingly being used by insurance companies like Allstate and State Farm to track drivers' behavior and protect them [6, 7]. Using the Internet of Behavior, it can be found out whether an accident that has happened is a certain event or it is a false belief generated by it.

2.3 WORKING PROCESS OF IOB

The stages of operating flow method of comprehending the web of Behavior for client necessities and creating those methods to feel happier with their shopping for is solely mirrored. The standard enhancement journey starts with assembling data from all relevant sources. The information primarily supported facts were then collection of varied sources then analysis as needs data then sensing data and final compile all data and serving to customer. Once plotting pro re nata data graphs, and last the ultimate section is to implement the gathering and analysis data front for the realization of IoB for customer satisfaction in any relevant services the information may be obtained from many completely different shops. There are various methodologies of IoB that provide client services. Industrial shopper data to the welfare media and additional data is also accessible to all. That mixes numerous technologies for visual recognition, location monitoring, and intensive data that focuses directly on the person and connects the data to behavioral events. IoB is regarding how data can be higher understood and the way it can turn out and sell new merchandise from human psychology. The IoB provides digital analysis from different outlets and may be used to manipulate behavior. This has led to new insights into the IoT through behavioral analysis and psychology. IoB can become a tool for corporations and organizations worldwide for sales and promotion [8–11]. Corporations effectively link all primary devices to the web and keep them on their tracking list. All the information is currently being employed for advertising business and non-commercial products. Digital transformation methods will considerably impact the automotive sector, and here the IoB is taking its position among IoT growth, artificial intelligence, and artificial intelligence technologies utilized in manufacturing. In the industrial sector, the IoB is being used to track employer operating capability [12]. With an outsized quantity of data, distribution mechanisms for sales merchandise and services to interested people may be strategically implemented. It will additionally be ready to meet individuals who are at the top of the acquisition chain who access instruments for behavioral analysis and explanations. Digital marketing is being employed more conspicuously by individuals for whole ads, lead generation, and sales generation [13]. One can modify people's lives by opening up new technological fronts. it's go with several excitations and brings power and get to the technical environment. Business can be expedited to include new solutions with the help of IoB and a huge quantity of user information for client analysis, product analysis, observation research, experimental research, and simulation results [14]. So as to develop careful strategies, the research business will help contemplate the business demands. This allows the tracking, monitoring, and operation of physical devices through the Internet [15, 16]. IoB expands this by connecting these instruments and therefore the information they gather to regulate personal conduct. The processes are as follows:

- Dataset – collect from various sources – analysis of collected required data – sensing data and its behavior – collect data in various terms – serve data as required.

If we follow the India web platform, when someone interacts with any other device from a user's laptop, then IoB analyses clearly how the user is interacting with the resource, for example, which button they are clicking. Internet of Behavior is a process in which the data received by the user is analyzed in the context of psychology and the analysis obtained from the user experience, search experience optimization, knowing the user's interests, we develop new concepts to promote the growth of the company makes.

We are currently taking full advantage of this by integrating the Internet of Behavior with machine learning. In the self driving process, machine learning via artificial intelligence and Internet of Behavior is able to choose the better option by remembering the data of past experiences. By analyzing the experience gained by other human beings in a psychological way, it brings efficiency to the work.

2.4 DISCUSSION: THE IMPORTANCE OF IOB

It is even easier to explain it with an example: we go to any shopping mall and buy different types of things, then pay, and then, according to a survey, he tries to know that your experience was cash. Here we use the IoT, but as we know, IoB works one step ahead of it. In contrast, IoB does not require a survey. IoB also tracks the behavior of the employees of the company according to it and according to them it understands the behavior of the customers on its own. And then it works to improve all kinds of collected data to the customers and the employees [17–19].

We know very well how important someone's data is in today's era. We know any human being by their behavior; in the same way, IoB also explains to the public and understands a user's identity and activities in daily life and its usefulness according to human data. Even an organization named gather also made a prediction and said that in the year 2021–2022 Internet of Behavior in the world will get the best place in the world and its use and development will be very fast [19, 20].

With the help of the Internet of Behavior, all the companies and businesses will put four moons in their progress, its use will improve human life by making progress in every field from the pandemic to climate change [21]. IoB is completely new in today's world, and on top of that, there are a lot of applications being developed and work going on right now.

IoB, in its own way, collects all the activities done by humans on the Internet, analyses them thoroughly. It enables a user to track the usage of any device, provides additional touch-points per the user's purchase decisions, and thus provides better products to the customer. The Internet of Behavior is considered a better source of getting complete information about the user. The data received through all kinds of approaches promotes the quality of service and the value chain and interest of the people towards it. With the efficiency of understanding the intention of the users described by natural language statements in search engines and playing a vital role in enhancing the product features [22, 23].

The IoB will further improve the quality and efficiency of services. With the help of Internet of Behavior, the goals of increasing the quality of all the data being collected and keeping data secure become very important. In such a situation, it also becomes very important for the user to be aware of their security and privacy [24].

- **Security:** Both the customer and the company need to be aware of security because there are many criminals who will constantly try to steal user data. In this case, it is also the user's responsibility to keep their data safe. In which off behavior can play an important role or say that it is playing. They need to be careful about this. As we know, the Internet of Behavior is capable of identifying someone's behavior from the data received. If we imagine that a person searches for informal data on a search engine, then with the help of Internet of Behavior, we can analyze his behavior and identify him easily. We are able to trace any kind of informal activities of such a user. We can take care of them by getting the data of their equipment [25, 26].

- **Health:** The Internet of Behavior will prove to be a boon in the health field. In which we can analyze them with different help and make them more efficient by the many types of mistakes being made by the doctor. Tracking patients in real time enables providing better treatment to them by which they can meet the needs of their body by tracking daily life through the device. With the help of Internet of Behavior, we are able to predict their health by giving them the best possible treatment and help them live much longer. Or as if we cannot allow humans to get sick [27].

Since the beginning of advertising, marketing and science have coexisted. In this way, the knowledge gathered through the Internet of Things has been enhanced by activity analysis and psychology. IoB has the potential to be a powerful new marketing and sales tool for companies and organizations all around the world. Utilizing this tool can help you develop a thorough understanding of your clients, which is crucial for any organization.

Undoubtedly, corporations have used analytics, A/B testing, SWOT analysis, and many other tactics to design their products and selling strategies over the years in order to develop and market products that customers will want to purchase. IoB is anticipated to make a significant impact in the sales sector.

With this idea, businesses want to be able to look at past results and make predictions about the future. Companies' development, marketing, and sales operations will be reorganized as a result of the knowledge amassed through the Internet of Things. It basically consists of dynamic industries and dealing techniques, as well as digital marketing. Modern society can no longer ignore the effects of advanced technology and the IoB because they will have an impact on consumer behavior and the success of established sales channels [28].

Therefore, it's crucial to start integrating the Internet of Behavior into your digital marketing plan in order to profit and quickly gather a significant amount of the most satisfied customers. Access information from various points of contact with the Internet of Things. You are able to examine the entire client journey this way.

In other words, you'll be able to identify the customer's initial point of interest in the product, their path toward purchase, and the goal of purchase, indicating you may be able to create a significant number of touch points for a positive engagement with customers. Additionally, you'll be able to learn new techniques for communicating with clients so that you can establish a connection with them earlier than at the time of purchase [18, 29].

An investigation of consumer activity on social networks and other platforms, as well as details about their everyday lives, are all part of the idea of IoB. Information is gathered using the Internet of Things, which the average consumer can use to access occasional makers, thermostats, home automation systems, and wearable devices. Since each of these devices is a part of our daily lives, it is likely that they will be able to collect data on lifestyle trends, which will help us understand how and when particular products and services are used [30].

Because it feels more comfortable and natural when we lift devices before entering queries into Google, SEO pros see huge potential in IoB. Google Home, Apple Siri, and Amazon Alexa are examples of AI-enabled devices that demonstrate how search engines can understand human intent, not just recognize keywords. This suggests that information processing system pages won't be evaluated solely on the basis of their keyword content but also on the language used in those pages. Therefore, we have a tendency to see that it's important to change the SEO content approach so that it can support intent. Businesses, diverse non-profit groups that care for the community, and government agencies that uphold the rule of law all benefit from IoB. Let's see how this concept is used in modern society [31].

- During the epidemic, groups using portable computer vision started to employ IoB to determine whether a person was wearing a mask. Additionally, thermal imagers were sometimes used to produce images of humans with higher body temperatures.
- Because you can track someone's whereabouts using a smart phone, the system can tell whether you've visited a market or a beauty parlor as well as how long you stayed there. Uber analyzes IoT data to better understand its audience's preferences and find new ways to reach out to customers. Large brands today are familiar with almost everything about consumers, from hobbies to the reasoning behind purchases [32].
- In China, the introduction of a social credit score system was made feasible with the use of AI, particularly face recognition. Remember that the advent of AI during the Chinese era was intended to verify the protection of the organization of data that is loyalty to the present regime.
- The Directorix Barista for residential homes successfully included a biometric authentication system in 2018. Thus, sex, age, and mood are determined by goods purchased. The system evaluates the findings and provides the customer with the appropriate beverage. The same technology might be used in shops for customized advertising [33].

2.5 CONCLUSION: PROSPECTS FOR THE FUTURE

The Internet of Behavior is based on assessment data and is geared toward dynamic models and the modern era of behavior. Record analytics may be employed for well-timed modeling and behavior modification due to its networked nature. The resulting device complexity may be managed with the aid of illustration and access capabilities. The proposed approach adopts a science-based, improvement approach. It targets organizational systems that, as a result of the choreographic conduct encapsulation of useful entities, may be progressed to IoB transformation. The transformation technique starts off by describing the behavior that is, in my opinion, thought to be role or task specific as a part of mutual interplay styles that may be challenged with a particular purpose. The identified conduct encapsulations and interplay styles are subtly included into executable method models in a subsequent phase. In this way, businesses can experiment with IoB device solutions and tailor the development of analytical intelligence to their own requirements.

Many pieces of software that only link users to a whole community from a single application continue to be made available without Google, Facebook, or Amazon's consent.

Additionally, there are significant criminal and safety risks to the right to privacy that may be distinct among states globally. Future research may reveal that customers enjoy the entire experience. This will control the customer's interest in the product as it develops, their shopping experience leading up to the point of purchase, and the creation of additional contact points to promote positive customer engagement. Additionally, it might research fresh ways to communicate with customers so they can interact with the brand prior to making a purchase. The top-level view of human behavior included in the idea of Internet behavior incorporates knowledge about how people interact with social networks and other media.

Data from everyday users, such as from coffee makers, thermostats, home control systems, wearable technology, and so on, is collected online. It is employed for gathering information on lifestyle trends that, in turn, might provide a focus on using such goods and services. IoB will supply enough records for the market analysis. Additionally, it will be utilized to improve the security of well-known public places. It might present more opportunities for people in the market. It might lower the price of corporate tracking. This provides a better customized product and service focused on delivering a higher-quality customer experience, and new initiatives and solutions are emerging [29].

Deep behavioral patterns and consumer insights can be recognized and turned into practical ways to influence human behavior. Since a large number of people are practically tethered to our computers, our technology is the most readily available tool for businesses to analyze and extrapolate consumer behavior.

IoB has quickly evolved into a global setting that defines human behavior in just a few years. To connect people and computer systems for behavior analysis, a milestone is needed. IoB uses behavioral data records and then assesses their potential. Businesses have examined, tested, and put into practice a variety of techniques to expand their tactics for offering and promoting goods to consumers. The data can serve as a foundation for growth, promotion, and revenue strategies for businesses. The industries may also investigate a variety of new materials and records. Additionally, it helps consumers feel more brand loyalty and make more money [34]. The IoB makes it easier to examine the complete experience by using data gathered from several touch points. More information is produced in this way, as are fresh methods of communicating with customers. IoB is utilized for marketing and advertising purposes and could help business people improve their businesses. It will boost sales of devices that connect to the Internet and acquire and transfer data across wireless networks without human assistance. The IoB takes the gathering of records and converts it into insight. It integrates behavioral psychology and links people to their behaviors. IoB issues a warning if there is a bad situation and offers suggestions for reversing the course of action. It gathers behavioral and user data obtained through the use of Internet-connected devices and gives users insights into their motivations, interests, and behaviors.

All kinds of technology have its advantages as well as disadvantages. It is true that the prediction made by Gartner became true today, in 2022, and we can say that by 2025, 70% of the world's population will participate in the IoB [35]. But even with all the convenience of using IoB, this trend raises many questions related to security. Companies will have to implement cyber security education and awareness programs, after which Internet of Behavior will play a role in writing a new story in its future.

REFERENCES

1. C. Arnold, D. Kiel, K.I. Voigt, How the industrial Internet of Things changes business models in different manufacturing industries, *Int. J. Innov. Manag.* 20(8), 1640015 (2016).
2. M. Augl, C. Stary, Adjusting capabilities rather than deeds in computer-supported daily workforce planning. In: Ackerman, M.S., Goggins, S.P., Herrmann, T., Prilla, M., Stary, C. (eds.) *Designing Healthcare that Works. A Sociotechnical Approach*, pp. 175–188. Academic Press/Elsevier, Cambridge (2017).
3. S.M. Li, T.M. Chung, Internet function and Internet addictive behavior, *Comput. Hum. Behav.* 22 (6) (2006 Nov 1) 1067–1071.
4. W. Buente, A. Robbin, Trends in Internet information behavior, 2000–2004, *J. Am. Soc. Inf. Sci. Technol.* 59 (11) (2008 Sep) 1743–1760.
5. H.P. Shih, Extended technology acceptance model of Internet utilisation behavior, *Inf. Manag.* 41 (6) (2004 Jul 1) 719–729.
6. S.Y. Yousafzai, G.R. Foxall, J.G. Pallister, Explaining Internet banking behavior: Theory of reasoned action, theory of planned behavior, or technology acceptance model? *J. Appl. Soc. Psychol.* 40 (5) (2010 May) 1172–1202.

7. G. Guzman, Internet search behavior as an economic forecasting tool: The case of inflation expectations, *J. Econ. Soc. Meas.* 36 (3) (2011 Jan 1) 119–167.

8. T. De Vass, H. Shee, S.J. Miah, The effect of "Internet of Things" on supply chain integration and performance: An organisational capability perspective, *Austr. J. Informat. Syst.* (2018 Jun 27) 22.

9. C. Perera, C.H. Liu, S. Jayawardena, M. Chen, A survey on Internet of Things from industrial market perspective, *IEEE Access.* 2 (2014) 1660–1679.

10. S. Wachter, Normative challenges of identification in the Internet of Things: Privacy, profiling, discrimination, and the GDPR, *Comput. Law Secur. Rep.* 34 (3) (2018 Jun 1) 436–449.

11. J. Chin, V. Callaghan, Educational living labs: A novel Internet-of-Things based approach to teaching and research. In: *2013 9th International Conference on Intelligent Environments*, pp. 92–99. IEEE (2013 Jul 16). doi: 10.1109/IE.2013.48.

12. C. Kidd, *What Is the Internet-of-Behavior.* IoB Explained, The Business of IT Blog, BMC (2019). www.bmc.com/blogs/iob-internet-of-behavior/. Accessed 10 Feb 2020.

13. V. Lala, V. Arnold, S.G. Sutton, L. Guan, The impact of relative information quality of e-commerce assurance seals on Internet purchasing behavior, *Int. J. Account. Inf. Syst.* 3 (4) (2002 Dec 1) 237–253.

14. C. Stary, Non-disruptive knowledge and business processing in knowledge life cycles – aligning value network analysis to process management, *J. Knowl. Manag.* 18 (4) (2014) 651–686.

15. D. Jani, J.H. Jang, Y.H. Hwang, Big five factors of personality and tourists' Internet search behavior, *Asia Pac. J. Tourism Res.* 19 (5) (2014 May 4) 600–615.

16. A.H. Turan, Internet shopping behavior of Turkish customers: Comparison of two competing models, *J. Theoret. Appl. Electr. Comm. Res.* 7 (1) (2012 Apr) 77–93.

17. S. Rab, S. Yadav, S.K. Jaiswal, A. Haleem, D.K. Aswal, *Quality Infrastructure of National Metrology Institutes: A Comparative Study* (2021).

18. Y. Do, J.Y. Kim, M. Lineman, D.K. Kim, G.J. Joo, Using Internet search behavior to assess public awareness of protected wetlands, *Conserv. Biol.* 29 (1) (2015 Feb) 271–279.

19. Z. Pan, W. Yan, G. Jing, J. Zheng, Exploring structured inequality in Internet use behavior, *Asian J. Commun.* 21 (2) (2011 Apr 1) 116–132.

20. L. Lancieri, N. Durand, Internet user behavior: Compared study of the access traces and application to the discovery of communities, *IEEE Trans. Syst. Man Cybern. Syst. Hum.* 36 (1) (2005 Dec 19) 208–219.

21. C.L. Hsu, K.C. Chang, M.C. Chen, Flow experience and Internet shopping behavior: Investigating the moderating effect of consumer characteristics, *Syst. Res. Behav. Sci.* 29 (3) (2012 May) 317–332.

22. H.P. Breivold, K. Sandstrom, Internet of Things for industrial automation € –challenges and technical solutions. In: *2015 IEEE International Conference on Data Science and Data Intensive Systems*, pp. 532–539. IEEE (2015 Dec 11).

23. C. Metallo, R. Agrifoglio, F. Schiavone, J. Mueller, Understanding business model in the Internet of Things industry, *Technol. Forecast. Soc. Change.* 136 (2018 Nov 1) 298–306.

24. Y. Lu, S. Papagiannidis, E. Alamanos, Internet of Things: A systematic review of the business literature from the user and organisational perspectives, *Technol. Forecast. Soc. Change.* 136 (2018 Nov 1) 285–297.

25. D.N. Smith, K. Sivakumar, Flow and Internet shopping behavior: A conceptual model and research propositions, *J. Bus. Res.* 57 (10) (2004 Oct 1) 1199–1208.

26. A. Tsitsika, M. Janikian, T.M. Schoenmakers, E.C. Tzavela, K. Olafsson, S. Wojcik, G.F. Macarie, C. Tzavara, EU NET ADB Consortium, C. Richardson, Internet addictive behavior in adolescence: A cross-sectional study in seven European countries, *Cyberpsychol. Behav. Soc. Netw.* 17 (8) (2014 Aug 1) 528–535.

27. D. Langford, Ethics and the Internet: Appropriate behavior in electronic communication, *Ethics Behav.* 6 (2) (1996 Jun 1) 91–106.

28. A.H. Crespo, I.R. Del Bosque, M.G. de los Salmones Sanchez, The influence of perceived risk on Internet shopping behavior: A multidimensional perspective, *J. Risk Res.* 12 (2) (2009 Mar 1) 259–277.

29. M. Javaid, et al., *Sensors Int.* 2 (2021) 100122 6 [8] T.K. Yu, G.S. Wu, Determinants of Internet shopping behavior: An application of reasoned behaviour theory, *Int. J. Manag.* 24 (4) (2007 Dec 1) 744.

30. L.A. Ho, T.H. Kuo, B. Lin, The mediating effect of website quality on Internet searching behavior, *Comput. Hum. Behav.* 28 (3) (2012 May 1) 840–848.

31. G. Schuh, V. Zeller, J. Hicking, A. Bernardy, Introducing a methodology for smartification of products in manufacturing industry. *Procedia CIRP.* 81 (2019) 228–233.

32. A. Sodero, Y.H. Jin, M. Barratt, The social process of big data and predictive analytics use for logistics and supply chain management. *Int. J. Phys. Distrib. Logistics Manag.* 49 (7) (2019) 706–726. https://doi.org/10.1108/IJPDLM-01-2018-0041.

33. L. Andrews, C. Bianchi, Consumer Internet purchasing behavior in Chile, *J. Bus. Res.* 66 (10) (2013 Oct 1) 1791–1799.

34. C. Perera, A. Zaslavsky, P. Christen, D. Georgakopoulos, Context-aware computing for the Internet of Things: A survey, *IEEE Commun. Surv. Tutorials.* 16 (1) (2013 May 3) 414–454.

35. S. Rab, S. Yadav, N. Garg, S. Rajput, D.K. Aswal, Evolution of measurement system and SI units in India, *MAPAN* (2020) 1–16.

Chapter 3

A Detailed Study to Increase Business Value

P. Devisivasankari, R. Vijayakumar,
and Vijayalakshmi V

CONTENTS

3.1 INTRODUCTION

The Internet of Behavior (IoB) [1] helps to analyze how information is better utilized to develop new products from the outlook of human psychology. The concept of IoB can be utilized in different ways by the various sectors. The IoB is defined as the technology that collects and processes information based on the behavior of users to provide quality of life for users. The IoB [2] may be a network of interconnected physical objects that collect and exchange information and data over the Internet, called the Internet of Things (IoT). Within the Internet of Things, the range of complexity is consistently expanding and evolving. The way devices are connected and the calculations which will be performed autonomously by those objects and therefore the data stored in the cloud are constantly evolving in increasingly complex ways [3]. It's called the Internet of Behavior because it provides useful information about customer behavior, interests, and preferences collected through various data collection methods (business intelligence, big data, customer data platform, etc.). The Internet

DOI: 10.1201/9781003305170-3

27

of Things aims to analyze data from consumers' online activities in terms of behavior. It seeks to answer all the questions on the way to interpret the data and how this understanding can be applied to the development and commercialization of new products, all from the attitude of human psychology and cognitive science. The term "Internet of Things" [2] describes a way to look at user-controlled data from a behavioral psychological point of view. Supported by the results of this survey, companies can develop new user experiences (UX), search experience optimization (SXO), and ways to promote their final products and services [4]. As a result, implementing IoB within a corporation is technically simple but psychologically difficult. Thanks to ethical and legal considerations, it's necessary to conduct statistical surveys that map daily habits and activities without fully disclosing the personal information of consumers. Aside from that, the Internet of Things integrates existing personally targeted technologies with big data, like facial recognition and location tracking. This area consists of three areas: technology, data analysis, and behavioral psychology [5]. Because of big data, you'll get information from various contacts. This enables you to explore the customer experience from start to finish and understand where the customer's interest in the product begins, how the customer makes a buying decision, and the way to complete the transaction. This provides you the opportunity to generate more touch points with your consumers and increases your chances of active involvement. The power to personalize a service is critical to the efficiency of the service [6]. Users can still operate the service and, if the service is efficient, change behavior supported by that efficiency. Human behavior is often captured, analyzed, and understood using new innovations and developments in machine learning algorithms [7–10]. The Internet of Things helps us track and interpret people's behavior. A survey by IBM has come up with the prediction that by 2030, each person might own ten devices. The IoT is a trendy topic that connects devices for the exchange of information. Now the Internet of Behavior is an emerging topic with the new concept where companies use the huge amounts of data collected through the IoT to analyze customer behavior [11, 12]. The result of the analysis is used to predict the buying pattern of the customers, which in turn is used to give them suggestions and recommendations [13, 14]. This concept will have a great influence on the marketing side of the product. This chapter discusses:

1) Pattern of Shopping Using Customer Purchase Behavior
2) Analysis of Sentiment on Social Media
3) Decision Making Based on Wearable Dataset
4) IoB in the Insurance Industry

3.2 PATTERN OF SHOPPING USING CUSTOMER PURCHASE BEHAVIOR

Customer buying behavior refers to the typical way in which customers will purchase goods and benefit from services. This depends on the quantity, duration, frequency and timing. This buying pattern can be used to predict how customers will buy goods and services [15]. But this is sensitive data and is highly expected to change.

3.2.1 A Priori Algorithm

This algorithm is used for mining frequently used item sets and their corresponding association rules. The two major steps of this algorithm are join and prune. This refers to the occurrence frequency and the conditional probability. This algorithm uses prior knowledge of frequently occurring item set properties.

```
# importing dataset
data("Groc")

# using the apri function
rules <- apriori(Groc, param = list(sup = 0.02, conf = 0.3))

# using the function inspect ()
inspect(rules[1:10])

# using the function itemFrequencyPlot()
arules::itemFrequencyPlot(Groc, topN = 30, col = brewer.
  pal(9, 'Pastel2'), main = 'Relative Item Frequency Plot',
  type = "relative", ylab = "Item Frequency (Relative)")
```

Figure 3.1 shows the relative frequency plot of grocery items. The graph shows that people will have a buying pattern and follow it every time with slight variation. The customer who buys rolls or buns is expected to buy pastry. Similarly customers buying diapers are expected to buy baby soap and shampoo.

3.3 ANALYSIS OF SENTIMENT ON SOCIAL MEDIA

The Twitter dataset for Apple is taken for implementation. This dataset contains feedback from users about Apple and was collected in 2017.

This dataset contains 16 attributes and around 1000 records. An image of the dataset is shown in Figure 3.2. The first attribute, 'Text', contains

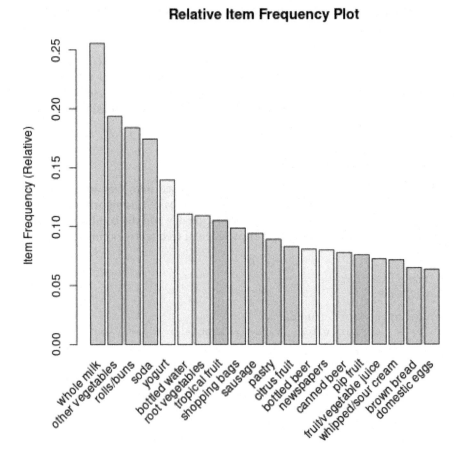

Figure 3.1 Relative frequency plot.

text	favorited	favoriteC	replyToSI	created	truncatec	replyToSI	id	replyToU st
RT @option_snipper: $AAPL beat on both eps and revenues. SEES 4Q REV. $49B-$5;	FALSE	0	NA	01-08-2017 20:31	FALSE	NA	8.92E+17	NA <;
RT @option_snipper: $AAPL beat on both eps and revenues. SEES 4Q REV. $49B-$5;	FALSE	0	NA	01-08-2017 20:31	FALSE	NA	8.92E+17	NA <;
Let's see this break all timers. $AAPL 156.89	FALSE	0	NA	01-08-2017 20:31	FALSE	NA	8.92E+17	NA <;
RT @SylvaCap: Things might get ugly for $aapl with the iphone delay. With $aapl do'	FALSE	0	NA	01-08-2017 20:31	FALSE	NA	8.92E+17	NA <;
$AAPL - wow! This was supposed to be a throw-away quarter and AAPL beats by ov	FALSE	0	NA	01-08-2017 20:31	FALSE	NA	8.92E+17	NA <;
RT @CNBCnow: EARNINGS: Apple Q3 EPS $1.67 vs. $1.57 Est.; Q3 Revs. $45.4B vs. !	FALSE	0	NA	01-08-2017 20:31	FALSE	NA	8.92E+17	NA <;
RT @CNBCnow: EARNINGS: Apple Q3 EPS $1.67 vs. $1.57 Est.; Q3 Revs. $45.4B vs. !	FALSE	0	NA	01-08-2017 20:31	FALSE	NA	8.92E+17	NA <;
RT @Selerity: #BREAKING: Apple $AAPL Q3 Earnings Per Share (EPS), $1.67 vs. $1.57	FALSE	0	NA	01-08-2017 20:31	FALSE	NA	8.92E+17	NA <;
RT @Selerity: #BREAKING: Apple $AAPL Q3 Revenue, $45.41B vs. $44.9B expected	FALSE	0	NA	01-08-2017 20:31	FALSE	NA	8.92E+17	NA <;
RT @JackWangCFA: #Apple @apple $aapl #earnings #RealTime #BREAKING Rev $45	FALSE	0	NA	01-08-2017 20:31	FALSE	NA	8.92E+17	NA <;
RT @Selerity: #BREAKING: Apple $AAPL Q3 iPhone Shipments, 41.03M vs. 40.5M ex|	FALSE	0	NA	01-08-2017 20:31	FALSE	NA	8.92E+17	NA <;
$AAPL probably tanks tomorrow lol	FALSE	0	NA	01-08-2017 20:31	FALSE	NA	8.92E+17	NA <;
$AAPL Actual 1.67 E, 45.4 B Rev https://t.co/YY4XTrHdP7	FALSE	0	NA	01-08-2017 20:31	FALSE	NA	8.92E+17	NA <;
RT @Super1NYC: $AAPL Apple Reports Q3 EPS $1.67 vs $1.57 Est., Sales $45.4B vs $	FALSE	0	NA	01-08-2017 20:31	FALSE	NA	8.92E+17	NA <;
RT @SylvaCap: Things might get ugly for $aapl with the iphone delay. With $aapl do'	FALSE	0	NA	01-08-2017 20:31	FALSE	NA	8.92E+17	NA <;

Figure 3.2 Dataset of the company.

feedback from the customers. Sentiment analysis is done for the dataset using the R package.

```
apple <- read.csv(file.choose(), header = T)
str(apple)
```

The dataset is read using the previous command. The STR function in R is used to show the internal structure of the object.

```
# Clean text
corpus <- tm_map(corpus, tolower)
corpus <- tm_map(corpus, removePunctuation)
inspect(corpus[1:5])
```

The tolower function is used to convert all the text in the dataset to lowercase and, removePunctuation is used to remove the punctuation marks in the dataset. So tolower and removePunctuation are used to clean the dataset and prepare it for processing. The result of these commands on the data is shown in Figure 3.3.

Functions from the tm package are used for cleaning the dataset in R.

1. Remove words
2. Stopwords
3. Remove URL
4. Cleanset
5. stripWhitespace

```
# Term document matrix
tdm <- TermDocumentMatrix(cleanset)
tdm
```

```
<<SimpleCorpus>>
Metadata:  corpus specific: 1, document level (indexed): 0
Content:  documents: 5

[1] rt options nipper aapl beat on both eps and revenues sees
    4q rev 49b52b est 491b httpstcohfhxqj0iob
[2] rt options nipper aapl beat on both eps and revenues sees
    4q rev 49b52b est 491b httpstcohfhxqj0iob
[3] lets see this break all timers aapl 15689
[4] <NA>
[5] aapl wow this was supposed to be a throwaway quarter and
    aapl beats by over 500 million in revenue trillion dollar
    company by 2018
```

Figure 3.3 Result of cleaning the dataset.

Terms	Docs																			
	1	2	3	4	5	6	7	8	9	10	11	12	13	14	15	16	17	18	19	20
beat	1	1	0	0	0	0	0	0	0	0	0	0	0	0	0	0	0	0	1	0
eps	1	1	0	0	0	0	0	1	0	0	0	0	0	1	0	0	0	0	0	0
est	1	1	0	0	0	0	0	0	0	0	0	0	0	2	0	0	0	0	0	0
options nipper	1	1	0	0	0	0	0	0	0	0	0	0	0	0	0	0	0	0	0	0
rev	1	1	0	0	0	0	0	0	0	0	0	0	1	0	0	0	0	0	0	0
revenues	1	1	0	0	0	0	0	0	0	0	0	0	0	0	0	0	0	0	0	0
sees	1	1	0	0	0	0	0	0	0	0	0	0	0	0	0	0	0	0	0	0
break	0	0	1	0	0	0	0	0	0	0	0	0	0	0	0	0	0	0	0	0
lets	0	0	1	0	0	0	0	0	0	0	0	0	0	0	0	0	0	0	0	0
see	0	0	1	0	0	0	0	0	0	0	0	0	0	0	0	0	0	0	0	0

Figure 3.4 Matrix format.

```
tdm <- as.matrix(tdm)
tdm[1:10, 1:20]
```

The raw text is converted into matrix format, as shown in Figure 3.4, using the function matrix().

This matrix represents the frequency of all words appearing in the dataset. The frequency count represents the number of times the word has been used in the dataset. The resulting matrix is shown in Figure 3.5, which shows that the word 'earnings' appeared 250 times in the dataset.

The function word cloud is used to generate a word cloud with the words present in the dataset. The required package for generating the word cloud is word cloud, and it has to be installed along with the cleaned file. The word cloud is used to analyze the data in the view. The word cloud shows the importance of the words given their frequency or the number of times they are repeated in the dataset.

The Syuzhet package is used to extract sentiments from the words used in the dataset. barplot represents the result graphically.

```
barplot(colSums(s),
las = 2,
col = rainbow(10),
ylab = 'Count',
```

Figure 3.7 shows that people have a positive attitude towards Apple.

From the figure, it is clear that the behavior of people and their sentiments are taken into account and decide the buying patterns for the item.

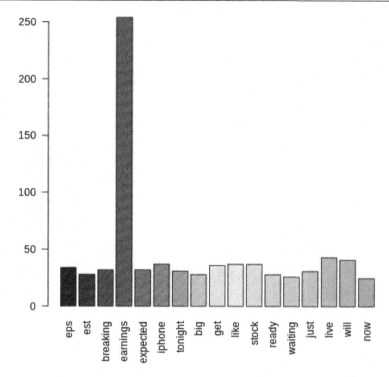

Figure 3.5 Word frequency bar chart.

Figure 3.6 Wordcloud.

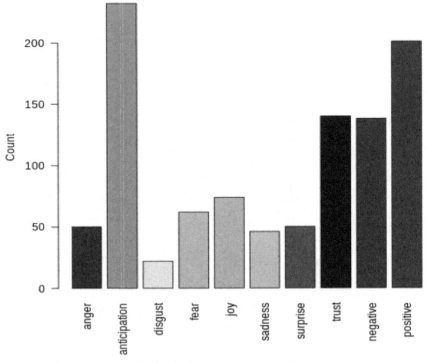

Figure 3.7 Sentiment scores for Apple Tweets.

3.4 DECISION MAKING BASED ON WEARABLE DATASETS

Today, many customers are using various wearables like smart watches and smart goggles. Smart devices used to give samples like heart rate, glucose level and regular blood pressure (BP) level. If a person wants to consume a drink, these wearable dataset values are cross-checked to see how much sugar can be added, or, if it is soup, how much salt can be added. All these decisions are purely based on the IoB [12, 16], since all the values will be tracked and regularly monitored by the cloud database. Any changes in BP levels or variations in heart rate can immediately be brought to the attention of a medical practitioner to give first aid. Mostly the IoB can be effectively used to track elderly people [17, 18]. The Internet of Behavior can be seen as a fusion of the three domains of technology, data analytics, and behavioral science, all working together. In terms of technology [19], behavioral sciences are often divided into four categories. Choice, emotions, expansion, and proficiency are all part of the game. For instance, the health app on your smart phone can facilitate monitoring your sleep rhythm, blood glucose, pulse, and more. This app can provide you with a warning about potentially dangerous health conditions and recommend behavioral changes [20, 21] that lead to positive and desirable results. In 2021, there are many IoB applications that are often personalized and applied. A variety of companies use Internet advertising to reach their customers in today's information technology era. They will use the Internet of Behavior to discover and target specific individuals or groups that may benefit from their products and services. For instance, Google and Facebook are social media sites that both use behavioral data to serve ads to users who are already using the platform and are susceptible to behavioral changes through it. This enables marketers to use 'click-through' statistics to interact with the ideal consumer and track their behavior in response to ads. YouTube uses behavioral analytics to enhance the viewer's experience by recommending or promoting only videos and topics that are relevant to the viewer, supported by the viewer's past viewing history and activity. The epidemic has raised awareness of the precautionary measures that need to be taken during this time. Employers can use sensors or radio frequency identification tags to assess whether employees are inconsistent in how they follow safety rules. In fact, restaurants and food delivery apps used their knowledge of the protocol to continue working after receiving the protocol. In a number of more imaginative use cases, a driver's temperature was tracked and showed to reassure the customer of safety [13].

3.5 THE INTERNET OF THINGS IN THE INSURANCE INDUSTRY

The majority well-known insurance companies are currently utilizing user monitoring solutions in order to investigate and collect information regarding user behavior and performance. Here, with the assistance of IoB, they will investigate behavior and most likely come to a conclusion as to whether a particular occurrence was the result of an accident or individual error. Accidents that are caused by drivers who are under the influence of alcohol or drugs, drivers who are under the effect of prescribed medication, drivers who are under the age of 18, or drivers who are retired can be avoided if this is done. I hope that the preceding example was clear enough for everyone to understand how IoB [22] would be utilized in 2023. If not, feel free to devise your own use case that addresses your specific needs.

The Internet of Thing is a network of connected devices that collects, analyses, and interprets data in order to recognize patterns in user behavior and then make use of that information to produce the required action depending on the behavior [23]. These initiatives have resulted in improved outcomes for large businesses, such as increased sales, which have been accomplished by targeting the appropriate viewers and successfully appealing to them. Because it offers customization to an unprecedented degree, this technology that will shape the future of product and service design, as well as marketing [22]. How can one bring about the appropriate feelings that will direct a person to make the decisions that they want? The solutions can be found through data mining and behavioral science [24]. The idea of the Internet of Things gave rise to the concept of the Internet of Business as a natural progression of that idea: if there is too much data, you want to know how to use it to your benefit [22]. The Internet of Things has a promising future in the longer term because people want their belongings to be 'smart'. This includes smart houses, smart cities, and eventually smart lives, in which everything in our environment is secure. You can be productive while still having plenty of time for your hobbies and creative endeavors. Although IoB is still a relatively young technology, it has already demonstrated its potential as a potent new tool for online and digitally based businesses. The practice of conducting market research and user profiling can be challenging for many businesses unless those businesses are Facebook or Google. The more gadgets that are connected to the web, the more in-depth the behavioral insights can be. And as a consequence of this, the businesses that will most likely give financial incentives to customers will open the door to their own universe, which may include their routines, lives, hobbies, and even dreams. The message may say that we will utilize this information about you to better your life in some way, such as by delivering the most relevant financial products, providing individualized health advice, helping you reach your goals, and so on. Learning how to put one's faith in other people is an extremely important skill. At the end of the day, it's supported by numbers and research, not guesswork. There is no requirement to construct the perfect user persona when utilizing IoB. The use of big data makes it possible to conduct multi-faceted analyses of potential clients. You will generate a map of your client journey that is exceedingly thorough, take an approach that is highly tailored, and increase your overall engagement score. Using this strategy will make it much simpler to sell specialized items aimed at smaller markets. Voice-enabled gadgets will become more common in people's daily lives, which will shift the focus of search engine optimization to natural language and intent-based queries. Behavioral insights will assist in optimizing the content of the website accordingly. Geographical locations, which may be retrieved through the user's smart phone, are going to be increasingly essential. Ratings of restaurants and beauty salons will also depend on the number of times a user has visited and how long they have stayed there.

3.6 DISCUSSION OF VARIOUS APPLICATIONS

IoB is mainly used to analyze human activities [25], and it is used in culture change like scanning people's accounts from social media and contacts for better forecast of behaviors regarding market products and to analyze customer habits through Google search, Facebook posts or Amazon ordering. This leads to phishing attacks by cyber criminals. Nowadays corporate firms are also implementing principles and guidelines for IoB. This project mainly focuses on enhancing skills using various apps on a smart phone and to monitor wearable devices, as well as to learn new techniques [25]. IoB is mainly used to track and archive trends that are characteristic of customers' decisions in purchasing items. In our day-to-day activities and jobs, more awareness is provided by the Internet.

It incorporates existing technology, focusing mainly on the customer/user to fetch data, such as monitoring the location where the user is, and combining the data to relate behavioral activities like money transactions or smart phone usage. The approach is straightforward for organizations to influence all of human behavior. For example, the system can check whether the workforce follows protocols by using IoB using computer vision methods. IoB links all the data related to those individual behaviors, like purchasing an item or a particular brand. In IoB, values are mainly used to create the optimal state of activities for behavioral events. IoB is mainly used to review businesses results from the past and forecast future activities. Currently it's used to track employees and to plan for various products, services, and ways to market them. A few companies choose this approach for a cyber protection policy to protect all responsive data. IoB understand and relates the data obtained by the IoT to a person's behaviors like selection of a brand. This collects data; then, though analytics, it retrieves information from the collected data. This knowledge is subsequently used to investigate and influence human behavior. Sensors are used to collect all behavioral data and suggest insight into consumers' activities, requirements, and expectations.

3.7 CHALLENGES

IoB data are vulnerable to cyber attacks; the data can easily get into attackers' hands and expose the behavior patterns of customers. In the long run, all these sensitive data can be collected and sold to other parties. It's quite dangerous to the people who are using IoT technology. IoB may create more cyber criminals to generate sophisticated scams. IoB can help cyber criminals generate scams customized to the behavior of individual users and thus increase the probability of users getting scammed. This advanced technology has certainly been quite helpful for businesses; it allows users or customers to optimize their relations with other users based on the data collected based on their lifestyle and living patterns. Finally, we can come to the conclusion that IoB is definitely a modern technique used to transform information into authentic perceptions.

3.8 CONCLUSION

Within few years, the IoB trend has changed the worldwide environment that defines a person's behavior. It's a milestone in analyzing the behavior of computers with humans. IoB mainly uses behavioral data and then evaluates its prospects. Various companies have analyzed, experienced, and applied this approach to sell goods to customers by developing techniques to produce new trends. One way it increases income is by connecting objects via the Internet. This connects various behaviors with individuals and uses behavioral psychology. This can instruct us about undesirable scenarios and offer guidelines to alter actions for scenario change. IoB collects behavioral and user information which can be obtained from smart devices and provides insights about their needs, interests, and behaviors. The Internet of Behavior provides companies with innovative strategies for promoting their products and services as well as influencing the behavior of their customers and employees. This technology is extremely beneficial to businesses because it enables them to improve the quality of their consumer connections in response to the information that is obtained.

REFERENCES

1. Li SM, Chung TM. Internet function and Internet addictive behavior. *Comput Hum Behav*. 2006 Nov 1;22(6):1067–1071.
2. Hernández B, Julio J, Martín MJ. Customer behavior in electronic commerce: The moderating effect of e-purchasing experience. *J Bus Res*. 2010;63(9–10): 964–971.
3. Andrews L, Bianchi C. Consumer Internet purchasing behavior in Chile. *J Bus Res*. 2013 Oct 1;66(10):1791–1799.
4. Wayne Buente, Alice Robbin, Trends in Internet information behavior, 2000–2004. *J Am Soc Inf Sci Technol*. 2008 Sep;59(11):1743–1760.
5. Lu, Y, Papagiannidis, S, Alamanos, E. Internet of Things: A systematic review of the business literature from the user and organisational perspectives. *Technological Forecasting and Social Change* 2018;136(C):285–297.
6. Breivold HP, Sandström K. Internet of Things for industrial automation – challenges and technical solutions. 2015 IEEE International Conference on Data Science and Data Intensive Systems, IEEE (2015 Dec 11), pp. 532–539.
7. Perera C, Zaslavsky A, Christen P, Georgakopoulos D. Context-aware computing for the Internet of Things: A survey IEEE. *Commun Surv Tutorials*. 2013 May 3;16(1):414–454.
8. Choi H, Youngchan K, Jinwoo K. Driving factors of post adoption behavior in mobile data services. *J Bus Res*. 2011;64(11):1212–1217.
9. Farrell AM. Insufficient discriminant validity: A comment on Bove, Pervan, Beatty, and Shiu (2009). *J Bus Res*. 2010;63(3):324–327.
10. Garbarino E, Michal S. Gender differences in the perceived risk of buying online and the effects of receiving a site recommendation. *J Bus Res*. 2004;57(7): 768–775.

11. McCole P, Elaine R, John W. Trust considerations on attitudes towards online purchasing: The moderating effect of privacy and security concerns. *J Bus Res*. 2010;63(9–10):1018–1024.
12. Nasco SA, Elizabeth GT, Peter PM. Predicting electronic commerce adoption in Chilean SMEs. *J Bus Res*. 2008;61(6):697–705.
13. Son M, Kyesook H. Beyond the technology adoption: Technology readiness effects on post-adoption behavior. *J Bus Res*. 2011;64(11):1178–1182.
14. Wang X, Chunling Y, Yujie W. Social media peer communication and impacts on purchase intentions: A consumer socialization framework. *J Interact Mark*. 2012;26(4):198–208.
15. Oliver RL, William OB. Crossover effects in the theory of reasoned action: A moderating influence attempt. *J Consum Res*. 1985;12(3):324–340.
16. Rohm AJ, Vanitha S. A typology of online shoppers based on shopping motivations. *J Bus Res*. 2004;57(7):748–757.
17. Davis RA. A cognitive-behavioral model of pathological Internet use. *Comput Hum Commun*. 2001;17:187–195. [Google Scholar]
18. Alavi SS, Maracy MR, Jannatifard F, Eslami M, Haghighi M. A survey relationship between psychiatric symptoms and Internet addiction disorder in students of Isfahan universities. *Sci J Hamadan Univ Medi Sci Health Serv*. 2010;17:57–65. [Google Scholar]
19. Chebb PI, Koong KS, Liu L, Prasanna C, et al. Some observations on Internet addiction disorder research. *J Info Syst Educ*. 2000;11:97–104. [Google Scholar]
20. Young KS, Rogers RC. The relationship between depression and Internet addiction. *Cyberpsychol Behav*. 1998;1:25–28. [Google Scholar]
21. Noble EP, Zhang X, Ritchie T, Lawford BR, Grosser SC, Young RM, et al. D2dopamine receptor and GABA-A receptor beta3 subunit genes and alcoholism. *Psychiatr Res*. 1998;81:133–147. [PubMed] [Google Scholar]
22. Kulviwat S, Gordon CB, Obaid A-S. The role of social influence on adoption of high tech innovations: The moderating effect of public/private consumption. *J Bus Res*. 2009;62(7):706–712.
23. Holden C. "Behavioral" addictions: Do they exist? *Science*. 2001;294:980–982. [PubMed] [Google Scholar]
24. Potenza MN. Should addictive disorders include non-substance-related conditions? *Addiction*. 2006;101:142–151. [PubMed] [Google Scholar]
25. Mohd Javaid, Abid Haleem, Ravi Pratap Singh, Shanay Rab, Rajiv Suman Internet of Behaviors (IoB) and its role in customer services. https://doi.org/10.1016/j.sintl.2021.100122.

Websites

1. www.analyticssteps.com/blogs/introduction-Internet-behaviour-iob
2. www.financialexpress.com/industry/technology/Internet-of-behaviours-more-power-to-digital-marketing/2371247/
3. www.techfunnel.com/information-technology/Internet-of-behaviors/
4. www.vectoritcgroup.com/en/tech-magazine-en/user-experience-En/what-is-the-Internet-of-behaviour-iob-and-why-is-it-the-future/

Chapter 4

Analytical Study on Consumer Social and Behavioral Psychology and Its Influence on Online Purchasing

Parth Rainchwar, Rishikesh Mate, Soham Wattamwar, Aditya Gaisamudre, Pratyush Jha, and Shilpa Sonawani

CONTENTS

4.1 INTRODUCTION

Digital markets, easily accessible Internet, and the increase in purchasing power of the consumer have changed the way consumer purchasing works. With the spontaneous rise in the Internet and rapid increase in accessibility of the Internet, common consumer utilization of the Internet and gaining knowledge from the Internet have become cheap. With the rise of Web 2.0 [1] and online purchasing platforms [2], it has become very easy to buy and sell products. The research done by [3] identifies that nationality, education, family upbringing, and lifestyle have a significant impact on online purchases and online purchasing behavior. With the ability to access and use the Internet, Internet addiction has become a problem. The authors in [4] give a brief discussion on addictive behavior related to the Internet. A detailed survey was taken of students regarding addictive Internet behavior with an average age of participants of 19 years and 71% male participants, who tend to have Internet consumption of an average of 3.3 hours in a single day. After analysis, the results showed that social interaction was the key factor of internet addiction, which leads to the most severe internet addictions. Those who use the internet for information-gathering purposes tend to face interpersonal and health problems. From the study, it became clear that social media–based utilization of the Internet is critical and has the potential to lead an individual to Internet addiction. With potential Internet addiction, a detailed study to understand the reason for Internet addiction and how consumers find comfort on the Internet begin. The authors [5] did a study finding that entertainment, sociality, information, and trust positively influence the attitude of a consumer to perform online interactions. Freely available Internet is not a curse at all; it has also opened a lot of opportunities. In [6], the authors did a detailed study of Internet information behavior from 2000 to 2004. The research revealed that the internet has the potential to reinforce disparities between those who use information effectively and those who are under-informed and make less effective use of information in their daily lives, which, in turn, could influence how the Internet is situated in everyday life. Looking at the positive side of the Internet-based market, social media and freely available knowledge can provide equal opportunity to all. Currently the online purchasing market is the most quickly growing field of investment. E-commerce is the new normal. Every vendor with a physical shop is able to establish itself as an individual on those platforms. Platforms such as Amazon, Flipkart, Myntra, and multiple region specific e-commerce platforms have given local vendors the confidence to display their products to the global market. With this, Internet of Behavior (IoB) has emerged as a field of study and research to understand the evolution of consumer purchasing trends and habits. Internet of Behavior is a combination of the Internet of Things, edge analytics, and behavioral science. IoB systems are made to collect, combine, and analyze data created from many different sources, such as wearables, computers, home digital devices, and people's online activities. The information is then examined through the lens of behavioral psychology to look for trends that marketing and sales teams might use to shape future consumer behavior. From the perspective of human psychology, Internet of Behavior aims to discuss how data is better understood and used to develop and market new products. Public or private organizations can use IoB in a variety of ways. For businesses and organizations around the world, this technology will develop into a fascinating new marketing and distribution platform. The IoB platform enables the deep client awareness that any business needs. The authors in [7] have talked about the role of Internet of Behavior in customer service. The authors states that the ultimate objective of Internet of Behavior is to improve the reliability and consistency of the consumer based upon the knowledge gained from customer data. Analysis is a major aspect of product development, and Internet of Behavior plays a critical role in shaping products based on consumer psychology. IoB seeks to explain the data obtained from a behavioral, psychological standpoint from people's web interactions. It addresses how data is understood and used in developing and marketing new goods from human psychology. IoB can affect customer choice, and it also restructures the supply chain with a goal to provide a clean and streamlined solution. With the help of machine learning technology, prediction and classification have become easy to use and implement in day-to-day life problems. Consumer data is a rich source for prediction and analysis. While giving a clear understanding of the impact the Internet has in our day-to-day lives, we present a detailed analytical study on the Internet and its consumption and online purchasing and its relationship with behavior and decision-making psychology.

4.2 LITERATURE REVIEW

The technology research company Gartner is credited with coining the term "IoB," which is defined in Gartner's "Top Strategic Technology Trends for 2021." Göte Nyman, a psychology professor at the University of Helsinki, is credited by Gartner with developing the idea of leveraging IoT data to affect behavior [8]. Internet of Behavior has risen to a totally different level; with extensive customer data and spontaneous demand for products, IoB acts as a backbone for recommendations systems [9], analytics, and decision making. Based upon the research done by [10], the Internet of Behavior has the potential to become a powerful new marketing and sales tool. Companies are able to examine previous performance and forecast the future using the IoB concept. Companies can organize their development, marketing, and sales operations using data obtained through the IoT. Companies can utilize IoB to cater to their customers' demands by using data, information, and behavior patterns. Data may come from various places, including our social media activity, smart phone geolocation data, credit card purchases, and even food preferences. The IoB will gather more information about consumers' behavioral patterns and choices when more can be obtained from our everyday actions, as stated by [11]. With the interpretation of data, interested parties can potentially obtain far more detailed insight into people's behavior than was previously possible, allowing them to utilize it for several purposes such as recommending products, maintaining demand and supply patterns, and identifying consumer sentiment, and they can use those parameters in development of new products in the market. Many companies use data collected by their systems for tracking consumer health as well. Organizations have created health apps for cell phones that track food habits, sleep habits, heart rate, and blood sugar levels in the medical field. The software may detect problems with the user's health and recommend behavioral changes that would lead to a better outcome [12]. With these types of advances provided by the Internet of Behavior, psychological study has also been raised to a completely new level, with studies revolving around the topics of decision-making psychology [13], behavior psychology [14], social psychology [15], and organizational psychology [16]. Internet-based psychological studies have taken place, and new findings and observations are consistently made regarding socio-Internet psychology [17]. Excessive use of the Internet has led to addiction and fear of missing out [18]. With social media platforms becoming a new individual identity platform [19], it has become critical for an individual to be perfect, or at least portray themselves as perfect [20]. This type of comparison-based living has made people act the way others want them to be in society. Clothing and confidence are some the first things to be looked at by a person while interacting [21], and social media platforms have some of the most rapid interaction for an individual. With such a psychologically observant world, it becomes very important to understand modern trends based upon the psychology that can suit someone. Likes, dislikes, choices, and quick decisions are huge pillars in identifying what a consumer wants, and this is what Internet of Behavior is successfully able to identify, which has given it stupendous growth.

4.3 SURVEY

A detailed study was performed in the field of decision making, behavioral psychology, and internet-based purchasing. The research was performed in India from January 2021 to March 2022. With around 1500 responses received, a total of 1438 filtered responses were taken for study. Based upon unverified and invalid responses, around 62 responses were discarded and hence 1438 verified responses were taken into consideration. The responders belonged to various age groups, and the majority of them were adults (ages 18 to 25). Table 4.1 is a representation of responders from various age groups.

A total of three classes were created to classify age: responders under 18 were considered teens, responders 18 to 25 were classified as adults, and responders above age 25 were considered mature. Around 65% of responders belonged to the adult group, 23.03% to the mature age group, and 11.97% to the teen age group.

A total of 30 questions were asked to 1438 responders. Table 4.2 shows some of the selective questions asked and the responses received to them.

Table 4.1 Age and Gender-Based Respondent Classification

Age Group	Gender	Percentage (%)	Summed Total (%)
Teen	Male	6.12%	11.97%
	Female	5.85%	
Adult	Male	32.99%	65%
	Female	32.01%	
Mature	Male	12.60%	23.03%
	Female	10.44%	
Grand Total		100%	100%

Table 4.2 Detailed Responses and Results

Question	Choices	Total (In%)
Are you present on Instagram?	Yes	75.50%
	No	24.50%
Are you present on Facebook?	Yes	51.01%
	No	48.99%
Are you present on Snapchat?	Yes	67.50%
	No	32.50%
Are you present on LinkedIn?	Yes	65.97%
	No	34.03%
How much time do you spend on social media platforms in a day?	Less than 1 hour	30.34%
	1 to 2 hours	29.37%
	More than 2 hours	40.29%
Are you an introvert or an extrovert?	Introvert	42.17%
	Extrovert	39.46%
	Prefer not to say	18,37%
Does social media have an influence in your personal life?	Yes	41.61%
	No	37.72%
	Maybe	20.67%
How are you in nature?	Angry	20.53%
	Balanced	21.02%
	Calm	19.90%
	Emotional	18.72%
	Submissive	19.83%
Do you prefer to listen to music while doing important work?	Yes	38.97%
	No	32.85%
	Maybe	28.18%

(*Continued*)

Table 4.2 (Continued)

Question	Choices	Total (In%)
Do you prefer to stay in or go out?	Stay in	46.90%
	Go out	53.10%
Are you a foodie by nature?	Yes	57.06%
	No	42.94%
Are you concerned about your looks?	Yes	35.42%
	No	34.03%
	Not sure	30.55%
Are you health conscious?	Yes	55.39%
	No	44.61%
Do you prefer to read books or go to a club?	Read books	27.95%
	Visit a Club	72.05%
Do you purchase products online?	Yes	99.16%
	No	0.84%
Do you purchase clothes online?	Yes	46.83%
	No	53.17%
Do you purchase electronics online?	Yes	50.87%
	No	49.13%
Do you purchase home appliances online?	Yes	47.32%
	No	52.68%
Do you purchase groceries online?	Yes	47.74%
	No	52.26%
Your general online purchasing budget?	No online purchases	0.84%
	Less than INR 1000	17.54%
	INR 1000–INR 4000	2.23%
	INR 4000 and above	79.40%

Based upon the responses gathered, it became clear that there is a relationship between psychological behavior, social media, and online product consumption.

4.4 RESULTS AND ANALYSIS

The analysis was done with the help of Apriori Algorithm [22] for identifying associated pairs and heatmap [23] for getting a clear understanding of possible relationships. Tableau [24], Power BI [25], and Excel [26] were used to plot the insight and relationship tables.

4.4.1 Social Media and Its Influence

Social media is a critical tool that has a huge impact on decision making, and it is clear that social media has a strong influence on behavioral psychology. It becomes very important to understand the importance of those platforms and where crowd deviation exists.

Figure 4.1 clearly gives a strong idea about social media and its interaction rate in different age groups. The result clearly shows that Instagram has the highest interaction rate in all age groups, with an average of around 75%, whereas Facebook has the lowest interaction rate in comparison. On average, 75% of responders claim to be active on Instagram, whereas around 50% of people are on Facebook, and Snapchat and LinkedIn have comparatively more active users than Facebook.

4.4.2 Online Purchasing Trends by Month

Table 4.3 shows the relationship between purchasing products online to the month of the year. From the table, it is very clear that, based upon the season, online purchasing increases, and the month of November has 13.64% of online orders, which is the maximum for the year. The most often stated reason for orders in the month of November is related to the holidays occurring in that specific month. Money-saving offers, free deals and easy equated monthly installment (EMI) options are provided to consumers based upon the holiday season [27] to increase sales. With appreciable and affordable deals placed in front of consumers, they end up purchasing products.

4.4.3 Relationship of Age Group to the Trait of Being a Foodie and Being Concerned With Health

The following analysis shows the relationship between a person being a foodie and its impact on health consciousness. In the pie charts, the light shade indicates the person being health conscious, and the dark shade indicates the person not being health conscious.

The Figure 4.2 pie chart gives the insight that 64.89% of mature people who are foodies tend to be health conscious, whereas 56.64% of mature people who are not foodies tend to be health conscious.

The Figure 4.3 pie chart gives the insight that 53.40% of adult people who are foodies tend to be health conscious, whereas 54.43% of adult people who are not foodies tend to be health conscious.

The Figure 4.4 pie chart gives the insight that 53.84% of teens who are foodies tend to be health conscious, whereas 50.00% of teens who are not foodies tend to be health conscious.

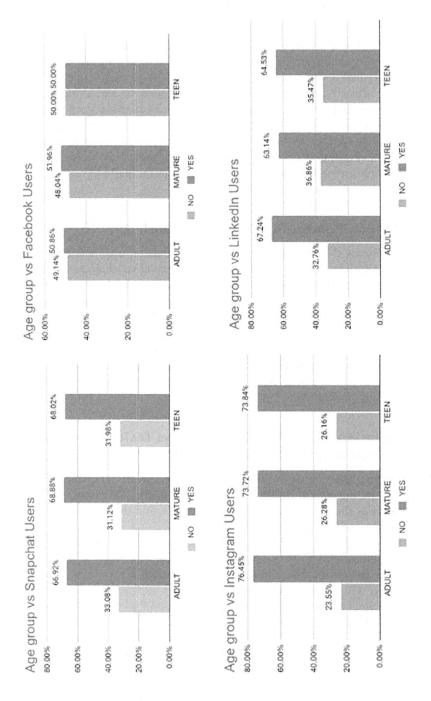

Figure 4.1 Social media interaction in different age groups.

Table 4.3 Monthly Online Purchasing Chart

Month	Orders (%)
January	6.26%
February	6.61%
March	5.64%
April	7.17%
May	6.12%
June	7.59%
July	11.69%
August	6.47%
September	9.67%
October	7.79%
November	13.64%
December	10.51%
Grand Total	100%

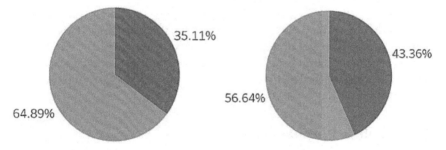

Figure 4.2 Relationship of a person being mature (above the age of 25) to the trait of the person being a foodie and being health conscious. Left: Person is a foodie and health conscious. Right: Person is not a foodie and health conscious.

Figure 4.3 Relationship of a person being adult (aged between 18 and 25) to the trait of the person being a foodie and being health conscious. Left: Person is a foodie and health conscious. Right: Person is not a foodie and health conscious.

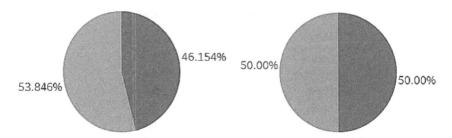

Figure 4.4 Relationship of a person being a teen (aged below 18) to the trait of the person being a foodie and being health conscious. Left: Person is a foodie and health conscious. Right: Person is not a foodie and health conscious.

From this result, we get a clear idea that with respect to age, there is a certain relationship with being health conscious. A person above the age of 25 is more conscious about their health in comparison to a person below the age of 25. There is a slightly lower-confidence relationship between a person being a foodie and being health conscious, but a person who tends not to be a foodie is also less health conscious. This trait of being a foodie impacts online food ordering patterns, and it has a close relationship with being health conscious; hence online food ordering and health tracking platforms tend to be useful for analyzing online purchasing patterns.

4.4.4 Online Purchasing Budget

Figure 4.5 represents the relationship between online purchasing budget and frequency of online purchasing. Around 78.28% of responders claimed to have spent more than 4000 INR while purchasing online, 19.15% stated they spent less than 1000 INR on online purchasing, and only 1.54% stated they spent in the range of 1000 to 4000 INR on online purchases. From this it is clear to see that online ordering reliability has increased a lot and there is scope for consumers to spend a higher amount of money for a certain products they want.

4.4.5 Relationship of Time Spent on Social Media and Its Influence

Figure 4.6 shows that based upon the time spent on social media, it is clear that social media can influence a person. Around 45.08% of people who claim to spend more than 2 hours per day on social media have accepted being influenced by social media.

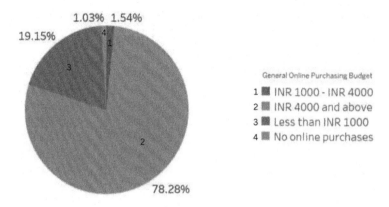

Figure 4.5 General online purchasing budget.

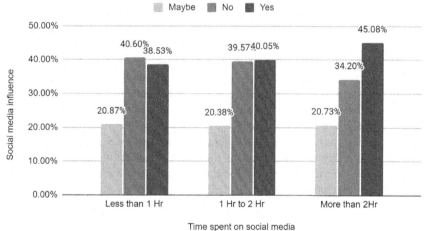

Figure 4.6 Relationship of time spent on social media and possibility of its influence on an individual.

4.4.6 Online Ordering Patterns by Age Group and Gender

Table 4.4 shows the total orders in a year with respect to the count of orders done by age group. From this, we can see that people from the adult age group tend to order more as compared to teens and mature people. A total of 72.36% of orders were placed by adults.

Table 4.4 Frequency of Online Ordering Based Upon Gender and Age Group

Age Group	Gender	Online Orders in a Year	Total (%)
Teen	Male	149	0.83%
	Female	239	1.33%
Adult	Male	6,782	37.62%
	Female	6,264	34.74%
Mature	Male	2,632	14.60%
	Female	1,964	10.89%
Grand Total		18,030	100%

Figure 4.7 shows how the frequency of online purchase changes from the previous graph with respect to age group. We learn that at 16 years and above, online purchases begin, but a sharp decline can be observed after the age of 25. People 20 to 24 place the most orders, 9.116% in comparison to all age groups. From this, a clear conclusion can be drawn that there is a sharp relationship between the age group and online ordering [28]. The most obvious reason for a relationship like this comes from the point that the age group from 16 to 25 represents people who began to access the Internet from an early age, and with early availability of the Internet, their confidence in using the Internet became higher than that of older people. With the potential to start earning, which in general begins from the age of 21 for a well-educated person, online purchasing power increased for individuals like this, which eventually gave them authority to purchase online products. Compared to an older person, later interaction with the Internet gave them fewer opportunities to explore it as fully as the age group of 15 to 25; due to this, those 25 and above, even with a stable income and better purchasing power, ended up with fewer online transactions and purchases.

4.4.7 Online Purchasing Genre and Gender and Age-Based Classification

When asked about electronics purchases with respect to age group and gender, the observation was clearly made that males from all age groups tend to purchase electronics more frequently compared to females. Figure 4.8 shows the online ordering pattern for electronic products with respect to age group and gender.

Figure 4.9 shows the online ordering pattern for grocery products with respect to age group and gender. When asked for grocery purchases with

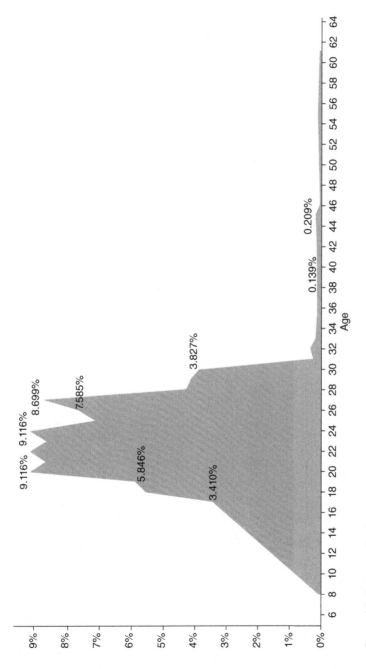

Figure 4.7 Online order frequency with respect to age.

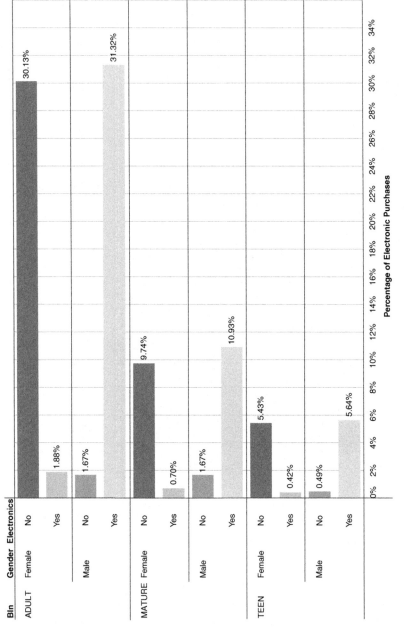

Figure 4.8 Online ordering pattern for electronic products with respect to age group and gender.

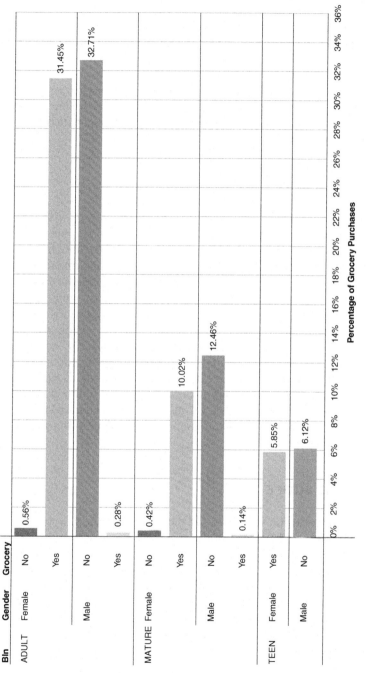

Figure 4.9 Online ordering pattern for grocery products with respect to age group and gender.

respect to age group and gender, females tend to purchase groceries more frequently compared to males.

Figure 4.10 illustrates the online ordering pattern for clothing products with respect to age group and gender. When asked for clothes purchases with respect to age group and gender, females tend to purchase clothes more frequently compared to males.

When asked for home appliance purchases with respect to age group and gender, females tend to purchase home appliances more frequently as compared to males. Figure 4.11 shows the online ordering pattern for home appliances with respect to age group and gender.

4.5 CONCLUSION

From the detailed study and analysis, it becomes very clear that there is a strong relationship between age group, use of the Internet, and confidence in using the Internet to make a consumer active enough to perform an online purchase. Seasons and holidays have a strong impact on online purchases based upon offers, discounts, and deals provided. People tend to purchase products online, they are confident and trust online purchases, and they are ready to spend a healthy amount on them. As the market becomes more expansive, opportunities are increasing for vendors and consumers. New adult consumers are the biggest source of income in the online market. Adults tend to make the most frequent purchases. Social media and judgmental psychology have a strong hold on decision making, and based upon looks and social media impressions, online purchases are actively being performed. Males are more dominant purchasers of electronic goods compared to females being more dominant purchasers of groceries and clothes.

4.6 FUTURE SCOPE

This entire study revolves around the data and consumer experience gathered in the last year. With changing times, there is a possibility there will be a change and a new way to look at online product consumption. With the current advancements and deep learning approaches, a more enhanced and insightful study can be performed. With help of natural language processing technology, an inference generation system can be created to analyze and provide a better representation than the current scenario in the field of online product consumption. We aim at working more effectively in this field and covering more aspects in coming studies.

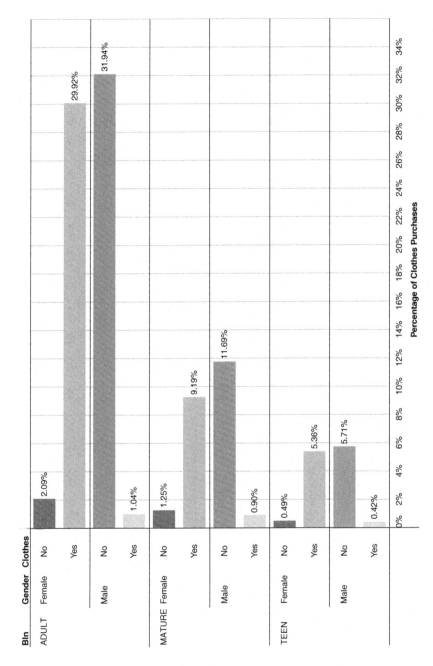

Figure 4.10 Online ordering pattern for clothing products with respect to age group and gender.

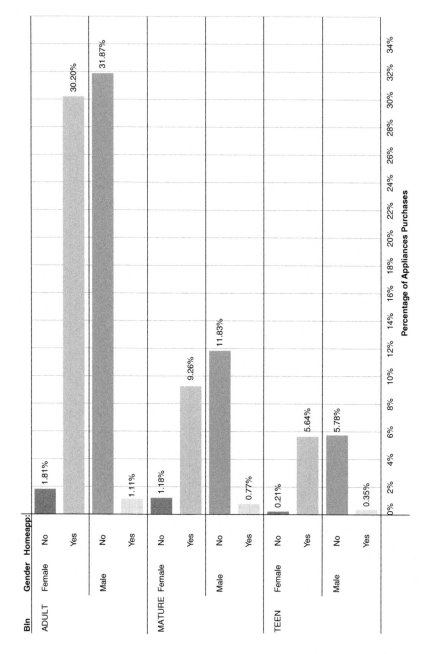

Figure 4.11 Online ordering pattern for home appliances with respect to age group and gender.

REFERENCES

1. Wilson, David W., Lin, Xiaolin, Longstreet, Phil, & Sarker, Saonee. (2011). Web 2.0: A definition, literature review, and directions for future research. *AMCIS 2011 Proceedings – All Submissions, 368.*
2. Yan, Hou, Chen, Huafei, & Yang, Shuling. (2016). Research on the business model of e-commerce platform based on value co-creation theory. *International Journal of u- and e-Service, Science and Technology,* 9.415–424. doi:10.14257/ijunesst.2016.9.3.39.
3. Peña-García, N., Gil-Saura, I., Rodríguez-Orejuela, A., & Siqueira-Junior, J. R. (2020). Purchase intention and purchase behavior online: A cross-cultural approach. *Heliyon,* 6.6: e04284. doi:10.1016/j.heliyon.2020.e04284
4. Li, S.-M., & Chung, T.-M. (2006). Internet function and Internet addictive behavior. *Computers in Human Behavior,* 22.6: 1067–1071. doi:10.1016/j.chb.2004.03.030.
5. Lien, C. H., & Cao, Y. (2014). Examining WeChat users' motivations, trust, attitudes, and positive word-of-mouth: Evidence from China. *Computers in Human Behavior,* 41: 104–111. doi:10.1016/j.chb.2014.08.013.
6. Buente, W., & Robbin, A. (2008). Trends in Internet information behavior, 2000–2004. *Journal of the American Society for Information Science and Technology,* 59.11: 1743–1760. doi:10.1002/asi.20883
7. Javaid, M., Haleem, A., Singh, R. P., Rab, S., & Suman, R. (2021). Internet of Behaviours (IoB) and its role in customer services. *Sensors International,* 2: 100122. doi:10.1016/j.sintl.2021.100122.
8. https://emtemp.gcom.cloud/ngw/globalassets/en/information-technology/documents/insights/top-tech-trends-ebook-2021.pdf, 2021.
9. Isinkaye, Folasade Olubusola, Folajimi, Yetunde O., & Ojokoh, Bolande Adefowoke. (2015). Recommendation systems: Principles, methods and evaluation. *Egyptian Informatics Journal,* 16.3: 261–273.
10. Turan, Aykut Hamit. (2012). Internet shopping behavior of Turkish customers: Comparison of two competing models. *Journal of Theoretical and Applied Electronic Commerce Research,* 7.1: 77–93.
11. Ali, Azmat, Ul Haq, Junaid, Hussain, Sajjad, Qadir, Alia, & Arsalan Haider Bukhari, Syed. (2022). OCEAN traits: Who shares more word of mouth? *Journal of Promotion Management,* 28.6: 749–773.
12. Haleem, A., Javaid, M., Singh, R. P., & Suman, R. (2021). Telemedicine for healthcare: Capabilities, features, barriers, and applications. *Sense International,* 2: 100117. doi:10.1016/j.sintl.2021.100117. Epub 2021 Jul 24. PMID: 34806053; PMCID: PMC8590973.
13. Edwards, W. (1954). The theory of decision making. *Psychological Bulletin,* 51.4: 380–417. https://doi.org/10.1037/h0053870.
14. Rachlin, Howard, Battalio, Ray, Kagel, John, & Green, Leonard. (1981). Maximization theory in behavioral psychology. *Behavioral and Brain Sciences.* 4: 371–388. doi:10.1017/S0140525X00009407.
15. Ajzen, I. (1996). The social psychology of decision making. In E. T. Higgins & A. W. Kruglanski (Eds.), *Social Psychology: Handbook of Basic Principles* (pp. 297–325). The Guilford Press.

16. Triandis, H. C. (1994). Cross-cultural industrial and organizational psychology. In H. C. Triandis, M. D. Dunnette, & L. M. Hough (Eds.), *Handbook of Industrial and Organizational Psychology* (pp. 103–172). Consulting Psychologists Press.
17. Dhir, Amandeep, et al. (2018). Online social media fatigue and psychological wellbeing – A study of compulsive use, fear of missing out, fatigue, anxiety and depression. *International Journal of Information Management*, 40: 141–152.
18. Reer, Felix, Tang, Wai Yen, & Quandt, Thorsten. (2019). Psychosocial well-being and social media engagement: The mediating roles of social comparison orientation and fear of missing out. *New Media & Society*, 21.7: 1486–1505.
19. Swar, Bobby, & Hameed, Tahir. (2017). Fear of missing out, social media engagement, smartphone addiction and distraction: Moderating role of self-help mobile apps-based interventions in the youth. *International Conference on Health Informatics*, 6. SCITEPRESS.
20. Bloemen, Noor, & De Coninck, David. (2020). Social media and fear of missing out in adolescents: The role of family characteristics. *Social Media + Society*, October. doi:10.1177/2056305120965517.
21. Nadeem, Waqar, Andreini, Daniela, Salo, Jari, & Laukkanen, Tommi. (2015). Engaging consumers online through websites and social media: A gender study of Italian Generation Y clothing consumers. *International Journal of Information Management*, Elsevier, 35.4: 432–442.
22. Al-Maolegi, Mohammed, & Arkok, Bassam. (2014). An improved apriori algorithm for association rules. *International Journal on Natural Language Computing*, 3. doi:10.5121/ijnlc.2014.3103.
23. Wilkinson, Leland, & Friendly, Michael. (2009). The history of the cluster heat map. *The American Statistician*, 63: 179–184. doi:10.1198/tas.2009.0033.
24. D'Agostino, Marcello, et al., eds. (2013). *Handbook of Tableau Methods.* Springer Science & Business Media.
25. Ferrari, Alberto, & Russo, Marco. (2016). *Introducing Microsoft Power BI.* Microsoft Press.
26. McCullough, B. D., & Wilson, B. (2002). On the accuracy of statistical procedures in Microsoft excel 2000 and excel XP. *Computational Statistics & Data Analysis*, 40.4: 713–721.
27. Shailashree, V. and Aithal, P. S. and Shenoy, Surekha. (December 22, 2018). A study on online consumer buying behavior during festive seasons in India. In *Proceedings of National Conference on Advances in Information Technology, Management, Social Sciences and Education* (pp. 188–195). ISBN No.: 978-81-938040-8-7.
28. Wan, Yun, Nakayama, Makoto, & Sutcliffe, Norma. (2012). The impact of age and shopping experiences on the classification of search, experience, and credence goods in online shopping. *Information Systems E-Business Management.* 10: 135–148. doi:10.1007/s10257-010-0156-y.

Chapter 5

Role of Internet of Behavior in Shaping Customer Service

Jaspreet Kaur and Harpreet Singh

CONTENTS

5.1 INTRODUCTION

Several decades into the Information Age, technology is having a greater impact on how people behave than ever before. Governments, corporations, and businesses have exploited the technologies available in each century to monitor, manage, and shape people's behavior for their own gain (Elayan et al., 2021). In this modern world, huge amounts of data are being created every day. More than 90% of data have been created in just the last 2–3 years.[1] According to Statista, global data generation, capture, copying, and consumption increased by a staggering 5000 % between 2010 and 2020. From 2021 to 2024, growth will continue at a compounded annual growth rate (CAGR) of 26%. There are currently over 4.66 billion Internet users globally, who will collectively log onto the Internet for more than "1.3 billion years of human time in 2021." Imagine how much data the Internet will produce in the next ten years at this incremental speed. In fact, data today are considered a treasure by companies. Analysis of this huge amount of data, also known as "Big Data," gives an opportunity to create personalized experiences as well as to generate high-impact solutions for both consumers and organizations. Personalization is therefore a key to achieving excellence in services and to driving sustainable growth of organizations in the future.[2] Internet of Behavior (IoB) is one of the latest concepts and organizes and analyzes data to create personalize experiences.

Internet of Behavior is an extension of Internet of Things (IoT), an interconnected network of physical objects that collect and exchange data and information online. IoT, therefore, relies on data, information, and the interconnectedness of many devices. More than 10 billion IoT devices are active now, and the number is predicted to be triple by 2025.[3] The number of networked devices is growing exponentially (Figure 5.1). According to McKinsey[4] and IBM,[5] there will be around ten IoT (intelligent) devices per person by 2030.[6] According to IDC, the number of Internet of Things devices, estimated to create over 90 zettabytes of data by 2025, will result in an average connected individual having one digital data encounter every 18 seconds. These data interactions influence our daily activities, including how we work, learn, shop, and take care of our health and wellbeing.[7]

With availability of mammoth amounts of data about user interactions, IoT expands to become the Internet of Behavior at this point. Companies can readily understand their consumers' behavior if they have fast access to consumer data and the capacity to derive useful insights. This implies that they would find it simple to understand their preferences, routines, habits, requirements, goals, and more. These insights are essential for creating and providing clients with customized experiences.[8]

Similar to IoT, IoB also uses the same parameters, but in conjunction with user behaviors, and analyzes patterns and perceptions that shape the user experience. To understand the interaction, IoB connects technology and human behavior. Additionally, it has the capacity to create patterns that can be used to influence people's behavior. The market for Internet of Behavior is anticipated to expand at a CAGR of roughly 22% from 2021 to 2031. The Internet of Behavior is a theory that makes use of the Internet of Things and technology to study and affect people's attitudes about goods and services. Businesses can make use of cutting-edge techniques for marketing goods

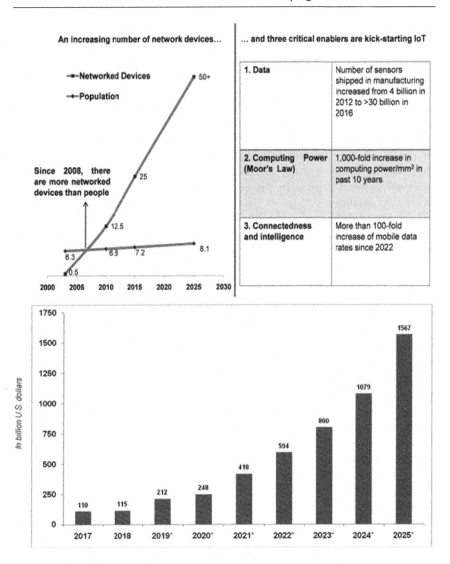

Figure 5.1 Overview of the growth of networked devices (in billions) and the three critical factors affecting the growth of IoT.

and services as well as influencing consumer and employee behavior thanks to the Internet of Behavior. In other words, it is a notion of new technology based on psychology's data mining of user online activity. Due to the ability to optimize consumer connections based on collected data, this technology is very beneficial to businesses.

5.2 INSIGHT INTO THE INTERNET OF BEHAVIOR

Göte Nyman, a psychology professor, was the first to introduce the idea of the Internet of Behavior. He stated in 2012 that there will be a chance to enhance profit from the knowledge discovered by evaluating the history of patterns in many business, societal, health, political, and other domains if the human behavioral pattern is assigned to devices (such as IoT devices) with unique addresses. The ability to collaborate or work with others can be predicted by a person's behavior, which is a psychological trait. Despite the other traits of cognition, emotion, personality, and intercommunication, behavior is what causes the propensity to act and depends heavily on the other four qualities.

Internet of Behavior is the interconnection of devices with web access to analyze the behavior of customers to help marketers and corporations manufacture and market products and services per the behavior portrayed by devices. Internet of Behavior is a development over the Internet of Things. Internet of Things is simply the interconnection of things with Internet access like mobile phones, laptops, desktops, and so on, and the information derived from this interconnection is used for certain purposes for which the connection has been established. For example, cameras have been established at various places like schools, colleges, roads, and so on. If there is a rush on a particular road, the Internet of Things will update the traffic police, and they will manage the traffic. Similarly, the Internet of Behavior is the application of this principle in marketing by corporate houses to manage their entire supply chain. The basic aim of this interconnection of devices and retrieval of information by marketers is to provide better products and services per the needs and desires of consumers and increase customer dependability, experience, loyalty, and gratification.

Before establishing interconnection, it is required to visualize the search patterns of consumers as well as contact points of consumers: websites, apps, portals, and so on. This technology is in development, and with it, marketers will be able to understand consumer needs and will try to meet their needs. Internet of Behavior analyzes the big data, that is, data that is very large, somewhat standardized, somewhat unstandardized, and very difficult to manage and handle. But with its aid, one can understand the behavioral and psychological aspects of consumers. Then this data is used for adding new features to products and services, and likewise, consumer needs revealed by the Internet of Behavior are also considered in the marketing of goods and services.

Businesses sell items using the Internet of Things, and these items access the behavioral data of consumers. Businesses also collect information from consumers as feedback. With these two techniques, marketers get information about consumers. For example, smart phones can also be used to trace the activities of various people on a real-time basis.

One can also link camcorders, conversational digital assistants, artificial intelligence assistants, and advanced data cleaners with desktops, LEDs, and smart phones to record and understand people's behavior. The author also analyzes facial expressions as well as tracking consumer visits at various places to understand their behavior (Javaid et al., 2021) [18]. In a nutshell, IoB can be considered an interaction between IoT, big data, artificial intelligence and behavioral sciences, and it is described in Figure 5.2.

IoB mainly uses devices to gather enormous amounts of information about how people behave and transform it into insightful knowledge. The knowledge can be used to modify interests, preferences, and behavior of users to bring improvements in user experience as well as search experience. As shown in the IoB pyramid in Figure 5.3, data and information represent the IoT, while the knowledge derived and its application in influencing the behavior of a person represent the IoB component.

It will be simpler, quicker, and more efficient to track behavioral data in the IoB process as a result of the growing number of IoT devices that are gathering enormous volumes of data (Elayan et al., 2021) [12]. IoB makes an effort to properly comprehend data and apply this understanding to develop new goods, market existing ones, remodel the value chain, boost revenue, or cut expenses from a psychological standpoint. Therefore, tracking user behavior from connected devices becomes the foremost step in an IoB workflow. A typical IoB workflow is shown in Figure 5.4.

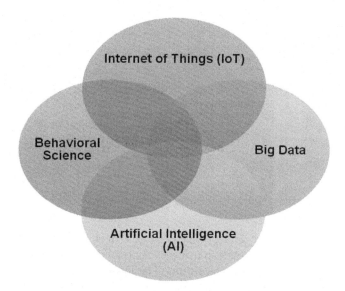

Figure 5.2 Various components of Internet of Behavior.

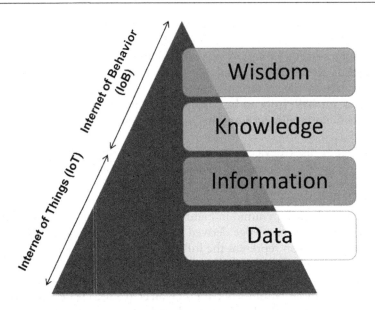

Figure 5.3 The IoB Pyramid.

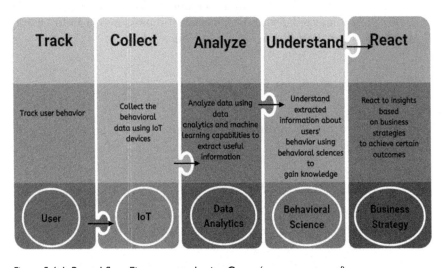

Figure 5.4 IoB workflow. Figure created using Canva (www.canva.com/).

The huge amount of data produced by IoT devices will be tracked and gathered, followed by its analysis using a variety of data analytics approaches and machine learning (ML) algorithms. The information obtained from the analysis stage will be helpful, but it must be properly comprehended from the standpoint of behavioral science. In the final stage, the acquired knowledge will be utilized to achieve specific goals, for example, to create appropriate business strategies to influence consumer behavior, to learn and respond to actual needs of patients, to develop more effective security solutions, to manage connected vehicles, to analyze personal energy consumption in smart cities and many more interesting applications.

5.3 PERSONALIZATION OF PRODUCTS AND SERVICES AND THE ROLE OF THE INTERNET OF BEHAVIOR IN SHAPING CONSUMER SERVICES

Customization of products and services is referred to as the design and manufacture of offerings by marketers per the needs, demands, and desires of individual consumers. Customization is also referred to as PSS: product-service system. It is a system of concrete products and imperceptible services that satisfy particular consumer needs and wants. This will ultimately result in increased customer contentedness, contentment, delectation, and delight. Customization and personalization are at the center of customer service. Mass customization at long last is taking shape.

Marketers, corporate houses, and service providers can reveal the needs, desires, and wants of consumers as well as satisfying their demands by customizing production procedures and resources. This ability has been provided to marketers by digital devices and social networks because consumers reveal their desires online on social sites. In short, they are asking marketers to provide them customized goods and services, and this also provides an opportunity to marketers to manufacture goods and services per the needs and wants of consumers. Furthermore, customers are prepared to pay a higher price for goods and services that are tailored to them.

Marketers who do not customize their goods and services bear the risk of loss of income as well as client dependability, reliability, and determination, and they will vanish over a period of time.

In the olden days, goods and services were customized per the needs and desires of the customers because the population was significantly lower, and there were no machines or automation. Everything was done by hand and with the aid of hand-made pieces of equipment to simplify the task. But with the change of era to industrialization, the concept of customization vanished, and the concept of mass production set in. In this era of mass production, both consumers and marketers have benefitted because, due to mass production, the cost per unit of output has decreased and there has been a large number of sellers selling goods with minute differences, so customers have been ensured a wide variety of goods with minimal prices due to competition among marketers.

But after 1980, the gap between the haves and have nots has increased. Wealthy people have been demanding customized products and services due to their status, to feel unique and to differentiate themselves from the throng. Exclusiveness used to be extremely costly. But due to the advancement of technology, customized goods and services have become cost effective and economical.

But now it's the era of personalization. There is a very thin line between personalization and customization. Customization is done by marketers at the request or command of the customer, but personalization—that is, manufacturing goods and services per the needs and requirements of customers— is done automatically by reviewing their online behavior. Personalization would not have been possible without the Internet. It is with the aid of the Internet and social sites that manufacturers have seen an overview of the behavior of people searching on the net and can use that information to produce goods and services per the needs and demands of consumers. Moreover, deals are offered to customers per their aspirations by watching their behavior. That is why personalized marketing has led to a personalized customer experience.

5.3.1 Means Used for Personalization

1. **Email and social media:** Customers see advertisements on social media. Advertisers through social media sites keep a watch on consumer search patterns. This information is then used to send personalized emails to customers and also to show items on social sites based on the personalized information of the customer to enhance their sales.
2. **Advertisement offers:** Based on the buying history of the customer either in the case of online or at-the-counter purchases, offers are made to customers to suit their needs. Customized offers are sent via messages, emails, Whatsapp, and so on by Dominoz, Metro shoes, Mochi shoes, Woodland, and others on the basis of the last purchases of customers. Like big store dealers sending a message two to three days before the birthday or anniversary of the customer, personalized offers to bring the customer to the store.
3. **Geographical personalization:** In this method, a device known as a beacon is used by sellers to track the geo-location of nearby customers and send them offers to attract them to the seller's store. In addition to this, if a person resident in one country surfs the website of a seller of another, the homepage of the website would lead them to a page specifically designed for that very country. For example, if an Indian surfs a US website, its homepage would lead him or her to the page specifically designed for Indians on the US website.

4. **IP address personalization:** When a customer accesses the seller portal, then based on the IP address of the customer, the portal personalizes itself to suit the needs and demands of the consumers.
5. **Customization of account:** When a consumer creates an account on a shopping site, he or she will become able to specify his or her preferences, that is, add or remove products or services or add a link to certain information by logging in. He or she can even do this without logging in with the aid of cookies.
6. **Related content:** This is usually done by shopping sites like Flipkart, Myntra, and Amazon to show items per the search and buying behavior of a consumer.

No doubt all this brings in personalization, but sometimes customers get irritated due to too many emails, calls, text messages, and notifications and they unsubscribe themselves to avoid the nuisance. So it is essential to send information to customers on a relevant and significant basis. Only then will sales be enhanced due to personalization.

Trust is also an important factor to be considered by marketer because if marketers maintain the secrecy of the information they get with the aid of various measures, only then will customer loyalty and satisfaction be enhanced. Moreover, they should use this information to serve their customer better by offering those personalized goods and services (Deloitte 2015).

A Deloitte survey has also revealed that:

1. Twenty percent of customers are willing to pay 20% more if they get personalized goods and services;
2. Forty-two out of 100 customers also look for brand names while purchasing personalized goods and services;
3. Twenty-two out of 100 customers are willing to share their personal information to get personalized goods and services;
4. People who are near retirement age plan for personalized holiday packages more than teenagers.

5.3.2 Factors Affecting Personalization

Since it is the era of personalization, every customer desires goods and services per his or her aspirations. Internet of Behavior, with the aid of artificial intelligence, machine learning, and intelligence analytics, performs the task of data mining about the behavior of consumers, and companies use the information gathered in manufacturing goods and delivering services. So the Internet of Behavior is the driving force behind personalization for customers and earning a profit for corporate houses.

1. **Business expansion and development:** Growth and development are musts for any business to survive and in today's era of personalization and customization, businesses are required to manufacture goods and provide services per the needs and requirements of customers. Internet of Behavior gathers information about customers, and manufacturers use that information while manufacturing and selling goods and providing services to customers. If a businessperson does not use IoB, he or she cannot survive, grow, and expand his or her business. For example: Texla brand TVs were very popular in India in the 1980s and 1990s. But this brand did not adapt, so it vanished over a period of time. Likewise, there were various brands of toothpastes like Colgate, Pepsodent, Close-Up, Babool, and others. Babool vanished over a period of time because it did not change.

2. **Information technology resurrection and software development:** The behavior of consumers varies regularly, and this variation alters their needs and demands. So businesses are required to modify their production and service delivery processes to achieve new heights and conquer gain consumer confidence by studying the behavior of consumers with the aid of application software and IT tools like software as a service (SaaS), application program interfaces, and so on.

3. **Reorganization of systems and tasks:** Businesses are required to reorganize their systems and tasks per data and information acquired with the aid of the Internet of Behavior. This will ultimately reduce risk and operational cost as well as enhancing the efficiency of business operations.

4. **People's perceptions:** To survive in a business, it is necessary to satisfy customers. For this, it is vital to study the perception of customers with the aid of IoB and satisfy their needs and wants.

5. **Digital strategies:** With the aid of IoB, businesses collect data about consumers, but this data has been saved online, so it can lead to data theft. So it is necessary to protect the data collected to harness the benefits, because hackers can gain its benefits without incurring any cost.

6. **Enhance customer experience:** IoB can gather and analyze customer data on a real-time basis, which was not possible earlier, and provide a better experience to customers by providing them offers and notifications per their point of purchase needs. Moreover, corporate houses are better able to understand customer concerns as well as satisfying them.

7. **Improve public hygiene:** With the help of cameras, companies can get real-time information on whether employees are following social safety protocols as well as COVID-19 directives while manufacturing and handling articles. This will ensure public health.

8. **Assist communal welfare and security:** IoB ensures community welfare and security. For example, the behavior of a car driver can be studied,

and if it is contrary to cab community welfare, a notification will be sent to him to avoid dangerous conduct for customer satisfaction.[9]

5.4 REVIEW OF LITERATURE: IOT, IOB, PERSONALIZATION, AND CONSUMER BEHAVIOR

IoB is currently a very active research area with an increasing number of applications in diverse areas. There is a wide range of related articles in the form of blogs, social media posts, and popular websites. However, there is a limited amount of work published in the form of systematic studies specifically related to the influence of IoB on consumer behavior. The current section reviews some of the viewpoints about IoT, IoB, and personalization and gives us an idea how IoB is expected to influence consumer behavior.

IoT can turn data into information. IoT gathers data about consumers with the help of their mobile phones and connects it to various smart devices like automobile cameras, laptops, home cameras, and virtual assistants. IoT gathers information about the health of consumers and driving-accident history, and IoB tries to alter the behavior by inculcating good values in consumers and also by sending alerts to them. Companies also suggest products that can help consumers to avoid bad behavior and follow good behavior. But sometimes consumers feel disturbed when they realize that companies are using their personal information for profit. Moreover, there is an issue of hacking as well: the personal information of consumers might be made public. The author concluded that there is no doubt IoT can convert data into information, but whether IoB will be able to convert this knowledge into wisdom is a question mark (Kidd, 2019).[10]

IoT gathers data from interconnected devices with Internet access, and when this interconnection is used to grasp knowledge about consumer behavior, it is referred to as the Internet of Behavior. IoB is composed of applied science and behavioral science and also analyzes behavioral data. Feelings, alternatives, enhancements, and fellowship are understood and studied with the aid of data analytics and applied in the real world to provide consumers with products and services they like. For example, diet habits, sleep, napping, blood glucose, pulse, and so on can be gauged by a smart phone, and if your mobile is a part of IoT, then this information would reach sellers and they will guide your behavior and also offer you products and services to keep all these things under control. Moreover, the seller also gauges the interest of consumers in various products and services based on their search history on Facebook, Instagram, Google, and others and sends customized offers to them to convert their interest into action. This is just the start of this technology (Mishra, 2021).[11] IoT collects the data, and IoB understands it and uses it for devising changes in products and services per the desire of customers or tries to change their behavior after understanding that satisfaction of their desire is not viable. Moreover, companies are also required to assure customers that their data will be secured. The conglomeration of big data and behavioral analysis has led to increased customer satisfaction and delight and has also led to the achievement of the objectives of producers, sellers, and marketers (Ortiz, 2021).[12] A McKinsey survey revealed that due to IoB, the sales of companies grew by 85% and profit increased by 25% because IoB provides data about consumer behavior and helps companies to provide goods and services per the needs of consumers. Organizations are also using it to increase the efficiency of employees at work, such as whether they are working, following hygiene norms, wearing masks, and so on. But this information needs to be protected from falling into the wrong hands to prevent its misuse. As it is just the start of Internet of Behavior, time will reveal whether it will become a blessing or a scourge (Vestian, 2021).[13]

Internet of Behavior acts as a research and development cell for an organization. Earlier data have been gathered by this cell but now are found with the help of IoB. IoB gathers data with the aid of digital devices; analyzes this data; and makes decisions about production, marketing, advertising, budgeting, and so on. IoB is the culmination of behavioral psychology and IoT edge computing. IoB is used to encourage good things and discourage bad things; for example, if a person is driving fast, an alert will be sent to him to drive cautiously (Davis, 2022).[14]

IoB gathers information about consumers using geo-location, health apps, travel history, creditworthiness, and so on and offers them campaigns and notifications per their interests. Moreover, these offers and discounts are offered to consumers on a real-time basis, that is, while they are shopping or are near the outlet. But there are issues of hacking, data leakage, and data sharing from one company to another. So consumers avoid sharing their personal information due to these risks. However, these risks exist because IoB is in the infancy stage. These risks will be reduced in time (Rao, 2022).[15]

Sales of companies have been badly affected due to customer preferences. In 2012, Göte Hyman the concept of IoB to understand human behavior and convince them. IoB is a combination of IoT, analytical science, and psychological science. A team of researchers has suggested assigning an address to each IoT device and then analyzing the data revealed by IoT like social sites, cameras, sensors, biometric devices, geo-location, and so on and sending updates to concerned persons per their interests, like sending a discount coupon to a customer while he or she is shopping in a nearby location so that he or she also visits the store or sending an update to a driver who is driving recklessly to drive slowly. This can enhance the volume of sales with various marketing efforts and enhance customer satisfaction and delight by providing personalized and customized goods and services to customers using IoB.

But there are security and privacy concerns that need to be regulated to make IoB a success (TEC Team, 2022).[16]

Sayol (2022) states that personalization is essential to satisfy the requirements, wants, and aspirations of consumers. A company or a marketer cannot survive without satisfying consumers. Therefore, they are required to change or adjust per consumer needs. Needs are revealed by IoT and IoB. IoT is an interconnection, and with this interconnection, IoB understands the behavior of users and consumers. IoB not only understands but also has the power to change customer and user behavior, such as in the case of a taxi service where the behavior of the driver can be studied, and from the study of the driver's behavior, one can easily reveal whether the customer would have been satisfied. If the customer would be unsatisfied, the driver could be asked to change his behavior to satisfy passengers. IoB gathers and uses two types of data: the data the company gathers while consumers interact with the company's website and data gathered with the aid of IoT (interconnection of smart devices) such as cameras, mobiles, cars, and so on. Corporate houses collect data using IoB from consumers, government agencies, digital media, social networking, administrative units with consumer or citizen data, geo-tracking, and interconnection with devices with artificial intelligence. Based on this information, companies personalize their products and services. But companies are also required to ensure network, computer, and data security to prevent information from getting into the hands of hackers.[17] The traditional strategies followed by business concerns for satisfying consumers have not been effective because companies have lacked knowledge about consumers and their issues. They have not been giving importance to buyer or end user needs and the timing of the needs. Marketers have not been answerable or responsible to consumers and have not been providing customized goods and services. But with the help of artificial intelligence and machine learning, companies have been better able to satisfy consumers' or end-users' needs, and their efforts have also been reduced because data is automatically generated through the IoT. This has also reduced customer attrition because businesses can now spot unsatisfied customers and convert them into loyal customers by providing them customized and personalized goods and services, resolving their issues, engaging with them, and so on (Kshatriya, 2022).[18]

IoB is a blend of mechanization, statistics analytics, and behavioral psychology. It has the power to elucidate the behavioral patterns of consumers and also change their behavior with the aid of IoT. IoT is an interconnection of various devices like cameras, mobiles, and so on, which have the power to reveal consumer behavior. Advertisements are shown to consumers by the Google search engine, Facebook, and so on based on their behavior grasped by that site. These behavioral patterns also form the base of product development and service quality delivery to satisfy consumers. Moreover, while consumers are shopping offline, their location is traced with the aid of geo-location of mobile devices, and customized value-added propositions are mailed or messaged to enhance their shopping experience. In addition to this, companies also make efforts to protect the private information of consumers to ensure privacy and security (Ganesh, 2021).[19]

IoB is an offshoot of IoT, and with its help, companies gather data about consumers' desires. Companies gather the data, that is, track human behavior, and convert it into information by noticing consumer conduct and using this information as knowledge to better serve consumers and lead to wisdom – satisfying consumers as well as corporate houses by earning profit and enhancing sales as a result of this whole process. IoB can enhance the production sector by manufacturing goods and services per the needs of consumers and by reducing idle time and nonessential tasks of employees and laborers and increasing their productivity. It will also improve sales activity by targeting consumers better and satisfying their needs, and all this is done online. Moreover, the research department will better understand the needs and requirements of consumers and try to satisfy their needs. By the end of 2025, there will be no need for employees at the checkout counter at malls and shopping outlets; all this will be automatic. No doubt IoB has made our life easier, but it has certain disadvantages as well. Data is not safe. Moreover, as data is quite large, it is required to be managed to reduce cyber attacks.[20]

The interconnection of things with Internet connectivity provides valuable insights into the behavior of consumers. With its aid, corporate houses can focus on the production of those goods which are in demand by consumers and can also ensure their employees are following COVID-19 protocols while manufacturing goods and delivering services. IoB has made everything digital. The behavior of consumers is seen online with Internet access, and customized offers are sent online to consumers while they are shopping online or offline. In online shopping, it is easier, but in offline purchasing, their location is traced, and on that basis, marketing campaigns and notifications are targeted to them. This enhances the customer experience. Moreover, manufacturing concerns also check online whether safety standards are being followed by employees while manufacturing and delivering goods. IoB has the potential to satisfy consumer needs and achieve business objectives in a better way. But there is a requirement to maintain equilibrium between personalized data and cyber risks.[21] IoB is a culmination of facts, mechanization, and social anthropology. Social anthropology is composed of sentiments, resolutions, addenda, and togetherness. Consumer behavior is grasped via IoB to satisfy them and enhance sales and profitability, avoid consumer surveys, and send them real-time offers while they are shopping as well as helping the government provide better services to citizens and natives. In addition to this, there is a dire need to secure personalized data. Moreover, there should be an equilibrium between individualized sales promotion initiatives and excessive contact with consumers to keep them from unwanted responses.[22]

5.5 APPLICATIONS OF IOB

The following sections highlight some of the major application areas of IoB.

5.5.1 Health: Smart Disease Surveillance and Management Systems

Although the field of IoB has been evolving very actively for the last few years with a wide range of applications, it has gained the most widespread public recognition during the COVID-19 pandemic. To cope with the challenge of avoiding direct contact and reducing infection, several researchers developed numerous face mask recognition systems (Brown et al., 2021) and socially distant surveillance systems (Hoeben et al., 2021). Governments have deployed a variety of mobile applications and smart networked devices to stop the virus's spread. For instance, the China Health Code Alipay app keeps track of a user's contacts, travels, and bodily biometrics like temperature. A colorful QR code is then generated to show the user's current health status. As a result, the user may be subject to limitations that have an impact on his or her behavior, such as travel authorization or quarantining at home or in a central location.[23] Apart from COVID-19–related applications, a number of mobile solutions and apps have been developed to deal with various health issues, including weight management, sleep management, mental health, stress management, and monitoring of chronic disorders. These software apps use biometrics, health and behavioral information measured via inbuilt sensors. For example, the Beddit health app monitors breathing rate, pulse rate, and sleep habits. The software delivers alarms, messages, and advice to improve the user's sleep after evaluating the observed behavior. It also encourages the user to fulfil daily goals for a more favorable outcome.[24] The mobile app Student Life[25] was used to measure and assess the level of anxiety and depression among college students in order to ascertain whether COVID-19 had an impact on their behavior and mental health (Huckins et al., 2020). Another application area of IoB is the management of chronic diseases to create smarter patient experiences. This is important because a large proportion of the world have been affected by chronic diseases such as cancer, diabetes, high blood pressure, and so on (for example, 60% of the adults in the United States suffer from at least one chronic disorder). The unavailability of sufficient physicians to take regular care of such a large number of patients has created the opportunity to invent smart IoT-based disease management systems, including sensors, software apps, and digital assistance per the specific needs and behavior of the patients. This remote digital assistance–based patient monitoring has reduced risk factors and reduced unnecessary hospital visits.[26] Some of the popular virtual care solutions include Amwell, Bright.md, eVisit, iConsult, Medocity, and others.[27]

5.5.2 Smart Cities and Transport

In an attempt to get an idea about individual-level energy consumption in smart buildings, researchers applied AI and ML algorithms to study the link between edge devices (Rafsanjani and Ghahramani, 2020). In another innovative attempt to reduce power consumption, conserve energy, and reduce cost, researchers implemented an IoB system using explainable artificial intelligence (XAI) to transform consumer behavior to environmentally friendly behavior (Elayan et al., 2021). An advanced deep learning framework for Internet of Behavior (ADLIoB) has been proposed to be applied to connected cars to advance research on driver assistance and self-driving car technology (Mezair et al., 2022). Researchers analyzed the information obtained from sensors as well as knowledge about abnormal traffic conditions to develop models to increase the prediction and detection rates of connected vehicles (Abdellatif et al., 2021). IoB can even be used to deal with behaviors of drivers as well as passengers. Uber has been experiencing a rising number of disagreements with its drivers, leading to a high turnover rate. Uber has come up with an innovative strategy to tackle such problems and settle disputes. Uber uses gamification to influence driver behavior in its favor. On the other hand, to compensate drivers or make them afraid of losing their earnings, Uber uses strategies like intrinsic motivation, loss aversion, and recognition.[28] Ford is also extending its customer reach by collaborating with Argo AI to create autonomous vehicles that can adjust and behave differently depending upon the road infrastructure and behavior of the driver.[29]

5.5.3 Digital/Retail Marketing and Personalized Customer Experiences

In 2021, the highest percentage was predicted to belong to the digital marketing sector. The IoB requires an Internet connection to function; hence, one of the industries that will benefit most from IoB technology is digital marketing. Data is the primary resource that the area of digital marketing uses to promote goods and services to customers all over the world. They will be in a better position to connect with those who are near the conclusion of the purchasing process if they have access to tools for behavioral analysis and interpretation. Globally, there will likely be a big rise in digital marketing. Lead generation, sales generation, and brand promotion will all be accomplished through digital marketing. Consider the advertising tools on social media platforms like Facebook and Instagram. Both platforms have the capacity to target users through IoB based on how they have interacted with that advertisement through "click rates." Brands will thus have an easier time connecting with their ideal audience. The same is true for YouTube, which uses behavioral analytics to suggest channels or videos based on user preferences to enhance the viewing experience.[30]

In addition to better customer experiences in the online world, retail marketing is also gearing up with some innovative ideas. For example, retail outlets are introducing smarter queuing systems as a first point of contact with customers, with digital notifications to give them a better retaining experience in stores with the aim to save customers' precious time and give them better guidance and overall service.[31] In addition, the use of dynamic signage is becoming popular among retailers to give their customers a better shopping experience. In addition, smart cameras with computer vision applications can be used to identify the products to which customers are being attracted. This information can then be used to give them relevant marketing offers.[32]

5.6 PERSONAL, ETHICAL, AND LEGAL ISSUES AND OTHER CHALLENGES OF THE INTERNET OF BEHAVIOR

Interconnection of devices poses the problem of contamination of data, such as viruses, worms, Trojans, spyware, adware, keyloggers, Klez, MSBlast, Netsky, and Spyware attacks. Most corporate houses are focusing on customer satisfaction and customer delight by understanding their needs and producing goods and rendering services per their desires. These houses gather information with the aid of the Internet. So, while getting information with the aid of interconnection, companies are exposed to the risks of malware. These types of risks force corporate houses to pull out all the stops to provide safety to consumers while gathering information about them. So there is a requirement to formulate, implement, and follow social, legal, and ethical sequestration concerns while using the information superhighway. No doubt the Internet of Behavior can satisfy the wide array of customer needs and bring in efficiency with the aid of artificial intelligence, but it is a Gordian Knot that ties within itself unethical and dangerous conduct, neglected and abandoned repercussions, and obtrusiveness.

There is a need for Internet of Behavior governance norms to strike a balance between its positive effects on customers, marketers, and society and the negative repercussions of cyber attacks and hacking personal information of the public at large. These norms should guide marketers, customers, and society about legal, ethical, and social issues while using IoB applied science for stimulating and enhancing reliability, dependability, and security.

While corporate houses and governments should not stifle technological advancement with excessive regulation, they also should not wait until the Internet of Behavior is fully developed before discussing policy and governance. There are various challenges of IoB. They include:

1. **Sequestration:** IoB requires striking a balance between information sequestration and the utilization of this individual data to advance efficiency, protection, and reliability. Networked seclusion and data virtue policies and procedures are quite hard to understand and impose. Individual details are of more use for a wide range of players, including corporate houses and governments, to formulate judgments about society, customers, and the public at large with the growth of IoB technologies. To reduce cyber attacks, an IoB "Bill of Rights" has been proposed. The public must have the ability to withdraw, quit, remove, or disguise their data from the Internet of Behavior system. But to restrict Internet of Behavior systems to create information about a person is impractical and technically may not be feasible.

   Another option can be to keep the particulars of participants anonymous or to encrypt their information so that nobody else can read it (Guerrero et al., 2016; Katapally et al., 2018; Acer et al., 2019; Komninos, 2019). But in the case of encryption, hackers will try to decrypt it using their techniques. Havinga et al. (2020) suggested aggregating the data of individuals so that individuals could not be traced personally.

   Moreover, there is also an option of excluding personal data that interferes with the privacy rights of the information provider by the information seeker. Let us understand it with the help of an example. A study was conducted by Acer and his investigative group in 2019. They collected data from the employees of the postage department of Belgium with the aid of a cyborg or humanoid clobber appliance that not only captured their geographic location but also their voice communication with their employees and customers. So, to protect their privacy, their audio was not made part of the experiment.

2. **The problem in fixing responsibility:** As self-driving automobiles make all the decisions without the intervention of human beings, if any of the systems fail, who shall be responsible? It will not be possible to assign anybody responsibility. Similarly, the Internet of Behavior operates as a self-governed system. So, if anything goes wrong, it becomes difficult to fix responsibility.

3. **Encouragement for moral application:** Moral values are missing in technology. Information collected with the aid of technology would no doubt be of great help for marketers and corporate houses, but

technology may make personal conduct visible to shady observers and invite unwelcome incursion.

Isaac Asimov proposed four regulations of artificial intelligence in his wildly successful and forward-thinking books on the fundamental tenet that computers should not hurt people. In these self-governed systems, artificial intelligence systems, there is a need to develop ethics so that system can identify what is good and bad as well as what should be done if any person tries to do a bad action (Berman and Cerf, 2017).

4. **Information standard and probity of information provided:** The customers from whom the information is collected might not reveal their actual behavior; this undermines the quality of data gathered. So information collected with the aid of a questionnaire might not reflect reality (Aoki et al., 2009; Andersson and Sternberg, 2016; Theunis et al., 2017; Barzyk et al., 2018; Vesnic-Alujevic et al., 2018; Scheibner et al., 2021). To avoid this issue, instead of single-time data collection, a longitudinal study can be conducted, due to which the issue of dishonesty will be resolved (Dema et al., 2019). Moreover, training could be provided to data collectors to improve the quality of information gathered (Ferster et al., 2013; Heiss and Matthes, 2017).

The quality of data collected can be improved using sensor-based systems. But these systems, such as Internet of Behavior devices, cannot be used by elderly people, people living in slums, and so on, which is why the information curve of data gathered will not be bell shaped but will be skewed due to demographic and socioeconomic differences (Havinga et al., 2020) because the study will not include these information sources.

5. **Conscious approval or explicit agreement:** The consumers about whom data have been collected should have the knowledge that information has been sought from them. They should also be told the purpose for which the data has been collected. In 2016, a woman from the United States filed suit against a corporate house that had been selling adult toys or marital aids with artificial intelligence system imbibed in its included. The intelligence system was gathering data about the favored oscillation rate, the number of times it had been used, and the days on which it had been used. This information was extremely private. So this kind of information should not be collected without the permission of the consumer (Allhoff and Henschke, 2018).

6. **Defending data and cyber security:** Many devices people use these days have intelligence systems like smart TVs, smart phones, smart watches, and other smart devices; that is, cameras and microphones collect the personal data of consumers. This information is provided to corporate houses, so there is no information security. Moreover, corporate houses, after collecting data, use it for the purposes for which they require it,

and this information is not kept safe. Cyber attackers and hackers use passwords because these passwords are publicly available online or can easily be hacked. So there is a requirement on the part of corporate houses to create 32-character passwords using letters, numerals, and special characters and change these daily. This will enhance the security of data. Moreover, the minimum data security standards should be set by regulators to be followed by information seekers so that they can also use the information for their benefit as well as for the benefit of information providers, and information should not move into the wrong hands.

7. **Physical well-being**: The IoB should not harm the physical well-being of customers. Things, products, goods, and services are provided per customers' aspirations, but the safety standards of these personalized items should also be checked. For example, toys are manufactured for children per the demand of children as well as their parents, but safety should be ensured: these toys should not harm children. Likewise, by understanding the behavior of consumers, corporate houses feel the need to develop vehicles having with intelligent systems that can run without drivers. In this case, as well as the security of people walking on the roads, the security of vehicles moving on the roads and safety of the individuals in the smart vehicles should be ensured before commercializing such vehicles. It is difficult to fix responsibility in these cases if something happens. For example, self-driven vehicles have an intelligent system and will move only when there is a green light, but if another person crosses against a red light while there is a green light for a self-driven vehicle, there would be a chance of an accident. So, all the standards of security should be installed in the vehicle. Moreover, users or customers must be informed beforehand about the security issues to avoid any problems later on.

8. **Confidence and faith:** Personalized items and services provided by corporate houses or marketers should be trustworthy. If customers lose trust in the services and goods provided by marketers, they will not purchase the goods and will not utilize the services. Let us take an example of a smart vehicle manufactured per the aspirations of consumers meeting with an accident; customers will lose confidence in the vehicle. If its brakes fail while it is moving on the road due to a hacker from a remote location, this can lead to a precarious and problematic situation: deaths, gashes, and property destruction. But if an artificial intelligence system makes better decisions than human beings, reliance on these expert systems will increase: if a self-driven car drives better than a car driven by a human being, then preference will be given to the vehicle with an expert system embedded in it (Allhoff and Henschke, 2018).

5.7 CONCLUSION

There has been an exponential increase in Internet users, connected Internet devices, and exchange of information among them, giving rise to a new concept called the Internet of Things (IoT). Such a huge network of connected devices generates an enormous amount of data (big data), which can be analyzed to derive extremely useful information about connected people, including their usage patterns, behavior, preferences, and so on. Access to such vital information about the behavior of users has given us an opportunity to develop models that can then be used to influence the behavior of an individual in a specific manner, giving rise to what we call Internet of Behavior. IoB has been evolving very fast with a rising number of applications in the field of health, education, energy, smart cities, and commerce. IoB can serve as the foundation for corporate growth, marketing, and sales strategy in the future. However, the long-term use of this technology needs to overcome associated risk factors as well as building more trust and reliability. In addition, various ethical and legal issues must also be taken care of as a priority.

NOTES

1. https://ignasisayol.com/en/data-science-the-companies-treasure-for-adding-value/
2. https://ignasisayol.com/en/behavioural-Internet-iob-the-evolution-of-personalization/
3. www.financialexpress.com/industry/technology/Internet-of-behaviours-more-power-to-digital-marketing/2371247/
4. www.mckinsey.com/industries/financial-services/our-insights/digital-ecosystems-for-insurers-opportunities-through-the-Internet-of-things
5. www.ibm.com/downloads/cas/WVG1BPYW
6. https://research.aimultiple.com/Internet-of-behaviours/
7. www.forbes.com/sites/forbesbusinessdevelopmentcouncil/2021/08/30/the-Internet-of-behaviour-smarter-technologys-next-frontier-is-our-human-experience/?sh=1662a2f44819
8. www.business-standard.com/content/specials/Internet-of-behaviours-is-critical-to-remodeling-customer-experience-and-business-innovation-121032400443_1.html
9. https://stefanini.com/en/trends/news/defining-Internet-of-behaviours-iob-and-4-ways-it-can-benefit-bus
10. www.bmc.com/blogs/iob-Internet-of-behaviour/
11. www.analyticssteps.com/blogs/introduction-Internet-behaviour-iob
12. https://citrodigital.com/blog/june-2021/Internet-of-behaviour-iob
13. www.vestian.com/blog/Internet-of-behaviour-providing-valuable-insights/
14. https://dzone.com/articles/Internet-of-behaviour-iob-is-it-the-future-of-custo
15. www.smartkarrot.com/resources/blog/Internet-of-behaviours/

16. https://www3.technologyevaluation.com/research/article/Internet-of-behaviour.html
17. https://ignasisayol.com/en/behavioural-Internet-iob-the-evolution-of-personalization/
18. www.smartkarrot.com/resources/blog/how-machine-learning-change-customer-success/
19. www.financialexpress.com/industry/technology/Internet-of-behaviours-more-power-to-digital-marketing/2371247/
20. www.tekkiwebsolutions.com/blog/Internet-of-behaviour/
21. www.terralogic.com/Internet-of-behaviours/
22. www.thequantumtech.com/the-evolution-of-personalization-Internet-of-behaviour-iob/
23. https://www:nytimes:com/2020/03/01/business/chinacoronavirus-surveillance:html
24. https://www:beddit:com/
25. https://studentlife.cs.dartmouth.edu/
26. www.forbes.com/sites/forbesbusinessdevelopmentcouncil/2021/08/30/the-Internet-of-behaviour-smarter-technologys-next-frontier-is-our-human-experience/?sh=7bb6a94b4819
27. www.gartner.com/reviews/market/virtual-care-solutions
28. https://www:nytimes:com/interactive/2017/04/02
29. https://www:ford-mobility:eu/autonomous-vehicles
30. www.persistencemarketresearch.com/market-research/Internet-of-behaviours-iob-market.asp#:~:text=Internet%20of%20Behaviours%20(IoB)%20Market%20to%20grow%20at%20a%20CAGR,the%20forecast%20period%202021%2D2031
31. www.delfi.com/solutions/breece-smart-queuing
32. www.forbes.com/sites/forbesbusinessdevelopmentcouncil/2021/08/30/the-Internet-of-behaviour-smarter-technologys-next-frontier-is-our-human-experience/?sh=7bb6a94b4819

REFERENCES

Abdellatif, A. A., Chiasserini, C. F., Malandrino, F., Mohamed, A., & Erbad, A. (2021). Active learning with noisy labelers for improving classification accuracy of connected vehicles. *IEEE Transactions on Vehicular Technology, 70*(4), 3059–3070.

Acer, U. G., Broeck, M. V. D., Forlivesi, C., Heller, F., & Kawsar, F. (2019). Scaling crowdsourcing with mobile workforce: A case study with Belgian postal service. *Proceedings of the ACM on Interactive, Mobile, Wearable and Ubiquitous Technologies, 3*(2), 1–32.

Allhoff, F., & Henschke, A. (2018). The Internet of Things: Foundational ethical issues. *Internet of Things, 1,* 55–66.

Andersson, M., & Sternberg, H. (2016, January). Informating transport transparency. In *49th Hawaii international conference on system sciences* (pp. 1841–1850). HICSS, Koloa, HI. doi:10.1109/HICSS. 2016.234.

Aoki, P. M., Honicky, R. J., Mainwaring, A., Myers, C., Paulos, E., Subramanian, S., & Woodruff, A. (2009, April). A vehicle for research: Using street sweepers to explore the landscape of environmental community action. In *Proceedings of the SIGCHI conference on human factors in computing systems* (pp. 375–384). USA.

Barzyk, T. M., Huang, H., Williams, R., Kaufman, A., & Essoka, J. (2018). Advice and frequently asked questions (FAQs) for citizen-science environmental health assessments. *International Journal of Environmental Research and Public Health, 15*(5), 960.

Berman, F., & Cerf, V. G. (2017). Social and ethical behaviour in the internet of things. *Communications of the ACM, 60*(2), 6–7.

Brown, M., Young, S. G., & Sacco, D. F. (2021). Competing motives in a pandemic: Interplays between fundamental social motives and technology use in predicting (non) compliance with social distancing guidelines. *Computers in Human Behaviour, 123*, 106892.

Deloitte, L. L. P. (2015). *The Deloitte consumer review made-to-order: The rise of mass personalization, UK.*

Dema, T., Brereton, M., & Roe, P. (2019, May). Designing participatory sensing with remote communities to conserve endangered species. In *Proceedings of the 2019 CHI conference on human factors in computing systems* (pp. 1–16).

Elayan, H., Aloqaily, M., & Guizani, M. (2021). Internet of Behaviour (IoB) and explainable AI systems for influencing IoT behaviour. *arXiv preprint arXiv:2109.07239.*

Ferster, C. J., Coops, N. C., Harshaw, H. W., Kozak, R. A., & Meitner, M. J. (2013). An exploratory assessment of a smartphone application for public participation in forest fuels measurement in the wildland-urban interface. *Forests, 4*(4), 1199–1219.

Guerrero, P., Møller, M. S., Olafsson, A. S., & Snizek, B. (2016). Revealing cultural ecosystem services through Instagram images: The potential of social media volunteered geographic information for urban green infrastructure planning and governance. *Urban Planning, 1*(2), 1–17.

Havinga, I., Bogaart, P. W., Hein, L., & Tuia, D. (2020). Defining and spatially modelling cultural ecosystem services using crowdsourced data. *Ecosystem Services, 43*, 101091.

Heiss, R., & Matthes, J. (2017). Citizen science in the social sciences: A call for more evidence. *GAIA-Ecological Perspectives for Science and Society, 26*(1), 22–26.

Hoeben, E. M., Bernasco, W., Suonperä Liebst, L., Van Baak, C., & Rosenkrantz Lindegaard, M. (2021). Social distancing compliance: A video observational analysis. *PLoS One, 16*(3), e0248221.

Huckins, J. F., Wang, W., Hedlund, E., Rogers, C., Nepal, S. K., Wu, J., Obuchi, M., Murphy, E. I., Meyer, M. L., Wagner, D. D., & Holtzheimer, P. E. (2020). Mental health and behaviour of college students during the early phases of the COVID-19 pandemic: Longitudinal smartphone and ecological momentary assessment study. *Journal of Medical Internet Research, 22*(6), e20185.

Javaid, M., Haleem, A., Singh, R. P., Rab, S., & Suman, R. (2021). Internet of Behaviours (IoB) and its role in customer services. *Sensors International, 2*, 100122.

Katapally, T. R., Bhawra, J., Leatherdale, S. T., Ferguson, L., Longo, J., Rainham, D., . . . Osgood, N. (2018). The SMART study, a mobile health and citizen science methodological platform for active living surveillance, integrated knowledge translation, and policy interventions: Longitudinal study. *JMIR Public Health and Surveillance, 4*(1), e8953.

Komninos, A. (2019). Pro-social behaviour in crowdsourcing systems: Experiences from a field deployment for beach monitoring. *International Journal of Human-Computer Studies, 124,* 93–115.

Mezair, T., Djenouri, Y., Belhadi, A., Srivastava, G., & Lin*, J. C. W. (2022). Towards an advanced deep learning for the Internet of Behaviours: Application to connected vehicle. *ACM Transactions on Sensor Networks (TOSN), 19*(2).

Rafsanjani, H. N., & Ghahramani, A. (2020). Towards utilizing Internet of Things (IoT) devices for understanding individual occupants' energy usage of personal and shared appliances in office buildings. *Journal of Building Engineering, 27,* 100948.

Scheibner, J., Jobin, A., & Vayena, E. (2021). Ethical issues with using Internet of Things devices in citizen science research: A scoping review. *Frontiers in Environmental Science, 9,* 629649.

Theunis, J., Peters, J., & Elen, B. (2017). Participatory air quality monitoring in urban environments: Reconciling technological challenges and participation. In *Participatory sensing, opinions and collective awareness* (pp. 255–271). Springer, Cham.

Vesnic-Alujevic, L., Breitegger, M., & Guimarães Pereira, Â. (2018). *Do-it-yourself* Healthcare? Quality of health and healthcare through wearable sensors. *Science and Engineering Ethics, 24,* 887–904. https://doi.org/10.1007/s11948-016-9771-4

Chapter 6

Dynamic Routing Mechanism to Reduce Energy Consumption in a Software-Defined Network

Viji Florance G

CONTENTS

6.1 INTRODUCTION

As network traffic increases, transmitted data reaches a point where managing it is a very challenging task, and the resources consumed for network devices also increase. Traffic can be created as normal traffic and attack traffic. One of the most widely created types of network traffic is attack traffic as a distributed denial of service (DDoS) attack [1]. A DDoS attack is done by either IP spoofing or real IP spoofing, and this attack not only causes traffic but is also used to deny service of for the entire network. When the attack is done by IP spoofing, attackers hide the original source IP address and use a fake IP address; one example is the SYN Floods attack [2]. Real IP spoofing uses a botnet master which in turn creates and floods the network.

Many approaches have been proposed for the solution of distributed denial of service attacks, such as applying the approach at the source, applying the

DOI: 10.1201/9781003305170-6

approach at the destination, and applying the approach at the intermediate router. For an approach at the source, only packets coming from a specific range of IP addresses are accepted, and packets coming from outside that range are filtered [3]. The solution for an intermediate router uses an IP trace back approach and packet filtering technique, but it is not practical because the network is widely spread [4]. The approach used at the destination is also not possible for small organizations due to being more expensive. Because of these approaches and a flooding attack, network energy will be consumed rapidly.

This problem is efficiently solved by applying a software-defined network (SDN) and network function virtualization (NFV). SDN is the paradigm to monitor, manage, and organize network activity in efficient ways. NFV is a technology that is enabled in each network, and it provides their spare resources to other networks when required.

Software-defined network is to make the network more flexible, efficient to administer, and programmable to monitor the traffic by separating the control plane and data plane. Advanced technologies like virtualization functions [5], hybrid networks, and controller trees provide innovative programmable network management. With this technology, when a huge amount of traffic is coming, all network devices are congested [6]. Therefore, when a large number of network devices and resources are connected, excessive usage of power will occur. In this context, one can create a virtual link between two hosts, and dynamic configuration is also available in the network infrastructure. The aim is to construct a model to minimize energy consumption without sacrificing efficiency.

In a traditional network, all network devices and resources, such as the data plane and control plane, are coupled together; it is very difficult to identify the optimal links in a congested network since it uses static routing, and it is not possible to change the network constraints. Moreover, the flow table should be modified according to a new optimal link, and the required numbers of resources and devices are connected to integrate usage of resources and capacity to reduce energy consumption.

A fault-finding aspect should be considered for energy savings [7] in an SDN-based virtual network, hybrid network [8], and controller tree [9]. However, different problems may arise when considering the router count (hop count) to do the data transfer and the shortest path to reduce delay and improve utilization, which account for energy savings. An energy consumption technique (ECT) is modeled to evaluate the shortest-path algorithm, virtual link capacity, and virtual routing [10]. The all-pair shortest-path (APSP) algorithm is used to find the shortest path between two nodes based on the number of routers connected. In this algorithm, if any networks are congested, then the nodes connected to the congested network are removed and the flow table updated based on modified network. After finding the shortest path, VSDN the virtual software-defined network (VSDN) creates the virtual controller used on each router and itself creates virtual links between all virtual controllers. Virtual controllers are coordinated by a centralized POX controller in Mininet.

The objective of this chapter is to perform an energy-saving technique to minimize energy consumption by finding the shortest path using the all-pair shortest-path algorithm, which results in removing the congested network; updating the flow table accordingly; and establishing virtual links between nodes using a virtual SDN connected to a centralized POX controller. If there is a link failure, then the system will first collect virtual path information, network topology, and the number of user requests. Second, there is a condition to verify the current request matches the resources allocated to the virtual link. Third, if the match is successful, the flow table is configured for the virtual link; if not, the VSDN recalculates the virtual link that satisfies the request.

6.2 MAIN CONTRIBUTION

The main motivation is to propose a new method for reducing energy consumption on a large-scale network, satisfy user requirements, and provide better performance in terms of number of routers in a congested network. The new methodology will develop a software-defined network with a POX controller through an OpenFlow protocol. This protocol provides communication among all three layers – data layer, control layer, and application layer – and it will take care of data transfer between those layers in a centralized manner. The main responsibility of the OpenFlow protocol is to perform actions, which may be either reactive or proactive. In the reactive method, the controller is responsible for transferring packets, whereas in the proactive method, the controller has given the premise to switches and routers to transfer packets [11].

The essential feature of the SDN is the centralized controller, which coordinates the logical decisions of the networking activity. The controller has the ability to determine the availability of resources and set of applications in the network infrastructure by using application program interfaces (APIs) as northbound and southbound interfaces [11]. API uses the advantages of the network infrastructure to provide services in the application layer, packet switching and forwarding of the data layer and reconfigurability, routing, managing, monitoring, and programmability. The control layer is shown in Figure 6.1.

SDN has the ability to decouple the data plane from the control plane to perform innovative routing mechanisms, congestion-avoiding techniques, and energy-saving methods according to quality of service (QOS) metrics. In this chapter, the proposed solution of an energy-saving method is an energy consumption technique used in a congested network to save energy

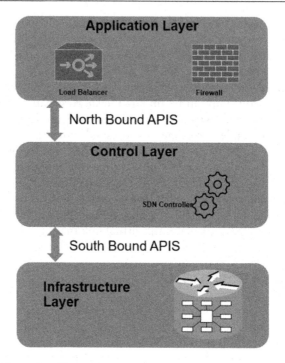

Figure 6.1 SDN layered architecture.

by applying the shortest path, virtual link capacity, and virtual routing. To establish this, we first identify the network that is not congested, then find the shortest path according to the network and update the flow table. Second, we create a virtual controller for all routers connected to the centralized controller to reduce traffic.

The rest of this chapter has six sections, structured as follows: Section 6.3 describes the related work of energy consumption techniques, Section 6.4 elaborates on the fundamental network routing framework, Section 6.5 explains the design considerations, Section 6.6 briefly explains the proposed solution for the energy-consumption challenge, Section 6.7 elaborates on the performance evaluation of the proposed solution as a model emulation and implementation and discusses the results, and finally, the conclusion of the article is given in Section 6.8.

6.3 RELATED WORKS

This section describes the various methods involved in saving techniques: energy saving by routing, energy saving by controller, and energy saving by virtualization.

6.3.1 Energy Saving by Routing

Routing is the process of forwarding data from one network to another through network devices. When there is a huge amount of data transfer within the network, there is a chance of having a huge volume of traffic. The typical energy reduction methods in routing are network traffic analysis, optimized methods of routing and having fewer active network devices [12–15]. An SDN network supports dynamic routing, and the controller has own capacity to configure. This way traffic could be reduced by doing configuration dynamically and creating fewer active network devices [16].

According to [17], it can be used to reduce traffic by identifying the throughput of flows, that is, how much data is transferred through the link for a specific time period, and making fewer hops among the network. Also using the Dijkstra-based routing (DBR) algorithm to find the shortest path and do routing with active devices [18].

Some parameter metrics have been found to determine the traffic of network. When the network is congested, the QoS is not stable, and it is maintained by applying routing techniques to modify network routing and minimize overloaded links, which leads to a non-congested network. In addition to that, we can obtain the shortest path and adjust the flow link cost where more traffic occurs. Therefore, minimizing traffic flow preserves the standard of QoS [19].

6.3.2 Energy Saving by Controller

An SDN network uses a controller to monitor the entire activity of the network. The main aim of a control plan is to activate the controller to save energy by decoupling the data plan and control plan. The centralized controller is connected to all the switches, which in turn create the virtual controller by using a VSDN. This virtual controller will be created to reduce load balancing; when the network is congested with traffic, the virtual controller redirects traffic to other networks to reach its destination. If the load is reduced by a virtual controller using routing techniques, latency will automatically be reduced [20].

Traffic is defined by congestion occurring in a particular time period. A centralized controller optimizes the congestion based on redirecting and creating a virtual link between the nodes. Controllers also initiate configuration in a device and assign specific resources needed to do optimization [21]. When the switches redirect the congestion by partitioning network device. Once the switch is partitioned, it is responsible for the configuration and routing of the network. Moreover, it is very important to take care of network devices such as routers, switches, links, and resources considered for energy saving. Therefore, a centralized controller is more useful to reduce energy consumption by implementing routing and virtual creation of controllers and links [22].

6.3.3 Energy Saving by Virtualization

The virtualization technique improves energy savings by allocating resources and load balancing an SDN network. This will focus on applying a model to choose a path that is more congested. The main objective of resource allocation is that resources that have already been helped already are distributed to the network that needs the resources. When resources are allocated to the network, all of the network flow will be controlled by the controller [23]. All the network functions are executed on hardware. There are some limitations of the virtualization function, such as allocation of resources, load assignment, and virtual link creation.

The integration technique used in an SDN network is resource allocation with respect to resources needed for specific data transfer and traffic minimization with respect to redirection of traffic to another network. Therefore, SDN-based virtualization specifies dynamic configuration, virtual creation of links between nodes, resource allocation, and load balancing to meet requests and energy savings efficiently [24].

6.4 THE NETWORK ROUTING FRAMEWORK

Energy consumption techniques focus on the shortest-path routing mechanism applied to every request by the centralized controller, which effectively reduces the energy consumed in active devices, active links, and resources used for data transfer between different networks [25].

The centralized controller is connected to the data plane and control plane through southbound and northbound interfaces. Each plane has corresponding resources such as computation capacity and memory capacity consume lot of server power [26]. This increases network infrastructure; applying the shortest-path mechanism on the network will reduce the load balancing of the controller by minimizing the number of active states. SDN networks consist of three layers, the data layer, control layer, and application layer. Each of these layers is managed by a centralized controller that controls all underlying network devices. The routing mechanism is applied to the routing path, which will minimize the flow route with all nodes based on energy consumption techniques [27]. This technique consists of three states: first, the paths between the nodes in the network can exchange network traffic and manage in-bound and out-bound messages by applying the shortest-path routing technique done by the centralized controller. Second, the centralized controller will control the data transfer between all the routers in the network. Third, each router has a virtual controller to monitor heavy traffic between the nodes.

When the number of flows is congested with traffic and shares the same routers and switches, the centralized controller will direct the traffic to other flows after applying the shortest-path routing technique. In the case of an enormous amount of traffic in the network, the centralized controller accomplishes sufficient resource utilization; load balancing and path utilization are important approaches that must be explored to reduce traffic and energy consumption [28].

6.5 DESIGN CONSIDERATIONS

Traffic is a set of flow requests specified by a user.

The flow request can be for data flow or control flow, which must be forwarded between the network nodes and monitored by the controller. When data is routed between nodes, the link capacity should not go beyond the limit of the bandwidth. During data transfers, if the network is congested with traffic, energy usage will automatically be maximized to reduce energy consumption; routing polices and virtual networks are created, which reduces the traffic [29]. The energy consumption technique uses the shortest path to minimize energy consumption on multiple flows by providing a minimum cost path with more nodes.

Figure 6.2 shows data transferred from source to destination by using the shortest shortest-path calculation. There are three domains connected to a single SDN centralized controller: domain1 has routers R1, R2, R3, R4, and R5 connected; domain2 has routers R6, R7, R8, R9, R10, R11, and R12 connected; and domain3 has routers R13, R14, R15, R16, R17, R18, R19, and R20 connected with the cost value of each link. When an attacker sends a large number of packets to a destination, there is the possibility of congestion in a network link. Once the network becomes congested, all the network devices become involved to resolve the congested network, so much of the energy will be consumed.

Figure 6.2 shows that the source node sends an unexpected amount of data to the destination node through R1, R2, R3, R6, R7, R10, R12, R13, R14, R15, and R20. When an unexpected number of packets is transferred through these routers, networks become congested. This can be solved by applying the shortest-path algorithm, all-pair shortest path. According to this algorithm, the route found from the source to the destination is R1, R2, R3, R6, R9, R12, R13, R16, R19, R18, and R20. It also creates the virtual link between the source and destination using a virtual software-defined network shown in Figure 6.2 and assigns the resources needed to the link.

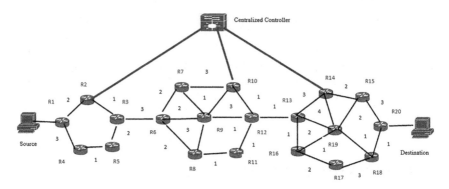

Figure 6.2 Shortest-path route from source to destination in network.

6.6 PROPOSED SOLUTION FOR ENERGY-CONSUMPTION PROBLEM

This section provides a proposed solution for the energy consumption technique. This technique consists of the shortest-path routing algorithm [30], virtual link capacity, and virtual routing, which will be managed by the centralized controller.

Routing in an SDN network finds the shortest path using the all-pair shortest-path algorithm [30] and determines the path length based the number of hops between the nodes. APSP is done in two main phases. In the first phase, when the network is congested with more requests, services of the network are denied. Therefore, we identify the networks that are highly congested and remove those links connected to the network. To remove a link, first identify the flow table of the highly congested switch in the network and remove the link along with the switch connected to the network. After removing the link and switch, modify the flow table according to the current network. In the second phase, update the shortest cost of allowable paths and routes identified for the upcoming request using the APSP approach. This approach only updates the shortest path after removing the congested link and switch. Therefore, the flow table of the congested link is not part of the new shortest path.

Once we make the shortest path between the nodes, allocate the sufficient capacity to the link. When the user sends a number of requests to the particular network, a virtual SDN is created to establish the virtual link between the nodes, where more congestion occurs. In this scenario, the VSDN allocates the resources needed for the specific virtual link. If any of the virtual links fail or lack link resources, then this problem is solved by the following three steps. First, collect information o virtual path allocation between the nodes, topology used for the network, and number of user requests. Second, check whether the current user request matches the resources allocated to the virtual link [31]. Third, if the match is successful, the flow table is configured for the virtual link; if not, the VSDN recalculates a virtual link that will satisfy the user's request [32]. Hence, the adjustment made to the shortest path and cost of the link is based on distance associated with linkability, so the ECT uses the minimum number of links to reduce network congestion.

Toward this goal, first, the all-pair shortest-path algorithm is used to remove networks that are highly congested and modify the flow table based on the current network. Then, using the APSP algorithm, find the shortest path that is not part of a congested link and update it in the upcoming request. Second, the virtual SDN is designed to assign the resources needed for the virtual link [33]. If any of the links fail, then verify the information collected from the network as path allocation, topology of the network, user requests, and whether the allocated resources are sufficient for the virtual link [32].

To coordinate the entire process of the ECT, a centralized controller is used. In traditional networks, a distributed controller is used to communicate with each node in network. But in SDN networks, a centralized controller is used. The controller monitors requests coming from the user; when there is a huge amount of requests to a particular network, energy consumption will increase automatically. To minimize energy consumption, the centralized controller uses the ECT technique. In this virtual controller associated with each router [34], when there is heavy traffic found in a particular path/network, the centralized controller directs traffic to the virtual controller, which will take care of the local network to minimize the energy consumption. The pseudocode of the proposed algorithm is given in the following:

```
Input: Graph, controller_capacity, link_capacity
Output: Number_of hops, number_of active_routes, energy_
   consumption.
Data transfer between set of nodes
Network is congested with traffic
If total traffic flow is greater than link capacity
Apply all-pair shortest-path algorithm
i. Identify and remove the links that are congested
ii. Update flow table and shortest path
VSDN is created to establish virtual link
If link fails
Collect information of virtual path allocation
Check the user request matches resource allocated for
   virtual link
If match is successful, flow table is configured for the
   virtual link
```

```
Else
Recalculate the virtual link and satisfy user request
End if
Else
No traffic and less energy consumption
End if
```

This algorithm takes as input the graph, controller capacity, and link capacity, and produces the number of hops, the number of active routes, and energy consumption.

In the first phase, the algorithm starts to transfer the huge number of data packets between the set of nodes in the data plane, and the network becomes congested with traffic. Once the network is congested, if total traffic flow is greater than link capacity, find the shortest path using the all-pair shortest-path algorithm. This algorithm identifies the links that are more congested and removes the switches along with the links from the network. Next, based on the available network, update the flow table and shortest path.

In the second phase, a virtual software-defined network is created to establish the virtual link and allocate the resources needed for the virtual link. If the link fails, analyze the information about the different nodes, topology used, and number of user requests already there to determine whether the network is congested.

Next check that the current user request matches the virtual link of resources. Then, if the match is successful, the flow table is configured for the virtual link; if not, the VSDN recalculates the virtual link that satisfies the user request, or else no traffic and lower energy consumption occur.

6.7 PERFORMANCE EVALUATION

This section describes the emulation setup of the proposed algorithm and its results. Model emulation is executed to monitor network traffic with a controller such as a POX controller through the energy utilization, path allocation, and path cost. The proposed algorithm was done using Mininet 2.2.1 executed using Ubuntu Linux on an HP laptop, Intel Core i7–4700MQ processor, and 16 GB of RAM.

6.7.1 Model Emulation

In this simulation model, a huge number of packets has been sent to the network to deny service of legitimate requests, which increases energy consumption. To reduce the energy consumption, the Mininet simulator has been used with a POX controller. In this Mininet simulator, networks with 15, 25, 35, and 45 hosts were first created using tree topology and applied the ECT. To consider the feasibility of the network in terms of size, we selected the tree topology and applied the ECT technique on each router, which is centrally managed by the POX controller. A virtual network has been created on each router, which is controlled by the centralized POX controller [35].

The efficiency of the ECT technique is compared with the existing energy aware routing model using the shortest-path routing technique. The energy-aware shortest-path routing (EASPR) algorithm uses the Dijkstra algorithm [36] with delay constraints. The typical SPR technique is used to find the number of routers (hop count) between the two hosts and the length of the route. However, when computing the shortest path between two hosts based on hop count, this algorithm found the shortest distance between the two hosts is established host by host and energy consumption technique also used host by host. Instead, the proposed ECT technique was applied to all routers using the POX controller in a centralized way [5]. So the efficiency of the algorithm is better than the existing algorithm.

6.7.2 Implementation and Results

To analyze the efficiency of proposed ECT algorithm, evaluation was carried out in terms of time and topology design. Networks were created with different hosts, and the ECT technique was applied. This model first finds the shortest path using the APSP algorithm by identifying the congested network and removing its links and switches. Once the links and switches are removed, the flow table is automatically updated according to the network. After finding the shortest path, resources are assigned to the link. When large numbers of packets are coming, the virtual SDN is created on each router to make the network flexible, which will redirect the traffic by the POX controller in a centralized way on the Mininet emulator. Energy consumption can be reduced by minimizing congestion, increasing the capacity of the network, and virtual routing will be concurrently monitored by the centralized POX controller.

According to the number of hosts in the network, path cost will decrease in the congested area after applying the APSP algorithm in the network. This could significantly decrease the energy consumption of the network. For analyzing the energy consumption of the network, two parameters, traffic and time, are considered. In addition, there are 15, 25, 35, and 45 hosts with given parameter readings in the network.

This section discuss the POX controller performance scenario. The tree topology was created with different numbers of hosts: 15, 25, 35, and 45. The energy consumption technique is applied, and the results are discussed as the tree topology uses the POX controller to reduce the traffic of the network with various hosts (15, 25, 35, and 45) in less time, as shown in Figure 6.3. The energy consumption is also measured for the same set of

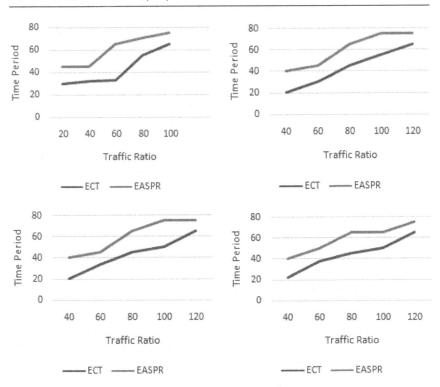

Figure 6.3 Analyzing traffic ratios for specific time periods. a) Tree topology with 15 nodes using POX controller. b) Tree topology with 25 nodes using POX controller. c) Tree topology with 35 nodes using POX controller. d) Tree topology with 45 nodes using POX controller.

networks for the existing algorithm with energy-aware shortest-path routing and the proposed algorithm energy consumption technique, as shown in Figure 6.4.

According to the analysis, energy consumption will increase when there is a large amount of traffic in a specific time period. This can be observed by tree topology using a POX controller with various nodes; 15, 25, 35, and 45 are shown in Figure 6.4. The experiment was compared the existing EASPR algorithm and proposed ECT algorithm. In the EASPR algorithm, traffic is found based on the shortest path, and it uses the Dijkstra algorithm, but the ECT technique uses all-pair shortest path and creates a virtual link whenever there is a huge volume of traffic. Therefore, the traffic ratio for a specific time period observed in Figure 6.3a shows a network with 15 nodes, Figure 6.3b shows a network with 25 nodes, Figure 6.3c shows a network with 35 nodes, and Figure 6.3d shows the network with 45 nodes.

On the other hand, increasing the network size makes the traffic increase along with overall hop count. So Figure 6.4 reveals the hop count for the

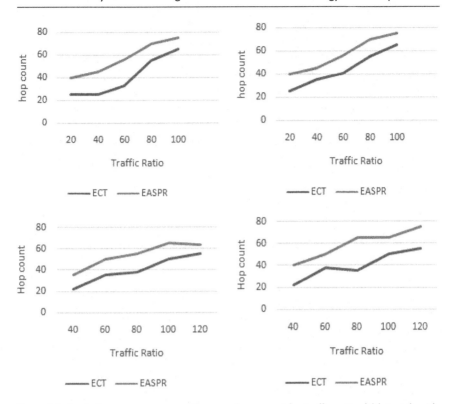

Figure 6.4 Analyzing energy consumption over hop count for traffic ratio. a) Network with 15 nodes. b) Network with 25 nodes. c) Network with 35 nodes. d) Network with 45 nodes.

traffic on the network with 15, 25, 35, and 45 nodes. It also shows the comparative analysis of the energy-aware shortest-path routing and energy consumption technique. By minimizing the number of congested nodes in the network, the ECT is able to maximize the utilization and reduce energy consumption. In comparison, the ECT technique raises the percentage of energy savings in a network of 15 nodes from 74% to 79%. As shown in the graph, the percentage level gradually changed for networks with 25 nodes, 35 nodes, and 45 nodes.

6.8 CONCLUSION

This chapter discuss the various ways traffic occurs, the drawbacks of traffic, and how these are solved for energy consumption using different techniques. Parameters such as traffic and time are computed with various hosts on the network using a POX controller in a Mininet emulator. To reduce energy consumption, the ECT technique uses the shortest-path algorithm, virtual link capacity, and virtual routing in a centralized way using a POX controller in Mininet, which uses a software-defined network. The tree topology was created with different numbers of hosts: 15, 25, 35, and 45, which uses a POX controller to reduce congestion by removing links connected to the congested network. Once we remove the links, the flow table is automatically updated accordingly. When there is a huge amount of traffic, the POX controller will create a virtual controller, which is associated with each router to reduce congestion. This reduces energy consumption using a POX controller in the Mininet emulator.

REFERENCES

1. B. Rashidi, C. Fung, and E. Bertino, "A collaborative DDoS defence framework using network function virtualization," *IEEE Trans. Inf. Forensics Secur.*, vol. 12, no. 10, pp. 2483–2497, October 2017, doi: 10.1109/TIFS.2017.2708693.

2. G. Florance, "Survey of IP traceback methods in distributed denial of service (DDoS) attacks," *IJIRSET*, vol. 4, no. 7, pp. 6319–6325, July 2015, doi: 10.15680/IJIRSET.2015.0407143.

3. P. Ferguson and D. Senie. "Network ingress filtering: Defeating denial of service attacks which employ IP source address spoofing (bcp 38)," http://tools.ietf.org/html/rfc2827.

4. A. John and T. Sivakumar. "DDoS: Survey of traceback methods," *IJRTE*, vol. 1, no. 2, pp. 241–245, 2009.

5. M. Alshammari and A. Rezgui, "POX-PLUS: An SDN controller with dynamic shortest path routing," 2020 IEEE 9th International Conference on Cloud Networking (CloudNet), 2020, pp. 1–4, doi: 10.1109/CloudNet51028.2020.9335792.

6. B. Rashidi, C. Fung, and E. Bertino, "A collaborative DDoS defence framework using network function virtualization," *IEEE Trans. Inf. Forensics Secur.*, vol. 12, no. 10, pp. 2483–2497, October 2017, doi: 10.1109/TIFS.2017.2708693.

7. A. A. Z. Ibrahim, F. Hashim, A. Sali, N. K. Noordin, and S. M. E. Fadul, "A multi-objective routing mechanism for energy management optimization in SDN multi-control architecture," *IEEE Access*, vol. 10, pp. 20312–20327, 2022, doi: 10.1109/ACCESS.2022.3149795.

8. Lei He, Xiaoning Zhang, Zijing Cheng, and Yajie Jiang, "Design and implementation of SDN/IP hybrid space information network prototype," 2016 IEEE/CIC International Conference on Communications in China (ICCC Workshops), 2016, pp. 1–6, doi: 10.1109/ICCChinaW.2016.7586705.

9. Z. Yang and K. L. Yeung, "An efficient algorithm for constructing controller trees in SDN," GLOBECOM 2017–2017 IEEE Global Communications Conference, 2017, pp. 1–6, doi: 10.1109/GLOCOM.2017.8254747.

10. A. M. Al-Sadi, A. Al-Sherbaz, J. Xue, and S. Turner, "Routing algorithm optimization for software defined network WAN," 2016 Al-Sadeq International Conference on Multidisciplinary in IT and Communication Science and Applications (AIC-MITCSA), 2016, pp. 1–6, doi: 10.1109/AIC-MITCSA.2016.7759945.

11. Florance G and R. J. Anandhi, "Study on SDN with security issues using Mininet," *Adv. Parallel Comput.*, vol. 39, pp. 104–113, December 2021, in IOS Press.
12. M. F. Tuysuz, Z. K. Ankarali, and D. Gözüpek, "A survey on energy efficiency in software defined networks," *Comput. Netw.*, vol. 113, pp. 188–204, 2017.
13. J. Zhang, M. Ye, Z. Guo, C. Y. Yen, and H. J. Chao, "CFR-RL: Traffic engineering with reinforcement learning in SDN," *IEEE J. Sel. Areas Commun.*, vol. 38, no. 10, pp. 2249–2259, 2020.
14. R. Maaloul, R. Taktak, L. Chaari, and B. Cousin, "Energy-aware routing in carrier-grade ethernet using SDN approach," *IEEE Trans. Green Commun. Netw.*, vol. 2, no. 3, pp. 844–858, 2018.
15. M. Priyadarsini and P. Bera, "Software defined networking architecture, traffic management, security, and placement: A survey," *Comput. Netw.*, vol. 192, December 2020, p. 108047, 2021.
16. A. Fernandez-Fernandez, C. Cervello-Pastor, L. Ochoa-Aday, and P. Grosso, "An online power-aware routing in SDN with congestion avoidance traffic reallocation," 2018 IFIP Networking Conference (IFIP Networking) and Workshops, 2018, pp. 1–9.
17. W. Wang, C. H. Wang, and T. Javidi, "Reliable shortest path routing with applications to wireless software-defined networking," 2018 IEEE Global Communication Conference GLOBECOM 2018 – Proceedings, 2018, pp. 1–6.
18. B. Özbek, Y. Aydogmuş, A. Ulaş, B. Gorkemli, and K. Ulusoy, "Energy aware routing and traffic management for software defined networks," 2016 IEEE NetSoft Conference and Workshops (NetSoft), 2016, pp. 73–77.
19. W. Sun, Z. Wang, and G. Zhang, "A QoS-guaranteed intelligent routing mechanism in software-defined networks," *Comput. Netw.*, vol. 185, November 2020, p. 107709, 2021.
20. J. Lu, Z. Zhang, T. Hu, P. Yi, and J. Lan, "A survey of controller placement problem in software-defined networking," *IEEE Access*, vol. 7, pp. 24290–24307, 2019.
21. A. Ouhab, T. Abreu, H. Slimani, and A. Mellouk, "Energy-efficient clustering and routing algorithm for large-scale SDN-based IoT monitoring," ICC 2020–2020 IEEE International Conference on Communications (ICC), 2020, pp. 1–6, doi: 10.1109/ICC40277.2020.9148659.
22. F. Li, X. Xu, X. Han, S. Gao, and Y. Wang, "Adaptive controller placement in software defined wireless networks," *China Commun.*, vol. 16, no. 11, pp. 81–92, 2019.
23. Y. Chai, G. Shou, Y. Liu, Y. Hu, and Z. Guo, "Towards dynamic bandwidth management optimization in VSDN networks," GLOBECOM 2017–2017 IEEE Global Communications Conference, 2017, pp. 1–6, doi: 10.1109/GLOCOM.2017.8254750.
24. Rafael L. Gomes, Luiz F. Bittencourt, Edmundo R. M. Madeira, Eduardo Cerqueira, and Mario Gerla, "Bandwidth-aware allocation of resilient virtual software defined networks," *Comput. Netw.*, vol. 100, pp. 179–194, May 2016.
25. S. Manzoor, Z. Chen, Y. Gao, X. Hei, and W. Cheng, "Towards QoS-aware load balancing for high density software defined wi-fi networks," *IEEE Access*, vol. 8, pp. 117623–117638, 2020.

26. Z. Chen, J. Bi, Y. Fu, Y. Wang, and A. Xu, "MLV: A multi-dimension routing information exchange mechanism for inter-domain SDN," 2015 IEEE 23rd International Conference on Network Protocols (ICNP), 2015, pp. 438–445, doi: 10.1109/ICNP.2015.34.
27. A. Ouhab, T. Abreu, H. Slimani, and A. Mellouk, "Energy-efficient clustering and routing algorithm for large-scale SDN-based IoT monitoring," ICC 2020–2020 IEEE International Conference on Communications (ICC), 2020, pp. 1–6, doi: 10.1109/ICC40277.2020.9148659.
28. Z. Guo et al., "Balancing flow table occupancy and link utilization in software-defined networks," *Futur. Gener. Comput. Syst.*, vol. 89, pp. 213–223, 2018.
29. M. N. Siraj, N. Javaid, Q. Shafi, Z. Ahmed, U. Qasim, and Z. A. Khan, "Energy aware dynamic routing using SDN for a campus network," 2016 19th International Conference on Network-Based Information Systems (NBiS), 2016, pp. 226–230, doi: 10.1109/NBiS.2016.80.
30. R. Jmal and L. Chaari Fourati, "Implementing shortest path routing mechanism using OpenFlow POX controller," The 2014 International Symposium on Networks, Computers and Communications, 2014, pp. 1–6, doi: 10.1109/SNCC.2014.6866528.
31. R. Mijumbi, J. Serrat, J. Rubio-Loyola, N. Bouten, F. D. Turck, and S. Latré, "Dynamic resource management in SDN-based virtualized networks," 10th International Conference on Network and Service Management (CNSM) and Workshop, Rio de Janeiro, 2014, pp. 412–417.
32. Y. Chai, G. Shou, Y. Liu, Y. Hu, and Z. Guo, "Towards dynamic bandwidth management optimization in VSDN networks," GLOBECOM 2017–2017 IEEE Global Communications Conference, 2017, pp. 1–6, doi: 10.1109/GLOCOM.2017.8254750.
33. H. T. Nguyen, A. V. Vu, D. L. Nguyen, V. H. Nguyen, M. N. Tran, Q. T. Ngo, T.-H. Truong, T. H. Nguyen, and T. Magedanz, "A generalized resource allocation framework in support of multi-layer virtual network embedding based on SDN," *Comput. Netw.*, vol. 92, pp. 251–269, December 2015.
34. R. Mijumbi, J. L. Gorricho, and J. Serrat, "Contributions to efficient resource management in virtual networks," in A. Sperotto, G. Doyen, S. Latr, M. Charalambides, and B. Stiller, editors, *Monitoring and Securing Virtualized Networks and Services, Volume 8508 of Lecture Notes in Computer Science*, Springer, Berlin, Heidelberg, pp. 47–51, 2014.
35. G. Schütz and J. A. Martins, "A comprehensive approach for optimizing controller placement in software-defined networks," *Comput. Commun.*, vol. 159, February, pp. 198–205, 2020.
36. J. Lu, Z. Zhang, T. Hu, P. Yi, and J. Lan, "A survey of controller placement problem in software-defined networking," *IEEE Access*, vol. 7, pp. 24290–24307, 2019.

## Chapter 7

A Deep Insight into IoT and IoB Security and Privacy Concerns – Applications and Future Challenges

Hina Bansal, Vusala Sri Sai Pravallika,
Shravani M. Phatak, and Veronica Kumar

CONTENTS

7.1 INTERNET OF THINGS

The Internet of Things (IoT) is a new paradigm that simplifies our lives, allowing electrical devices and sensors to communicate with each other over the Internet. IoT uses smart devices and the Internet to provide new solutions

DOI: 10.1201/9781003305170-7

to the challenges and problems facing businesses, governments, and public and private businesses around the world [1].

IoT is becoming an important part of our lives and can be felt all around us. IoT is a technology that combines various smart systems, frames, smart devices, and sensors. It also uses quantum and nanotechnology in previously unimaginable [2] areas of memory, sensors, and processing speed.

Extensive research has been conducted to demonstrate the potential effects and applications of IoT transformation, available in the form of scientific articles and press releases, both online and in print. It can be used as a basis for developing your own business concepts of security, reliability, and interactivity. With the increasing use of IoT devices and technologies, we are witnessing major changes in our daily lives.

Consisting of Internet-based devices, home automation systems, and reliable energy management systems [3], smart home systems (SHSS) and devices reflect the evolution of IoT. Another important achievement of the Internet of Things is the intelligent home security system, smart home security system (SHSS). SHSS involves the use of small smart devices [4] and technologies to support home security. The device allows you to monitor various health conditions, fitness levels, calories burned at the gym, and much more. It can be used both indoors and outdoors for detection and monitoring. It is also used in hospitals and trauma centers to diagnose serious health problems. As a result, state-of-the-art technology and smart devices facilitate changes in the overall healthcare environment.

In addition, IoT developers and researchers are actively interested in improving the lives of people with disabilities and the elderly. IoT has made great strides in this area, giving these people a new direction in their daily lives. Many people use these products and devices because they are relatively inexpensive to develop and are readily available at low prices [5]. Thanks to the Internet, people can now lead normal lives.

Transportation is another important part of our lives. The Internet of Things has led to many new innovations that make it more efficient, convenient, and reliable [6]. Smart sensors and drone devices are currently monitoring traffic at several signal nodes in major cities. Vehicles also have pre-installed sensors on the map that can detect oncoming traffic and provide a less crowded alternative route. As a result, IoT has a wide range of applications in both life and technology. IoT also demonstrates its usefulness and promise for economic and industrial development in developing countries. This is also a revolutionary development in trade.

On the other hand, data and information security is a key issue [7] and a desirable goal. The Internet offers hackers many opportunities to compromise data and information, a major source of security vulnerabilities and cyber-attacks. IoT, on the other hand, aims to provide the best available solutions to data and information security issues. Therefore, security is a

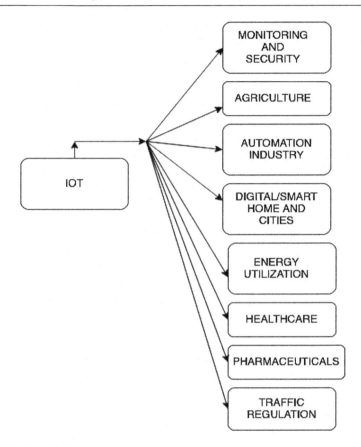

Figure 7.1 Use of IoT in various sectors.

key issue for IoT in commerce and enterprise and creating secure channels for collaboration on social media and addressing these privacy concerns is a topic for IoT developers. Therefore, it can be concluded that the Internet of Things has many features in terms of technological progress and ease of use.

7.2 INTERNET OF BEHAVIOR

Psychologically, the Internet of Behavior (IoB) aims to better understand data and discuss how data can be used to create and promote new products. It is also described as a solution for end users who can improve their behavior based on device suggestions. The Internet of Behavior can be used in a variety of ways by public and private organizations. It directly targets individuals, combining existing technologies such as facial recognition, location tracking, and big data. It combines science, data processing, and behavioral psychology [8, 9].

Before the application is built, IoB views user interaction patterns and contact points. This technology is used in the development process to meet the needs of users; to support a structured and consistent application interface; and to make navigation easy, intuitive, and valuable. It can also support multi-channel personalization, duplicate messages in a single center, distribution of personal ads for program customization, social media integration, and integrated design support [10, 11]. IoB aims to interpret psychologically the data collected from human interactions on the Internet. Marketers interpret and use the data to develop and market new products based on human psychology.

Studying consumer buying behavior over the network is one of the unique benefits of IoB. With easily viewed data on how your device interacts with your product, it gives you accurate information about where your customers [12] are in the buying process [13, 14]. Marketers use IoB to customize products and services based on the data they collect. Selected goods and services add value by encouraging consumers to stay with their products and services. Large files, location tracking, and facial recognition are all integrated so your data is connected to your smartphone. The purpose of IoB is not only to monitor and describe human behavior but also to monitor, analyze, recognize [8, 9], and respond to all types of human behavior, using new technologies and advances in machine learning. This is considered one of the most important technological advances of 2021.

The COVID-19 pandemic is primarily related to the emergence of IoB as a trend, as it has forced companies to rethink and change the way consumers interact with brands. They interact with customers. IoB principles have become more important in recent years due to the growing importance of communication in the production of goods and services and increased customer and user satisfaction. In a few years, the IoB will become a global environment that determines human behavior. A breakthrough has been made in connecting people and computers to analyze behavior. IoB assesses the potential of behavioral data. By collecting data from multiple contact points, you can explore the entire journey. This creates additional customer contact and new communication channels.

IoB is used to promote and advertise to help entrepreneurs improve their business. Next, we will look at the consumer experience from start to finish. We increase customer loyalty by creating additional contact points, taking into account the consumer's initial interest in the product and the customer's shopping experience to the point of purchase. You can also find innovative ways for people to interact with your company before making a purchase.

The concept of behavioral Internet includes an overview of user behavior and information about the use of (social) networks. Technology is becoming a new attractive marketing and sales platform [15] for companies and organizations around the world.

7.3 IOB AND IOT PRIVACY AND SECURITY CONCERNS

Privacy concerns refer to the amount of control a user has over his/her data while sharing personal information to others, in other words, he/she can choose who can see what part of their personal data without stealing [16]. One example is the browsing history of the user (IoB) [17]; through that, we can get to know the personal interests and choices of the user and understand their psychological way of thinking. Another example (IoT) is that of eavesdropping, which means that our data is being read by third-party users whose identity is unknown to us, and thus our data confidentiality is at risk [18].

Privacy in IoT is an important characteristic that must be present across all data service platforms because, in today's world, data needs to be collected daily or on a large scale, and it leads to over-accumulation of personal information let out in the open, which, if ignored or not handled properly, can lead to unpleasant consequences such as brand degeneration, reputation being questioned, and lawsuits [19].

Privacy in IoB is also a major factor for which strict measures have been taken from time to time. The behavior data of the users allows cyber-criminals to access, collect, and analyze behavior patterns of customers, thus leading them to fake websites and web pages which contain items/information of choice or interest of the user, prompting them to purchase the product, only to be scammed. This is the basis for fraud and scams [20]. One security concern is when the assets of a data service are vulnerable to theft. It is when a customer's data is vulnerable to hackers, which then leads to selling of personal information to unknown people who might extort from the customer [21]. An example is hackers (IoT) [18], when our information is left to be read without any safety locks, hackers might completely access our personal data and alter it per their own means, extorting resources (unknown transactions) for themselves through our data. One example is health data being stolen by smartwatches [22]. A smartwatch is used to tell our heart rate and blood count, but that also leaves the risk of any third-party organization knowing about our health records.

Security in IoT is also important, and data exchange must happen in an encrypted format, that is, encrypted communication, which prevents data breaches and data theft [23], which can further lead to financial loss and operational downtime [24]. Likewise, security in IoT is important when it comes to large-scale companies [25], as security lapses can lead to financial crimes because the data connected to home appliances, hospitals and healthcare, institutions, and large-scale smart factories is under the potential threat of data leakage [26].

7.3.1 Examples of IoB and IoB Privacy and Security Concerns

A. IoT Privacy Issues

1) **Unwanted public profile**: The privacy issue of a public profile is when data points about us have collected anonymously and used against our will through deception. Often IoT devices have a feature of collecting user data and giving access to third-party users, leading to unsafe ventures. For example, we have IoT systems being used in our cars, which record data about our driving performance and distance speed relationship that provides insurance companies data on our driving experience and can accordingly alter our interest rates [22].

2) **Consumer confidence**: In any forum or discussion, definitions are important because they enable a common understanding of words and topics. The world of technology is no exception, and discussions of technologies such as the Internet of Things are usually preceded by each party trying to understand how the other party defines the term being discussed [22]. Otherwise, it quickly becomes apparent that there is a gap between the use of the term on the one hand and the actual understanding on the other.

B. IoT Security Issues

1) **Incorrect access control**: IoT-associated devices must have permission to view personal data only by the user or the people that he or she has entrusted the device password to. But sometimes the system's security fails to provide that. It trusts the local network to such an extent that authentication is not even required, but this creates a problem, as anyone in the world can now access the functionality of the device. A common example is when systems have common default passwords such as "admin," "admin123," or "password123"; then access becomes much more vulnerable [27].

2) **Insecure default settings**: Devices such as smartwatches and smart TVs and systems such as smart homes or smart cars built with an insecure default setting can lead to the system becoming insecure and more open to potential threats.

Hackers hack our systems by starting from the motherboard, which is the deepest layer of our device. The hardware communication ports, such as inter-integrated circuit, joint test action group, universal asynchronous receiver/transmitter, virtual private network (VPN), and serial peripheral interface [26], are present here. This is the entry point for hidden backdoors, passwords, and major vulnerabilities of the firmware. Before installing apps on our devices, we must review/verify the permissions that the app requires and block the necessary important access. Using a VPN will help us solve this issue to a great extent.

C. IoB Privacy Issues

1) **COVID-19 smart health apps:** During 2020, that is, the COVID- era, the first real-world applications of IoB were beginning to be marketed globally; health care, and tracing apps had been developed with regard to COVID-19. Though the app's goal was to collect patient data and help them get better, a lot of organizations collected study information as part of studying COVID without the patient's consent. As an example, in the United Kingdom, the NHS contact-tracing app was launched but later suspended in March 2020, as it was said to have technical failings and concerns revolving around the centralization of the collected data [28].

2) **5G technology:** The computational power of fifth generation (5G) technology will have a major role in enhancing IoB. In 2021,22, a mobile operator confirmed its ultrafast 5G-based mobile broadband network had been live around 150 UK cities and towns, with plans of extending the region through the following year. The speed and functionality of 5G were amazing, but it led to concerns about cyber attackers attacking this harnessed energy. As data flow is a feature of the 5G infrastructure, both service providers and users should build and develop security measures and deal with trusted vendors only [29].

D. IoB Security Issues

1) **Shopping websites:** Online shopping sites such as Ebay, Amazon, Flipkart, Snapdeal, and Home Depot, use IoB to analyze user/customer activities. Does it happen that whenever you leave a restaurant or café, you are requested to give a rating or leave a review on Google? This is how your tastes are known by IoB technology. Uber uses the same logic to understand customer experiences and come up with better ideas to deal with them. All places where large numbers of people gather, not just shopping places, are monitored by IoB to promote an ordered protocol. By 2025, physical checkout process staff will be significantly

reduced, and automatic checkout systems will be installed in most shopping locations. But this has led to the psychological history of users being on the open net, which can lead to manipulation by cyber criminals and later extortion of assets from users [22].

2) **Location tracking (Uber):** After eating out at a restaurant, you often get a request to leave a review on Google, as that is how our preference is extracted. Uber applies the same method to find out about its customers' experiences/interests/choices and work on plans to improve its service. But this also gives the app access to your current/live location, which poses a threat to the user, as a third party has details about his or her travel history, and their office and home address. This is an important concern regarding security [30].

7.4 APPLICATIONS OF IOT

The Internet of Things has a wide range of potential uses, as it pervades almost every element of people's, institutions', and societies' daily lives. IoT applications play an important role in diverse sectors, including smart vehicles, smart homes, healthcare, manufacturing, agriculture, smart cities, home security, and disaster management and relief [31].

A. **Smart Cities**

The Internet of Things plays a critical role in developing city smartness and general infrastructure [32]. Smart transportation systems [33], smart infrastructure of buildings, traffic management [34], waste management [35], smart lighting, smart parking, and urban maps are some of the IoT application areas in constructing smart cities. This could include functions like monitoring available parking spots within the city, monitoring vibrations and material states of bridges and buildings, installing sound-monitoring devices in sensitive areas of cities, and monitoring pedestrian and vehicle levels.

B. **Healthcare**

Many countries' healthcare systems are slow and insufficient along with being vulnerable to mistakes. These problems can be addressed easily because the healthcare industry depends on a variety of technologies that are converted to automation and improved technology. Apart from this, we have technology that monitors activities such as sharing reports with numerous people and places, record maintenance, and medicine delivery that contribute to changing our healthcare industry [31]. Many of the advantages that IoT applications provide in our healthcare sector are classified as tracking of patient records, personnel, and items; authenticating and identifying persons; and autonomous data collection and sensing. Once the flow of patients is recorded, the hospital's workflow can be considerably improved.

C. **Smart Agriculture and Water Management**

The Internet of Things possesses the potential to develop and improve the agriculture industry by monitoring the moisture content of the soil, and in other cases, such as grapes, it is the diameter of the grapevine [36]. IoT can help in better management and preservation of vitamin content in agricultural products, along with maintaining proper micro-climate conditions for increasing fruit and vegetable quality and production. Furthermore, examining meteorological conditions enables forecasting of snow, rain, wind changes, drought, or information on ice formation, allowing humidity and temperature levels to be controlled, preventing fungal growth and other microbial pollutants.

D. **Retail and Logistics**

There are numerous advantages to applications of IoT in retail or supply chain management. Some examples include keeping track of storage parameters used in the supply chain, tracking products for traceability purposes, and processing of payments in public transportation, gyms, theme parks, and so on. In the retail environment, IoT is used in a wide range of applications, some of which are automatic check-out with biometrics, storage based on a pre-selected list to guide customers, detecting (potential) allergens in products, and controlling rotation of products and warehouses, which is helpful in automating procedures of restocking [37].

E. **Smart Living**

The smart living domain involves the use of IoT in devices to turn appliances on and off remotely, reducing the risk of accidents and conserving energy [38, 39]. Refrigerators with liquid crystal displays (LCDs) are another smart home appliance that allows users to see what is accessible within, what is old and about to expire, and what needs to be restocked. Also, the system data has the option of being connected to a smartphone application, allowing users to view it in and out of the house and accordingly purchase the required products. Moreover, washing machines can be used to monitor laundry from afar. Furthermore, a smartphone may be used as an interface with a wide range of kitchen gadgets, allowing temperature adjustments, such as an oven. There are ovens with self-cleaning capabilities that can be monitored easily. For home security, IoT is implemented through cameras and alarms that detect, monitor, and analyze windows, attic, or door openings and prevent home intrusion [39].

F. **Smart Environment**

Our environment has an important influence in all parts of existence; humans, microorganisms, birds, animals, and plants have been found to be affected in some manner by an unhealthy environment. Throughout history, countless efforts have been to establish to build a healthy environment in terms of minimizing all kinds of pollution and resource waste, but the presence of industrial and transportation wastes, as well as careless and dangerous human acts, are common factors that continually hurt the ecosystem. As a result, saving the environment needs clever and novel approaches in dealing with waste management and monitoring that generate large chunks of data responsible for driving governments to implement environmental protection networks.

7.5 APPLICATIONS OF IOB

Every day, the number of IoB applications grows significantly. For businesses, this is becoming a crucial marketing strategy. The "intelligence" of the Internet of Things can benefit both corporations and individuals. It arises as a novel technique of data transmission and storage [40–44] (Table 7.1).

The following are some examples of IoB applications.

A. Netflix

Netflix analyses user/customer watch data to predict what their choices might be in the future depending on likes and dislikes. It makes recommendations based on the users' choices, interests, preferences, and ratings for a particular series or movie. Imagine a scenario where it didn't analyze your previous watch history and began suggesting what to watch next without relying on your behavioral data to conclude what your preferences are. This will improve the user experience and push the project forward.

B. Insurance Sector

Insurance firms can examine behavior and determine if a certain incident was caused by an accident or by an insured person's error. This can help avoid situations of drunk driving, driving under the influence of drugs, or even underage or senior persons driving and causing an accident.

C. COVID-19 Pandemic

Employers could use radio frequency identification tags or sensors to see if there are any inconsistencies in following safety rules. Information about protocols is used by several restaurants and meal delivery applications, which subsequently carry out their plans.

D. Social Media Platforms

Online advertising is currently being used by a variety of organizations to reach their target audiences. Behavioral data is used by several social media companies, such as Facebook, to present ads to users on their

Table 7.1 Applications of IoB Resulting in Better Customer Service

Application	Description
1. Human Activity Analysis	The Internet of Behavior combines data with human activities to gain better knowledge about behavioral and psychological habits and preferences. After its development, integrated routing and bridging (IRB) is utilized by organizations to manage individual people's budgets, working circumstances, along with a variety of other domains relating to work-life. It has an impact on customer choice as well as supply chain reconfiguration in practically all industries. Companies are found to simply adopt novel ways to meet the needs of their customers.
2. Cultural Change	IoB connects data and decision-making together, necessitating adjustments in our cultural, legal, and ethical standards. It also scans social media profiles of individuals along with their contacts in order to forecast much better product usage. The IoB increases device connectivity, resulting in a plethora of novel data sources with the help of IoT. For emerging technology, we saw several opportunities for personal finance, industry, and the workplace. Data was important and crucial in determining what applications are used for accessing locations through the Internet. The IoB has led to an increase in the amount of data to be analyzed and collected. More data provides us a better understanding of consumer behavior.
3. Customer Habits	Cyber criminals have access to sensitive data about customers' habits. Their main task is to seize, sell, and access property along with the respective transmission routes. The result is that they would take their daily routine of phishing to the next level, as it led to the creation of more intricate fraud. Marketing analysis on Google, Facebook, and Amazon is growing more in-depth. Algorithms are tweaked to anticipate user desires and actions. The software alerts users about potentially harmful health scenarios and suggests changes in individual behavioral for an improved outcome. Software firms have added the idea of using the IoB principle as their company goal. The main goal of the project is improvement in skills in association with a smartphone app, wearable gadgets used in monitoring, and learning novel approaches.
4. Track Trends	The primary reason for employing tracking is to record trends in purchase decisions. Personalization is the key to a service's efficiency. Consumer and supply chain decisions are influenced by the Internet of Behavior. Consumer behavior followed by their response to a service, or a product can be accessed via concentrated sample analysis. The consumption of a service or a product is influenced by customers/buyers who have diverse viewpoints and experiences.

(Continued)

Table 7.1 (Continued)

Application	Description
5. Monitoring	Apps used for checking/monitoring nutrition, sleep habits, blood pressure, blood sugar levels, or heart rate on the smart phone affect behavior. The system would help notify you of any negative events and suggest behavior modifications that will lead to a good or more accurate outcome. As of today, marketers are largely taking the assistance of IoB for analysis and changing consumer behavior, usually to buy. Salespeople and behavior experts, on the other hand, are found to agree that has importance in service efficiency and that it is found to be more accurate when a client deals with it and even alters their behavior. This satisfies the need for personalization as well as consumer happiness.
6. Linking All Behavioral Activities	The Internet increases our awareness in our daily lives and at work. It relates data to associated behavioral activities such as smart phone use or cash transactions and incorporates current technology that focuses directly on the activities of the user, such as guarding a location and vast data. Organizations can easily affect human behavior using this method. The authorities, for example, will use IoB and computer vision to see if personnel follow protocols. IoB decodes instructions and connects these statements to specific actions, such as purchases relating to a certain brand. The state of behavior for behavioral events is constructed using values in IoB.
7. Review the Past and the Future	This enables businesses/companies to assess past performance, resulting in estimation of future outcomes. The information gathered by this technology will serve as the foundation for a company's success growth rate, marketing products, and sales efforts. The technology is used to optimize and automate a variety of procedures in various areas of life. Digital marketing is a rapidly changing sector with rapidly changing job practices. When changes are seen in customer/user behavior and marketing channels, the effects of such changes are analyzed with the help of IoB today. Integrating the IoB into a digital marketing plan is also critical. As a result, information from several points of connection can be simply obtained using this technique.
8. Employee Tracking During the Course of COVID-19	The method is used to keep a record of whether staff are following COVID-19 safety rules. Through IoB, infected people are constantly monitored. Because of the expanding number of cyber security dangers around the world, cyber criminals face serious risks to their personal security when accessing IoT data and combining it with behavioral data. Data including land access codes, bank access codes, and distribution routes is obtained by cyber attackers. IoB is used for tracking of health and fitness, healthy lifestyle, bad habit reduction, and more. This helps establish strict data protection and digital network security, keeping track of innovation's quick expansion.

Table 7.1 (Continued)

Application	Description
9. Product Planning, Service Planning, and Marketing	IoB can be used by any company that wants to plan products, service quality, and marketing efforts. This enables behavioral science information to effectively control behavior. For a strong cyber security policy that focuses on safeguarding all sensitive and important data, any organization can adopt an IoB approach. IoB interprets and connects data collected by IoT to individual/user/customer actions, an example is brand selection. Data is collected by technology, and then the data is analyzed to extract information. Following that, behavioral knowledge is a key aspect to study and understand the influence of human behavior. Sensors capture usage and behavior data points and provide inferences about users'/consumers' preferences, aspirations, needs, wants, and expectations.
10. Track Buying Habits of Users	In today's world, business is responsible for control of our behavior using data in a variety of ways. IoB uses technology which tracks the purchase habits of customer/user and advertise the choice of user products; for example, a person interested in mystery books will be shown ads on various mystery books along with their price and shopping websites during his/her browsing time on the Internet. This led to the evolution of a cutting-edge technology and a very accurate and effective marketing plan and distribution strategy for various enterprises. Our smart phone's IoB mobile fitness program allows us to track our nutrition, exercise, sleep routine, heartbeat, blood glucose, and other data. Our health care providers may utilize this information to suggest behavioral adjustments that will improve our health. This is something that health insurance suppliers may recommend to us. Our health care is presented in such a manner that it influences our health-related decisions.

platforms. This enables brands to communicate with their customers and track their responses to advertisements via "click rates" [45].

IoB, along with a huge volume of user data, can help the industry include new solutions used in customer choice analysis, service product research, experimental research, observation research, and stimulation findings [46–49]. The research sector can assist in the development of careful plans by taking into account corporate demands. This allows physical objects to be tracked, monitored, and controlled over the Internet. The Internet of Things expands the network by interconnecting devices along with the information they collect, which helps to manage people's behavior.

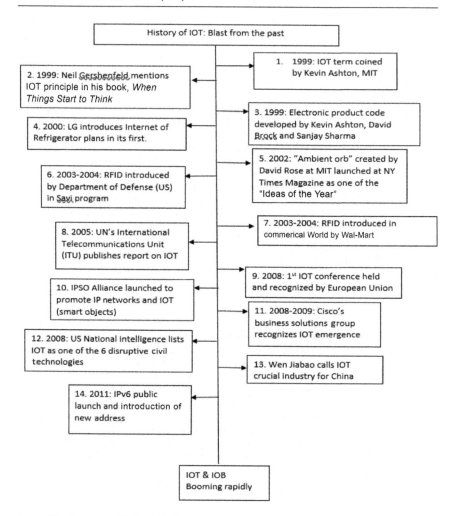

Figure 7.2 Progress of IoT and IoB.

7.6 CHALLENGES IN IOT

Machines, like technologies, are changing all the time. As a result of technical improvements, threats and privacy concerns occur. Smart devices will communicate with one another and exchange data in a network. The entire infrastructure is jeopardized if one device becomes compromised. If a machine is hacked, for example, production as well as the sensitive data stored on it may be jeopardized. Some major challenges like these are listed in the following.

7.6.1 Identification and Tracking Systems

The IoT's growing capabilities and technologies, as well as new IoT engagement platforms, have posed new privacy and security problems. Identification is one of the IoT's privacy and security issues, as it involves the risk of linking an identifier such as an address with a person and their data [50]. In this case, the main challenge is tying an individual's identity to a specific context, which compromises the user's privacy by releasing identifying information to entities beyond the user's personal sphere, hence increasing the number of potential cyber-attack vectors. Another privacy and security risk linked with the Internet of Things is monitoring and location. In this situation, the danger lies in determining and recording the individual's whereabouts over time and space. While localization and monitoring are currently possible using many methods such as Internet traffic and mobile phone GPS location, many users may perceive it as an invasion of privacy if their data is exploited or if they have no control over the sharing of their location data [50]. As a result, ensuring knowledge of location data monitoring and control is a challenge for the.

7.6.2 Outlining and Authentication

Profiling, interaction, and presentation, all of which undermine privacy, are all challenges raised by the Internet of Things. In terms of profiling, the Internet of Things raises concerns about gathering data on users in order to determine their interests through linkage with other data and profiles [51]. In this circumstance, profiling approaches could be employed in e-commerce for consumer customization as well as internal targeting and optimization based on customers' interests and demographics. Profiling, on the other hand, might lead to privacy violations if the data is used for unwanted advertising, price discrimination, or social engineering. Furthermore, the gathering and sale of user profiles in the data marketplace without the consent of the individual is considered a privacy infringement. As a result, the Internet of Things may present privacy and security problems, as private information about individual users may be mistakenly broadcast through public media, exposing the information to unexpected audiences. IoT applications that rely heavily on user participation include healthcare, transportation, and retail, to name a few. The vast majority of systems used to communicate with users and present feedback data are fundamentally public, creating a risk to an individual's privacy if other people have access to the information

[52]. As a result, the Internet of Things must handle the issue of easy access to personal data.

7.6.3 Inventory Attacks and Lifespan Transitions

IoT poses privacy and security issues when it comes to lifecycle transitions and inventory assault. In this case, with changes to the device's control spheres, users' private information obtained during the device's lifetime may be disclosed [53]. Smart devices interact with a wide range of services and people, and they keep track of their interactions in their history logs. Given that most consumer products have a lifecycle in which the customer owns the product for the remainder of his or her life, the sale or sharing of such devices could expose sensitive data about the previous owner, infringing on the individual's privacy. As a result, the potential for inventory attacks jeopardizes the privacy and security of the IoT. As the IoT connection capacity grows with the advent of end-to-end visions, smart devices can query from both legitimate and non-legitimate parties over the Internet. When a rogue entity queries an IoT device, the device can be used to retrieve rogue information about the properties and whereabouts of the user's personal belongings [54]. As a result, IoT enables the disclosure of a wealth of data about users' lives and property and poses security and privacy risks.

7.6.4 Ethics, Law, and Regulatory Rights

Legality, regulatory, and ethical rights are also concerns for IoT developers. There are special rules and regulations to adhere to standards and moral standards and prevent people from violating them. The only difference between ethics and law is that ethics refers to the norms that people adhere to, and law refers to the restrictions imposed by the government. Ethics and law aim to protect standards and quality and prevent people from engaging in criminal activity. As a result of IoT development, some real-life problems have been resolved, but it has also created significant ethical and legal challenges [55]. Some of these issues are data security, privacy, trust and security, and data usability. Due to the lack of trust in IoT devices, the majority of IoT consumers support government standards and laws related to data protection, privacy, and security. Therefore, this topic should be considered to maintain and improve public confidence in the use of IoT devices and systems.

7.6.5 Processing, Examination, and Supervision of Data

Processing, analysis, and data management techniques are exceedingly difficult due to the heterogeneous nature of IoT, and the massive amount of data created, particularly in this era of Big Data [56]. To offload data and perform computationally intensive processes on a global cloud platform, most systems now use centralized systems. Traditional cloud architectures, on the other hand, may not be capable of transmitting the massive volumes of data created and consumed by IoT-enabled devices, as well as maintaining the related processing load while fulfilling scheduling constraints [57]. Most systems rely on existing technologies like mobile cloud computing and fog computing, both of which are based on edge processing, to address this issue.

The usage of information-centric networking (ICN) on the Internet of Things is another field of data management study. Because they aid in effective content retrieval and access to services, these information-centric systems appear to be highly advantageous not only in accessing but also in transferring and managing generated material and its transmission. This technique, however, creates a number of difficulties, including how to successfully extend the ICN paradigm across the fixed network edge, how to incorporate static and mobile IoT devices, and how to apportion ICN functionality on resource-constrained devices [57].

Data analysis and its context are not only important to the success of the IoT but also pose serious problems. To achieve smart IoT capabilities, you need to collect data and use it in a meaningful way. Therefore, the development of artificial intelligence algorithms, machine learning techniques, genetic and evolutionary algorithms, and various other artificial intelligence systems derived from neural work is essential for automated decision-making.

7.6.6 Interoperability

Interoperability has always been an important core ideal, as the first requirement for an Internet connection shows that a "connected" system can "speak similar languages" in terms of encoding and protocol. Today, many standards are used to support applications in different industries. Due to the sheer volume and variety of data and heterogeneous devices, it is important to deploy standard interfaces to these heterogeneous entities, especially in applications that support collaboration between organizations and various system constraints. As a result, IoT systems are being developed to manage an ever-increasing level of interoperability [58].

7.6.7 Probable Solutions for Challenges in IoT

The most effective way to improve the privacy and security of the Internet of Things is to reduce the amount of user identification data available outside your personal environment. To achieve the goal of minimizing data availability, the IoT will focus on local data processing rather than centralized information processing and enhance horizontal communication between smart devices rather than vertical communication [59]. In addition, the latest methods for maintaining privacy and security apply to the IoT, Big Data interruption, client-side personalization, encryption, and data anonymity and obfuscation. On the other hand, such strategies need to be modified to account for the dispersibility of data in IoT networks. In addition, smart devices must be able to authenticate requests and respond only to legitimate requests [60].

7.6.8 Security by Design

The security of IoT devices depends on many factors, including the amount of sensitive data collected and the cost of patching vulnerabilities. Ramirez [61] suggested that companies need to consider the following key aspects to address these key issues: (1) running a security risk assessment throughout the design phase, (2) security measures for test equipment, (3) considering protecting sensitive data during transmission or storage, and (4) regularly monitor IoT devices and software upgrades. In addition, companies need to provide administrative and technical privileges by providing security training to their employees in order to achieve the desired security measures. According to Schaub et al. [62], the security measures taken from the beginning of the device provide a tamper-resistant and secure computing environment. The article states that the security of IoT devices needs to be considered throughout the device life cycle, from design to operation. This includes (1) secure boot, (2) access control, (3) device authentication, (4) firewalls and intrusion prevention systems, and (5) updates and patches.

7.7 CHALLENGES IN IOB

7.7.1 Negative Factors That Manipulate Vulnerabilities

Data security flaws are all too frequent, and they can disclose important information and patterns. There is a greater risk of online fraud, sophisticated theft, and identity theft. It's also feasible to collect delivery routes, banking codes, and other sensitive data. Companies can also persuade customers to spend more money on certain features.

7.7.2 The Utilization of Customer Data Raises Privacy Concerns

Because there is a lack of data regulation in the Internet realm, customer data or the usage of private data might be a privacy risk. These data privacy problems can make using the Internet of Behavior difficult. In terms of legal regulations, there is also some ambiguity in the space. This can result in a shortage of legal assistance in the future.

7.7.3 Cyberattacks Are a Danger

In current systems, cyberattacks are also very common. When the efficiency of digital technologies and the Internet of Things improves, you can predict and improve individual behavior. Top firms have admitted to sharing user data with other businesses. This could happen without the customer's knowledge or consent.

7.7.4 The Challenge of Persuading Users to Share Data

Many people may be hesitant to provide their personal information. According to Deloitte [63], more than 40% of vehicle insurance policyholders do not want their information shared. Many people are averse to sharing their personal information. This could be due to messages, marketing promotions, cyber security issues, and other factors.

The security of the Internet of Behavior is a major concern. There is a risk of personal information leaks and data theft, which could have a negative impact on individuals. The vast amount of data and information will be difficult to manage and secure. To combat crime, there will be a higher demand for cybersecurity. Because the Internet of Behavior is still in its early stages, many flaws that are currently hidden may surface in the future, and potential remedies are still being sought [64, 65].

7.8 FUTURE PROSPECTS

Our daily lives are changing dramatically as the use of IoT devices and technologies increases. Smart home systems and devices consisting of internet-based gadgets, home automation systems, and reliable energy management systems are examples of the evolution of IoT. Another big advancement in the Internet of Things is smart health sensor systems. SHSS involves the use of small smart devices and technology to support human health. As a result, they have transformed the entire healthcare landscape by making it easier with high tech and smart devices. Before building an application, IoB visualizes user interaction patterns and touch points. This technology is used in the development process to meet user needs. IoB aims to explain behavioral psychology approaches to data collected from people's internet interactions. It deals with the interpretation and application of data in the development and commercialization of new products based on human psychology. One of the unique advantages of IoB is the ability to explore consumer-buying behavior across all networks, easily see data about user device and product interactions. Marketers use IoB to personalize products and services based on the data they collect.

7.9 CONCLUSION

The Internet of Things is becoming an increasingly vital aspect of our lives, and it can be felt all around us. It employs quantum and nanotechnology in areas such as memory, sensing, and computing speed that were previously inconceivable. Furthermore, IoT developers and researchers are passionate about making the lives of persons with impairments and the elderly better. The Internet of Things strives to improve data understanding and debate how data may be used to develop and market new goods. It's also referred to as a solution for end users who want to modify their behavior by following device recommendations. Public and private enterprises can leverage the Internet of Things in a variety of ways.

Because data needs to be collected daily or on a large scale in today's world, privacy is an important characteristic that must be considered across all data service platforms. This leads to an overabundance of personal information being exposed in the open, which, if ignored or not handled properly, can result in unpleasant consequences such as brand degeneration, reputation questions, and lawsuits. Privacy has always been a vital concern in IoB, and strict procedures have been adopted from time to time. User behavior data allows cybercriminals to access, gather, and analyze consumers' behavior patterns, leading them to phony websites and web pages that feature items/information of the user's choosing, enticing them to buy a product only to be dumped. Scams and fraud are built on this foundation.

Security is particularly vital in IoB, and data must be exchanged in an encrypted format. This avoids data breaches and data theft, which can result in financial loss and operational disruption. Security in IoT is especially critical for large-scale businesses, as security flaws can lead to financial crimes because data connected to household appliances, hospitals and healthcare, institutions, and large-scale smart factories are vulnerable to data leakage. Because it affects practically every aspect of people's, institutions, and societies' daily existence, the Internet of Things offers a vast range of possible applications.

Smart automobiles, smart homes, healthcare, manufacturing, agriculture, smart cities, home security, and disaster management relief are just a few of the industries that use IoT applications. The quantity of IoB applications grows exponentially every day. It is quickly becoming a critical marketing technique for firms.

Machines, like technology, evolve rapidly. Threats and privacy issues arise as a result of technological advancements. In a network, smart devices will communicate and share data. If one device is compromised, the entire infrastructure is put in jeopardy. Reducing the quantity of user identity data available outside of your personal environment is the most effective strategy to increase the privacy and security of the Internet of Things. Furthermore, the

IoT benefits from the most up-to-date technologies for ensuring privacy and security. Big Data obfuscation, data interruption, client-side personalization, encryption, and data anonymity are some problems related to privacy and their solutions, on the other hand, must be changed to account for data dispersibility in IoT networks. Furthermore, smart devices must be able to authenticate requests and only react to those that are real.

Extensive research has been carried out to demonstrate the possible usefulness and applicability of IoT developments, which is available in the form of academic studies, news stories, and both online and printed reports. It can be utilized as a starting point for creating your own unique business model that is secure, reliable, and interoperable. We are seeing big changes in our daily lives as the adoption of IoT devices and technology grows.

One of IoB's unique benefits is the consumer study of its purchase behaviors across all networks. Data on user equipment and goods interactions is straightforward to review. It provides exact information about a customer's current purchasing status. Marketers use IoB to customize their products and services based on the information they collect. Customers are more likely to persist with a product, good, or service that has been customized for them.

REFERENCES

1. Sfar AR, Chtourou Z, Challal Y. A systemic and cognitive vision for IoT security: A case study of military live simulation and security challenges. In 2017 International Conference on Smart, Monitored and Controlled Cities (SM2C) 2017 Feb 17 (pp. 101–105). IEEE.
2. Gatsis K, Pappas GJ. Wireless control for the IoT: Power, spectrum, and security challenges. In 2017 IEEE/ACM Second International Conference on Internet-of-Things Design and Implementation (IoTDI) 2017 Apr 18 (pp. 341–342). IEEE.
3. Zhou J, Cao Z, Dong X, Vasilakos AV. Security and privacy for cloud-based IoT: Challenges. *IEEE Communications Magazine*. 2017 Jan 19;55(1):26–33.
4. Sfar AR, Natalizio E, Challal Y, Chtourou Z. A roadmap for security challenges in the Internet of Things. *Digital Communications and Networks*. 2018 Apr 1;4(2):118–137.
5. Montenegro-Marin CE, Gaona-García PA, Prieto JD, Nieto Acevedo YV. Analysis of security mechanisms based on clusters IoT environments. *Special Issue on Advances and Applications in the Internet of Things and Cloud Computing*.
6. Behrendt F. Cycling the smart and sustainable city: Analyzing EC policy documents on Internet of Things, mobility and transport, and smart cities. *Sustainability*. 2019 Jan;11(3):763.
7. Minoli D, Sohraby K, Kouns J. IoT security (IoTSec) considerations, requirements, and architectures. In 2017 14th IEEE Annual Consumer Communications & Networking Conference (CCNC) 2017 Jan 8 (pp. 1006–1007). IEEE.

8. Langford D. Ethics and the Internet: Appropriate behavior in electronic communication. *Ethics & Behavior*. 1996;6(2):91–106.
9. Hsu C, Chang K, Chen M. Flow experience and Internet shopping behavior: Investigating the moderating effect of consumer characteristics. *Systems Research and Behavioral Science*. 2011;29(3):317–332.
10. Afanasyev Y. PII of original article S0034–4257(00)00209–1. *Remote Sensing of Environment*. 2001;77(2):227–228.
11. Tsitsika A, Janikian M, Schoenmakers T, Tzavela E, Ólafsson K, Wójcik S, et al. Internet addictive behavior in adolescence: A cross-sectional study in Seven European Countries. *Cyberpsychology, Behavior, and Social Networking*. 2014;17(8):528–535.
12. Guzmán G. Internet search behavior as an economic forecasting tool: The case of inflation expectations. *Journal of Economic and Social Measurement*. 2022;36(3). doi:10.3233/JEM-2011-0342.
13. Griffin J. *Customer loyalty*. Jossey-Bass; 1995 Jan.
14. Crespo Á, del Bosque I, de los Salmones Sánchez M. The influence of perceived risk on Internet shopping behavior: A multidimensional perspective. *Journal of Risk Research*. 2009;12(2):259–277.
15. Javaid M, Haleem A, Singh R, Rab S, Suman R. Internet of Behaviours (IoB) and its role in customer services. *Sensors International*. 2021;2:100122.
16. www.igi-global.com/dictionary/enterprise-information-system-security/26096.
17. https://neeva.com/learn/data-privacy-4-common-issues-and-how-to-solve-them.
18. www.insiderintelligence.com/insights/iot-security-privacy/.
19. Weber RH. Internet of Things – new security and privacy challenges. *Computer Law & Security Review*. 2010 Jan 1;26(1):23–30.
20. https://softtek.eu/en/tech-magazine-en/user-experience-en/what-is-the-Internet-of-behaviour-iob-and-why-is-it-the-future/.
21. www.trellix.com/en-us/security-awareness/cybersecurity/what-is-Internet-security.html.
22. www.tekkiwebsolutions.com/blog/Internet-of-behavior/.
23. www.matellio.com/blog/Internet-of-behavior-and-its-effects-on-your-life-and-business/.
24. www.metacompliance.com/blog/5-damaging-consequences-of-a-data-breach/.
25. www.designrush.com/agency/software-development/trends/iot-security-issues.
26. https://www2.deloitte.com/content/dam/Deloitte/nl/Documents/financial-services/deloitte-nl-fsi-elevating-the-fight-against-financial-crime.pdf.
27. https://informer.io/resources/why-is-iot-security-important.
28. www.itproportal.com/features/could-cybercriminals-capitalize-on-renewed-interest-in-the-Internet-of-behavior-iob/.
29. Sekhar M, Bhat G, Vaishnavi S, Siddesh GM. Security and privacy in 5G-enabled Internet of Things: A data analysis perspective. 2021. doi:10.1007/978-3-030-67490-8_12.
30. www.iotforall.com/Internet-of-behavior.

31. Mano LY, Faiçal BS, Nakamura LH, Gomes PH, Libralon GL, Meneguete RI, Geraldo Filho PR, Giancristofaro GT, Pessin G, Krishnamachari B, Ueyama J. Exploiting IoT technologies for enhancing health smart homes through patient identification and emotion recognition. *Computer Communications*. 2016 Sep 1;89:178–190.

32. Zanjal SV, Talmale GR. Medicine reminder and monitoring system for secure health using IoT. *Procedia Computer Science*. 2016 Jan 1;78:471–476.

33. Jain R. A congestion control system based on VANET for small length roads. *arXiv preprint arXiv:1801.06448.2018 Jan 9*.

34. Soomro S, Miraz MH, Prasanth A, Abdullah M. Artificial intelligence enabled IoT: Traffic congestion reduction in smart cities. In Smart Cities Symposium 2018 (pp. 1–6), Bahrain. IEEE. doi:10.1049/cp.2018.1381.

35. Mahmud SH, Assan L, Islam R. Potentials of Internet of Things (IoT) in Malaysian construction industry. *Annals of Emerging Technologies in Computing (AETiC)*, Print ISSN. 2018 Oct 1:2516–0281.

36. Sundareswaran V, Null MS. Survey on smart agriculture using IoT. *International Journal of Innovative Research in Engineering & Management (IJIREM)*. 2018;5(2):62–66.

37. Tadejko P. Application of Internet of Things in logistics – current challenges. *Ekonomia i Zarządzanie*. 2015;7(4).

38. Miraz MH, Ali M, Excell PS, Picking R. A review on Internet of Things (IoT), Internet of everything (IoE) and Internet of nano things (IoNT). In 2015 Internet Technologies and Applications (ITA) 2015 Sep 8 (pp. 219–224). IEEE.

39. Miraz MH, Ali M, Peter S. Excell, and Richard Picking, "Internet of Nano-Things, Things and Everything: Future Growth Trends." (to be published) Future Internet. 2018 Jul.

40. Ammar M, Haleem A, Javaid M, Walia R, Bahl S. Improving material quality management and manufacturing organizations system through industry 4.0 technologies. *Materials Today: Proceedings*. 2021 Jan 1;45:5089–5096.

41. Gil D, Ferrández A, Mora-Mora H, Peral J. Internet of Things: A review of surveys based on context aware intelligent services. *Sensors*. 2016 Jul;16(7):1069.

42. Jia M, Komeily A, Wang Y, Srinivasan RS. Adopting Internet of Things for the development of smart buildings: A review of enabling technologies and applications. *Automation in Construction*. 2019 May 1;101:111–126.

43. Boos D, Guenter H, Grote H, Kinder K. Controllable accountabilities: The Internet of Things and its challenges for organisations. *Behaviour and Information Technology*. 2013 May 1;32(5):449–467.

44. Gu F, Ma B, Guo J, Summers PA, Hall P. Internet of Things and big data as potential solutions to the problems in waste electrical and electronic equipment management: An exploratory study. *Waste Management*. 2017 Oct 1;68:434–448.

45. www.geeksforgeeks.org/moving-beyond-iot-with-iob/.

46. Javaid M, Haleem A, Rab S, Singh RP, Suman R. Sensors for daily life: A review. *Sensors International*. 2021 Jan 1;2:100121.

47. Bagheri M, Movahed SH. The effect of the Internet of Things (IoT) on education business model. In 2016 12th International Conference on Signal-Image

Technology & Internet-Based Systems (SITIS) 2016 Nov 28 (pp. 435–441). IEEE.

48. Verdouw CN, Beulens AJ, Van Der Vorst JG. Virtualisation of floricultural supply chains: A review from an Internet of Things perspective. *Computers and Electronics in Agriculture*. 2013 Nov 1;99:160–175.

49. Al-Garadi MA, Mohamed A, Al-Ali AK, Du X, Ali I, Guizani M. A survey of machine and deep learning methods for Internet of Things (IoT) security. *IEEE Communications Surveys & Tutorials*. 2020 Apr 20;22(3):1646–1685.

50. Rose K, Eldridge S, Chapin L. The Internet of Things: An overview. *The Internet Society (ISOC)*. 2015 Oct 15;80:1–50.

51. Abomhara M, Køien GM. Cyber security and the Internet of Things: Vulnerabilities, threats, intruders and attacks. *Journal of Cyber Security and Mobility*. 2015 May 22:65–88.

52. Razzaq MA, Gill SH, Qureshi MA, Ullah S. Security issues in the Internet of Things (IoT): A comprehensive study. *International Journal of Advanced Computer Science and Applications*. 2017 Jan;8(6):383.

53. Baldini G, Botterman M, Neisse R, Tallacchini M. Ethical design in the Internet of Things. *Science and Engineering Ethics*. 2018 Jun;24(3):905–925.

54. Lin H, Bergmann NW. IoT privacy and security challenges for smart home environments. *Information*. 2016 Sep;7(3):44.

55. Tzafestas SG. Ethics and Law in the Internet of Things World. *Smart Cities*. 2018;1(1):98–120. https://doi.org/10.3390/smartcities1010006.

56. Alansari Z, Anuar NB, Kamsin A, Soomro S, Belgaum MR, Miraz MH, Alshaer J. Challenges of Internet of Things and big data integration. In International Conference for Emerging Technologies in Computing 2018 Aug 23 (pp. 47–55). Springer, Cham.

57. Cooper J, James A. Challenges for database management in the Internet of Things. *IETE Technical Review*. 2009 Sep 1;26(5):320–329.

58. Mazayev A, Martins JA, Correia N. Interoperability in IoT through the semantic profiling of objects. *IEEE Access*. 2017 Nov 10;6:19379–19385.

59. Borgia E, Gomes DG, Lagesse B, Lea RJ, Puccinelli D. Special issue on "Internet of Things: Research challenges and Solutions". *Computer Communications*. 2016 Sep 1;89:1–4.

60. Farooq MU, Waseem M, Mazhar S, Khairi A, Kamal T. A review on Internet of Things (IoT). *International Journal of Computer Applications*. 2015 Mar;113(1):1–7.

61. Shipley AJ. Security in the Internet of Things. *Wind River*, September 2014.

62. Schaub F, Balebako R, Durity AL, Cranor LF. A design space for effective privacy notices. In Eleventh Symposium on Usable Privacy and Security (SOUPS 2015) 2015 (pp. 1–17).

63. www.smartkarrot.com/resources/blog/Internet-of-behaviors/.

64. www.tekkiwebsolutions.com/blog/Internet-of-behavior/.

Chapter 8

Sentiment Analysis and Feature Reduction Using Arboreal Monkey Compression Algorithm with Deep Modified Neural Network Classifier

Rajalaxmi Hegde, Sandeep Kumar Hegde, Monica R. Mundada, and Seema S

CONTENTS

8.1 INTRODUCTION

Today there are many e-commerce stores running on online platforms. On business platforms, e-commerce stores are leading other types of business. Simple access to the Internet has led to this change in the business platform. Various other parameters also influence these achievements [1, 2]. One of the main factors for this standard of e-commerce is product reviews, which play an important role in elevating reputations [3]. The important role of e-commerce is to keep up the reputations of brands on e-commerce websites. Basically, it needs a lot of follow-ups to maintain its reputation [4, 5]. The natural way to keep up a brand's reputation is reviews. Reviews are a new standard for e-commerce websites because the Internet is available to everyone [6]. Things reviews are the primary source for determining the bond between customers and stores; they help to build better coordination between customers and stores, which leads a potential buyer to buy their product based on their perspective, regardless of what is left over [7, 8]. An e-commerce website that includes a many buyers' opinions shows a large number of opinions from a group of buyers.

Votes play a major role in making decisions on online platforms; for example, a customer will buy products by evaluating the reviews and ratings of the product by other customers who previously bought that product [9, 10]. However, we cannot determine every product through this type of circumstances only the legitimate client who utilize that item can enlighten the precise the insights about the product. This is the significance of reviews [11]. In present days, we are blindly wasting our cash in purchasing delegate items because of lack of information in system. This problem is addressed by the demonstration of sentiment analysis on reviews [12, 13]. The user's premium is only looked at for a short time. So, customer survey subjects can be delicate. For example, when buying a cellphone, different people will have different opinions [14].

Some will focus on the camera, while others will focus on the battery. Each has their own unique area of product enthusiasm [15, 16]. The significance of sentiment analysis is highlighted here. The method of evaluating the emotional state behind a series of words is known as sentiment analysis, also known as opinion mining [17, 18]. Sentiment classification is a very effective method for analyzing comments on e-commerce websites because it reveals the buyers' feelings about the product [19]. It helps brands know more about users' opinions about the product. Through natural language processing (NLP) and machine learning, reviews on e-commerce sites are written in natural languages such as English. This technique is proposed to analyze the sentiment or emotion connected to the underlying text. So if you want to know which type of emotion it includes in a line, for example, positive or negative, in this type of case we can apply the technique of sentiment analysis.

8.2 LITERATURE SURVEY

For traditional users, the e-commerce platform is complicated because of decision making, and it has plenty of samples and limited surveys scope, so we proposed this chapter [20] to approach a unique technique that is useful to evaluate comments from online platforms, to create upgrades indicating a system for products with an opinion analyzer and emotion analysis for online reviews. With this efficient method based on a large number of buyer opinions. In this case, prediction accuracy has only a 9.9% error. This process involves product estimation and upgrades with a search engine with plenty of user reviews. The field of emotion detection and sentiment analysis has seen rapid growth in order to investigate opinions and texts present in various social media platforms using machine learning techniques with sentiments, subjectivity analysis, or polarity calculation [21, 22]. The use of various machine learning techniques and tools for sentiment analysis during the listing process needs a different approach to manage this type of complication. This chapter contributes adaptation of a sentiment analyzer and includes an algorithm called naïve Bayes and support vector machine (SVM). This chapter also provides a comparison of techniques of sentiment analysis in the analysis of political views. This chapter focuses on adaptation of various sentiment analyzers with a machine learning algorithm to determine the approach with highest accuracy rate. In [23], sentiment analysis denotes the public opinion about products, which we are going to be figuring out and will play an important role in a brand's reputation. Users give feedback in online posts to the brands, like negative and positive thoughts, which are going to give different types of recognition for products. This process is going to separate sentiments into two different branches (positive or negative) that denote products as recommended or not recommended. In this process, fundamental OM approaches whether the comments are positive and negative. We first use a machine learning approach that is used in sentiment analysis, and we also use a lexicon or dictionary in the second approach to analyze the words and expressions in a comment.

In social media (SM), every brand has a significant impact on the emotional reaction of its users [24]. Companies understand the need and the realities that customers expect through the various types of posts. Based on those posts, companies design their future strategies. This case study analyzes how to use SM technologies, and a customer-oriented management system contributes to building a stable platform and upgrades to it in the future by means of social customer relationship management (CRM). The two brands involved in the study look at regular consumers of the goods by analyzing the interaction by customers with the posts that are posted on their official channels. They divide customers into two categories: normal and potential customers [25, 26]. The study aims to analyze posts in fixed social networks like Facebook, Twitter, Instagram, Pinterest, Google+, and YouTube. It shows the similarities and differences between the SM customer behaviors of two highly competitive brands. The study gives an output of measurement between brands' SM ability to understand customer expectations by using various statistical tools and sentiment analysis techniques on big sets of data. Big data performs a key role in a company's stable competitive advantage, and the customers' creation of a large amount of company-related content in social media gives the brand a capable value for advertising, and the more big data are created through user-generated content, the more likely they are to be created through online reviews [27, 28].

According to a recent study that uses sentiment analysis (SA) tools to examine the documented entirety of comments and classify buyer opinion, focusing on online comments that place greater emphasis on product marketing and a more stable position under these conditions, the star score ratings of brands are obtained. The SA tool categorizes feelings as either negative or positive, with different sites for each type of comment, because people may have differing opinions on each brand's attributes [29]. For product and brand managers, analyzing different product features can be extremely interesting. In this theory, we propose a technique that uses text analytics NLP techniques, such as sentiment analysis, data retrieval, and clustering techniques, in order to obtain new scores based on customer feelings on various product features. In order to obtain a new combination price and the aforementioned score, we must first define a new global score for the product, which will provide a proper ranking according to product feature. Products can also be classified according to their positive, neutral, or negative features in order to assist customers in their purchasing decisions. With the help of big data acquired from Amazon online evaluations (particularly cell phones), we were able to demonstrate the validity of our approach in a case study, yielding satisfying and promising results. After conducting the experiments, we came to the conclusion that our work has the potential to improve recommender systems by incorporating good, neutral, and negative customer evaluations, as well as by categorizing customers based on their remarks.

The main purpose of this process is to create a platform that helps companies analyze customer opinion on social media to maintain customer relationship management, marketing strategies, and course management. They are going to analyze the opinions from social media platforms like Instagram by analyzing comments, votes, and likes from users, which are recorded a in company database. They preprocess this data and use it in classification stages, so this process helps brands to make feature decisions [30].

The main purpose is to study the buyer's reaction, which can give more reasonable information, by analyzing sentiments on social platforms such as Instagram or Face-book. This is the main means to learn about user opinions. However, the stability of SA is abstracted by problems NLP. Several experiments have demonstrated the deep learning model is the best way to preprocess problems of NLP. So we analyzed how deep learning is used to resolve problems in sentiment analysis, such as sentiment differences. Models using term frequency–inverse document frequency (TF-IDF) and word fixation have used a set of data. A similar study applied experimental results to gain polarized different representations and input features In this work, the binary adaptation of a cuckoo search (nature-inspired, meta-heuristic algorithm) known as the binary cuckoo search is proposed for optimum feature selection for sentiment analysis of textual online content. The baseline supervised learning techniques, such as SVM and others, have first been implemented with the traditional TF-IDF model and then with the novel feature optimization model [31]. Sentiment analysis evaluates the opinion of a sentiment as either positive, negative, or neutral. Sentiments are very specific, and with respect to the underlying content, they play a crucial role in depicting real-world scenarios [32]. The objective of this work is to analyze sentiment and perform classification. In traditional feature selection methods, the word order in the given document is not considered; hence, it will be a tedious process to compute features [33].

8.3 RESEARCH GAPS

E-commerce advancements will increase the buying ratio. Nowadays, customers prefer to buy things online rather than traveling to physical stores because it saves them time and money. However, while purchasing things online may appear to be simple, purchasing through e-commerce sites is not. The main issue with e-commerce sites is deciding which product to buy from hundreds to thousands of options. Users' decisions are influenced by a variety of elements such as ratings, reviews, keywords, and so on. The user can select what he or she wants by looking at the rating, but it is not always worth it because there may be instances where there are concerns about fraud and bogus ratings, in which case reviews come into play. Because there are so many users or so many reviews, the product's data grows quickly. It is vital to efficiently classify these reviews. These reviews will have a direct impact on purchasing decisions and may alter attitudes in a positive or negative way. Users may become confused if a large number of both critical and positive evaluations are displayed to them without categorization, leading to a loss of interest in the e-commerce system and a preference for traditional purchasing. Positive reviews are commonly used to recruit clients, while bad evaluations are frequently used to aid in decision-making. If these reviews are appropriately categorized as good, negative, or neutral, the system can reach the highest level of customer satisfaction, as well as increasing product sales and value. So, with that in mind, we're putting feelings into action to solve the problem. User feedback on items is analyzed.

8.4 OBJECTIVES OF THE WORK

- **Preprocessing:** The reviews of the e-commerce websites are collected in the dataset are analyzed by performing symbolization, breaking, common word removal, and hash tag and user ID removal. First the analyzing step goes through symbolization, which is basically a plan of action to divide texts into compiled meaningful symbols. For example, a paragraph is divided into words or phrases; then the regular terms that are not necessary will be taken out. This process is called common word removal. Common terms like "the," "or," and "and" can be fetched out by analyzing text with a stop words list. Next the breaking process is performed; this process is used to remove words used as suffixes so that we can make words smaller. In final step, the URL, tags, and user ID are fetched out because these terms are used in social media to point to descriptions in messages, which make them easier to find. In this stage the tags denoted with the pound sign (#) in front of the text are fetched out from an input text. If a URL or user ID is present, then it will be fetched out. Finally, large words are truncated into small words.

- **Feature Extraction:** The features, for example, fear emoticon count, anger emoticon count, exclamation point count, question mark count, positive journal word occurrence count, negative journal word occurrence count, echograms, pictograms, cartograms, diagrams, phonograms, parts of speech, and tags from the analyzed data are fetched out.
- **Feature Selection:** By using the arboreal monkey compression algorithm (AMCA), the necessary characters are selected around the fitness values of fetched features. AMCA is a population-centered stochastic algorithm. AMCA is motivated by smart food behaviors Arboreal monkeys (AMs) in their food-finding process indicate that this AM belongs to the fission-fusion social structure (FFSS) class of animals. The minimization algorithm based on AM searching behavior could be well described with reference to FFSS. This follows the chief features of the FFSS.
- **Deep Learning Modified Neural Network Classifier:** After feature selection, the selected comments are listed using a sentiment analysis dictionary or opinion lexicon. Word Net, narrated as of the word net data collection, is primarily a dictionary in which every expression is denoted by numerical scores. It marks positive and negative sentiment data. The characteristic terms enclose positive and negative lists. The outcome's score value will be sent to DLMN and is classified as positive, neutral, or negative. As if positive lists indicate that the product is good and that the circumstances are favorable in the eyes of the customer.
- **Positive reviews appear first:** To make customers feel more positively, the positive reviews appear first when a user visits the e-commerce site to purchase a product.

8.5 METHODOLOGY

Take reviews as input first, and then begin the retrieval procedure for those reviews. After that, the preprocessing stage will be completed. In the preprocessing stage, the stop word, the management of contradictions, the fixing of misspellings, and the positive and negative word lists of each review are removed. The first step in preprocessing is to employ filtering to remove any extraneous information from the sentence. After that, the sentence is reviewed to remove any duplicated or repeated characters. The tokenization process is carried out during the preprocessing phase, with the goal of dividing the text into a collection of meaningful parts, or tokens, as the plan of action. A block of text is divided into words or sentences in this section. It will then be necessary to delete any undesired words that are not beneficial to learning, which is referred to as the stop word removal process. During the contradiction phase, the system will look for any discrepancies between the user evaluations that have been submitted. If any inconsistencies are discovered, they will be dealt with during the dealing with contradictions step. The most fundamental part is to compute a sentiment score. The underlying concept of sentiment scoring is to establish a relationship between the number of positive reviews and that of negative reviews. If the emotion score is greater than zero, the statement is believed to be accurate, which results in bad reviews being written. If the sentiment score is less than zero, the review is assumed to be false, and the review will be checked to see if it is a neutral review. Then, if the neutral review is correct, the positive review will be given.

8.5.1 Arboreal Monkey Compression Algorithm

The AMCA algorithm depicts the food searching process of female monkeys. If the leader has not been able to find the proper food resources, then the leader divides the all the monkeys into groups so that they can search for food independently, and each group will also have a leader.

1. Start
2. Initialize population: N potential solutions (each of dimension D) are uniformly seeded across the search space

$$N_{ab} = N_b^{min} + v(0,1) \times \left(N_b^{max} = N_b^{min}\right)$$

N_{ab} is the ath dimension of the ath arboreal monkey, where N^{max} and N^{min} are the
$b \rightarrow b$
maximum and minimum limits of the free parameters.
3. if $v > Ag$ is true
where N^{new} is the position update of the ath N that is the part of cth group is stated as where N_{ab} denotes the ath N in the bth direction, $_{cb}$ denotes the bth dimension of the cth local group leader position.

$$N_{ab}^{new} = N_{ab} + v(0,1) \times \left(M_{cb} - N_{ab}\right) + v(-1,1) \times \left(N_{db} - N_{ab}\right)$$

Arboreal Monkey Compression Algorithm

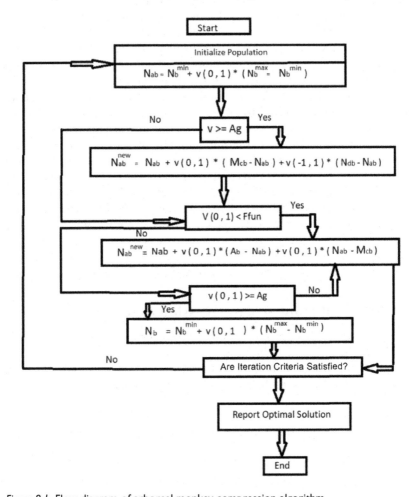

Figure 8.1 Flow diagram of arboreal monkey compression algorithm.

N_{db} specifies the bth dimension of the dth N that is randomly selected from the cth group in order that d does not equal a in the bth dimension

4. if $v > Ag$ is false, then it goes to $V(0,1) < F\,fun$

5. if $V(0,1) < F\,fun$ is true, $N_{ab}^{new} = Nab + v(0,1) \times (A_b - N_{ab}) + v(0,1) \times (N_{ab} - M_{cb})$ is executed, where ab denotes the a location in the bth dimension and b belongs

$\{1,2,\ldots,D\}$ specifies the arbitrary result

6. if $V(0,1) < F\,fun$ is false, it goes to $V(0,1) \geq Ag$

7. if $V(0,1) \geq Ag$ is false, $N_{ab}^{new} = Nab + v(0,1) \times (A_b - N_{ab}) + v(0,1)*(N_{ab} - M_{cb})$ is again executed

   if $V(0,1) \geq Ag$ is true, $N_b = N_b^{min} + v(0,1) \times (N_b^{max} - N_b^{min})$ is executed; then it goes to iteration criteria satisfy state and it report optimal solution and then end.

This subgroup leader can make the plans and a decision themselves. To avoid collision between the groups, subgroups can communicate between themselves, and by doing this, they can cover more area. Also, there will be high chances of finding more food resources.

8.5.2 Modified Deep Hybrid Neural Model

The purpose of this work is to examine the effectiveness of online product reviews using a deep learning modified neural network methodology. Deep learning customized neural networks can be used to output results as negative, positive, or neutral reviews, depending on the learning algorithm used. The arboreal monkey compression algorithm can be used to perform a weighting factor and feature analysis on a product in order to make a prediction about the product's future performance. A detailed overview of the suggested modified hybrid deep neural network classifier model for conducting classification is given in this part. It has been proposed that the arboreal monkey compression method results be fed into the proposed classifier model. The number of features is reduced, and this information is later incorporated into the suggested model. The input layer is responsible for passing the feature vectors from the input layer to the hidden layers. It is necessary to tune the hyper parameters of hidden layers, such as the learning rate, activation function, and so on, before the inputs are processed. In order to maximize the learning rate, an Adam optimizer is used. There is no vanishing gradient problem with the rectified linear unit (ReLU) activation function, unlike the sigmoid and tanh activation functions, which are also used in other types of activation functions. The suggested classifier model incorporates the ReLU activation function into the hidden layers. It is used for the output layer in order to classify the incoming network data using the Softmax classifier. During the training phase of the deep neural network (DNN), the accuracy and time complexity of the proposed system are examined to determine its overall performance. Furthermore, the suggested system's performance is evaluated in comparison to that of the DNN. The results of the experiment, as well as their interpretation, are addressed in the following section.

8.6 RESULTS AND DISCUSSION

The outcomes of the experiment are assessed and examined in this portion of the chapter. This section also includes an explanation of the results, as well as an evaluation of the proposed model's performance and a comparison of the proposed model with current models. The results of the basic model,

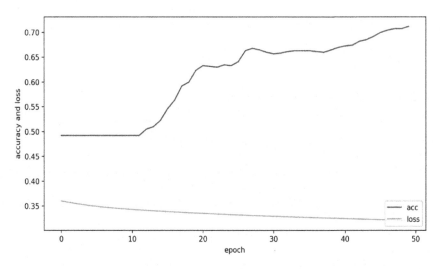

Figure 8.2 Accuracy and loss curve of basic DNN model.

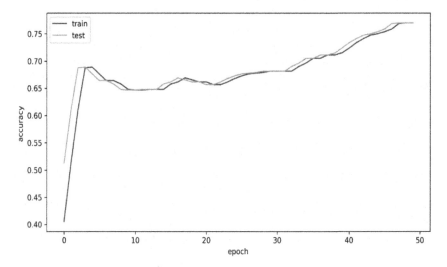

Figure 8.3 Epoch vs accuracy of basic DNN model.

as well as the results of the suggested modified deep hybrid neural model (MDHNM), are presented at length in this section. The evaluations are carried out with the use of the Amazon dataset.

The hyper parameters are used to tune the model's overall performance and accuracy. The grid search approach is employed in this case. The model

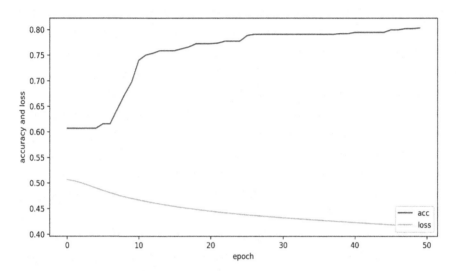

Figure 8.4 Accuracy and loss curve of basic DNN model.

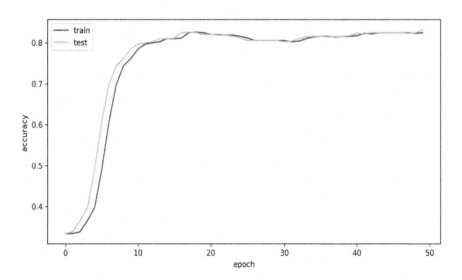

Figure 8.5 Epoch vs accuracy of the proposed model.

is subjected to a learning rate of 0.01 bits per second. The number of epochs used is 50, and the system is validated using a tenfold cross-validation procedure. The performance is compared with the basic DNN model and the MDHNM model. The performance of the system is evaluated using both the basic model and the proposed model.

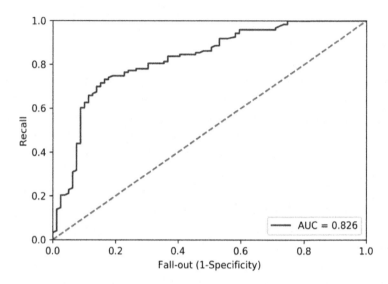

Figure 8.6 AUC curve of basic model.

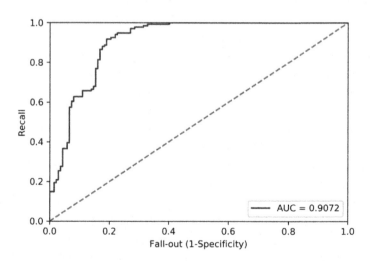

Figure 8.7 AUC curve of proposed model.

It has been noticed that the proposed model outperforms the baseline model in terms of precision, recall, and F1-score. The proposed approach achieved promising results in terms of accuracy. The area under the ROC (AUC) curve value is 0.9072 in the case of the proposed model, whereas the basic model has an AUC curve value of 0.826 and a score, among other measures of performance.

Also advantageous is the fact that the suggested system requires less time to train than other systems now available. As a result, when experimenting with the proposed modified deep hybrid neural model hybrid classifier system, it has been discovered that the time and complexity is significantly reduced when compared to the basic deep learning model.

8.7 CONCLUSIONS

In this chapter, an arboreal monkey compression algorithm is proposed for the purpose of lowering the number of features, and a deep hybrid classifier model is constructed for the purpose of classification. The proposed model was constructed and tested using a normal Amazon product review dataset. The results were encouraging. When the text is reduced to its bare essentials, this model computes the advantages of the arboreal monkey compression approach, and then it performs the binary classification process using the proposed deep hybrid neural network model. The accuracy, precision, recall, and F1-score performance measures were used to evaluate the suggested model, and the results were presented as a percentage of the total. Furthermore, when determining the performance of the proposed model, the training time for the DNN is taken into consideration. In addition, the results are compared to those obtained using the basic DNN model. The proposed model achieved improved accuracy of 90.23%, whereas the basic model gives an accuracy of 86.78%. The proposed model gives good results while requiring less training time than the basic deep learning model considered for comparison, according to the results. The proposed model has a restriction in that it can only be used for binary classification, which is not ideal. Adding multiclass classification to the study will allow researchers to evaluate its effectiveness in future studies.

REFERENCES

1. Verma, J. P., B. Patel, and A. Patel. *Big Data Analysis: Recommendation System with Hadoop framework*. IEEE, 2015. https:// doi.org/10.1109/CICT.2015.86.
2. Choudhary, M., and P. K. Choudhary. "Sentiment analysis of text reviewing algorithm using datamining." In International Conference on Smart Systems and Inventive Technology (ICSSIT), pp. 532–538, 2018.

3. Khuc, V. N., C. Shivade, R. Ramnath, and J. Ramanathan. "Towards building large-scale distributed systems for twitter sentiment analysis." Proceedings of the 27th Annual ACM Symposium on Applied Computing, ACM, 2012.

4. Vijayakumar, S., V. Vijayakumar, R. Logesh, and V. Indragandhi. "Unstructured data analysis on big data using map reduce." *Procedia Computer Science* 50 (2015): 456–465.

5. Gondaliya, V., and K. Mandaviya. "An improved approach for online trending forum detection based on sentiment analysis." *International Conference on Inventive Computation Technologies (ICICT)* 3 (2016): 1–5.

6. Xing, Fang, and Zhan Justin. "Sentiment analysis using product review data." *Journal of Big Data* 2.1 (2015): 5.

7. Vinodhini, G., and R. M. Chandrasekaran. "Sentiment analysis and opinion mining: A survey." *International Journal* 2.6 (2012): 282–292.

8. Severyn, A., and A. Moschitti. "Twitter sentiment analysis with deep convolutional neural networks." Proceedings of the 38th International ACM SIGIR Conference on Research and Development in Information Retrieval, ACM, 2015.

9. Kumar, K. S., J. Desai, and J. Majumdar. "Opinion mining and sentiment analysis on online customer review." In IEEE International Conference on Computational Intelligence and Computing Research (ICCIC), pp. 1–4, 2016.

10. Jagbir, Kaur, and Meenakshi Bansal. "Multi-layered sentiment analytical model for product review mining." In 4th International Conference on Parallel, Distributed and Grid Computing (PDGC), pp. 415–420, 2016.

11. Singla, Z., S. Randhawa, and S. Jain. "Statistical and sentiment analysis of consumer product reviews." In 8th International Conference on Computing, Communication and Networking Technologies (ICCCNT), pp. 1–6, 2017.

12. Hemmatian, F., and M. K. Sohrabi. "A survey on classification techniques for opinion mining and sentiment analysis." *Artificial Intelligence Review* (2017): 1–51.

13. Ronen, Feldman. "Techniques and applications for sentiment analysis." *Communications of the ACM* 56.4 (2013): 82–89.

14. Trupthi, M., P. Suresh, and G. Narasimha. "Sentiment analysis on twitter using streaming API." In IEEE 7th International Advance Computing Conference (IACC), pp. 915–919, 2017.

15. Lijuan, Wang Hongwei, and Gao Song. "Sentimental feature selection for sentiment analysis of Chinese online reviews." *International Journal of Machine Learning and Cybernetics* 9.1 (2018): 75–84.

16. Richard, S. et al. "Recursive deep models for semantic compositionality over a sentiment tree bank." Proceedings of the Conference on Empirical Methods in Natural Language Processing, 2013.

17. Xavier, G., B. Antoine, and B. Yoshua. "Domain adaptation for large-scale sentiment classification: A deep learning approach." Proceedings of the 28th International Conference on Machine Learning (ICML-11), 2011.

18. Rajalaxmi, H., and S. Seema. "Aspect based feature extraction and sentiment classification of review data sets using incremental machine learning algorithm." In 3rd International Conference on Advances in Electrical, Electronics,

Information, Communication and Bio-Informatics (AEEICB), pp. 122–125, 2017.

19. Saleh, M. R., M. T. Martín-Valdivia, A. Montejo-Ráez, and L. A. Ureña-López. "Experiments with SVM to classify opinions in different domains." *Expert Systems with Applications* 38.12 (2011): 14799–14804.

20. Krishna, M. H., K. Rahamathulla, and A. Akbar. "A feature based approach for sentiment analysis using SVM and conference resolution." In International Conference on Inventive Communication and Computational Technologies (ICICCT), IEEE, pp. 397–399, 2017.

21. Kumar, Akshi, et al. "Sentiment analysis using cuckoo search for optimized feature selection on Kaggle tweets." Research Anthology on Implementing Sentiment Analysis Across Multiple Disciplines. IGI Global, pp. 1203–1218, 2022.

22. Rajalaxmi, Hegde, and S. Seema. "Nearest neighbour-based feature selection and classification approach for analysing sentiments." *International Journal of Bioinformatics Research and Applications* 18.1–2 (2022): 16–29.

23. Kumar, R. Satheesh, et al. "Exploration of sentiment analysis and legitimate artistry for opinion mining." *Multimedia Tools and Applications* 81.9 (2022): 11989–12004.

24. Ramasamy, Madhumathi, and A. Meena Kowshalya. "Information gain based feature selection for improved textual sentiment analysis." *Wireless Personal Communications* (2022): 1–17.

25. Rohith, Pavirala, Ranga Sai, and Hemant Rathore. "Sentiment analysis of IMDb movie reviews: A comparative analysis of feature selection and feature extraction techniques." *Hybrid Intelligent Systems: 21st International Conference on Hybrid Intelligent Systems (HIS 2021), December 14–16, 2021* 420 (Springer Nature, 2022).

26. Deniz, Ayça, Merih Angin, and Pelin Angin. "Evolutionary multi objective feature selection for sentiment analysis." *IEEE Access* 9 (2021): 142982–142996.

27. Hussein, Mohammed, and Fatih Özyurt. "A new technique for sentiment analysis system based on deep learning using Chi-Square feature selection methods." *Balkan Journal of Electrical and Computer Engineering* 9.4 (2021): 320–326.

28. García, Maximiliano, Sebastián Maldonado, and Carla Vairetti. "Efficient n-gram construction for text categorization using feature selection techniques." *Intelligent Data Analysis* 25.3 (2021): 509–525.

29. Alharbi, Manal S. F., and El-Sayed M. El-kenawy. "Optimize machine learning programming algorithms for sentiment analysis in social media." *International Journal of Computer Applications* 174.25 (2021): 38–43.

30. Chen, Jie, et al. "A classified feature representation three-way decision model for sentiment analysis." *Applied Intelligence* 52.7 (2022): 7995–8007.

31. Birjali, Marouane, Mohammed Kasri, and Abderrahim Beni-Hssane. "A comprehensive survey on sentiment analysis: Approaches, challenges and trends." *Knowledge-Based Systems* 226 (2021): 107134.

32. Bhamare, Bhavana R., and Jeyanthi Prabhu. "A supervised scheme for aspect extraction in sentiment analysis using the hybrid feature set of word

dependency relations and lemmas." *Peer Journal of Computer Science* 7 (2021): e347.

33. Geethapriya, A., and S. Valli. "An enhanced approach to map domain-specific words in cross-domain sentiment analysis." *Information Systems Frontiers* 23.3 (2021): 791–805.

Chapter 9

Cyber Security Concerns for IoB

Sainath Patil, Ashish Vanmali, and Rajesh Bansode

CONTENTS

9.1 INTRODUCTION TO CYBER SECURITY

The last three decades have seen a massive increase in Internet activities. The term *cyber space* is commonly used to indicate these Internet activities. In today's world, almost everyone is connected to cyber space in one way or another, from surfing to gaming, from schooling to household activities, from banking to business; the uses are endless. This increasing number of cyber space users poses security issues for information stored on computers or data flowing through the network. The terms *cyber crime, computer crime, Internet crime* and so on are often used to indicate illegal activities that target the security of computer system(s) and data. These cybercrimes include spamming, spoofing, data manipulation, hacking, spying, password

Figure 9.1 CIA triad (adapted from [3]).

sniffing, online fraud and many more. Readers can refer to Godbole and Belapure [1] for a comprehensive list of cyber crimes and their details.

The terminology *cyber security*, *information security* or *computer security* is used for trying to safeguard user data in cyberspace. Cyber security is the practice of securing computer resources, computer networks and communication devices and protecting information stored therein from unauthorized access, disclosure, modification or destruction. Cyber security focuses on protecting electronic assets, including Internet, LAN, WAN and resources used to store and transmit information.

To provide a secure environment in cyber space, three core tenets considered are *confidentiality*, *integrity* and *availability* (CIA) [2–4]. They are considered broad and important aspects of cyber security. Confidentiality is protecting computer resources and stored data or information from unauthorized access. Integrity stands for authenticity and reliability of the data stored in computer resources. The information should not be altered or fabricated by attackers. Availability means the information or computer resources should be available to the authorized intended user(s) at any time. Combined, CIA is considered the triad of data security, as depicted in Figure 9.1.

9.1.1 Domains of Cyber Security

According to the security aspect, cyber security can be broadly considered in the following domains [2–5]:

- **Application Security**: While developing applications, the application developer, with a cyber security expert is expected to design a secure application architecture, write secure code and implement input validation checks to reduce the chances of unauthorized access or modification in application data resources.

- **Network Security**: This means protecting network infrastructure from unauthorized access, disruption or any other abuses. It may be a software- or hardware-based mechanism for network protection.
- **Cloud Security**: Organizations tend to use the cloud for their business. This domain requires design of a secure cloud architecture and applications for organizations that use the cloud.
- **Access Control and Data Security**: This domain relates to the authorization and authentication of legitimate users of information systems by controlling access. The measures involve implementing authorization protocols with an access control list (ACL), a powerful security mechanism for information storage, encryption for secure data transmission and so on.
- **Mobile Security**: The big challenge for security today is increasing use of mobile devices for various applications. This domain relates to protecting personal or organizational data stored on mobile devices like cellphones, tablets and laptops from attackers.

9.1.2 Threats of Cyber Security

Cyber security needs to deal with a variety of threats. Some common threats in cyber space are:[1–4, 6]

- **Malware**: Malware are programs by attackers to do malicious activity. It encompasses viruses, worms and spyware. These codes can block access to computer resources, disrupt the system or covertly transmit information from a computer to an attacker.
- **Trojan**: These are programs that fool users by doing useful work, but in the background. These programs look legitimate but perform malicious activities such as opening a back door to allow access to attackers.
- **Denial of Service (DoS) Attack**: This is an attack that blocks computer or network resources, making them inaccessible to authorized users.
- **Botnets**: Network computers infected with bot malware are remotely controlled by attackers. Botnets are basically used to distribute spam and launch distributed denial of service (DDoS) attacks.
- **SQL Injection**: This is a type of attack in which an attacker inserts malicious code into a SQL server to manipulate a database and gain access to confidential data.
- **Phishing**: This is a kind of social engineering attack where an attacker sends fraudulent emails which appear to come from reputable sources. They are designed to tempt the user to enter sensitive information.

9.2 IOT AND IOB INTERCONNECTION

Internet of Behavior (IoB) extends from Internet of Things (IoT), the interconnected physical devices that collect and exchange information over the Internet, which results in a vast amount and variety of data sources. IoB focuses on analyzing data with respect to user behavior, collected from people's daily activity through IoT devices. Organizations use IoB data to influence user behavior further and link to IoT applications so that users see recommendations according to their interests. Figure 9.2 depicts the interconnection between IoT and IoB.

Different types of data used for analyzing human behavior include tracking online/social networking activities of the user, browsing habits, purchase habits and so on. Along with these, data collected by various IoT sensors like biometric data, location data, activity data and so on is also used to understand behavioral patterns. With IoB, companies not only connect to their potential customers but also track the behavior of other customers for recommendations and services. Google, Facebook and other companies make use of behavioral data so that they can display relevant product advertisements. For example, if you search for any product online, the different brands, offers of that product will be shown to you during your browsing. Alexa and Siri are also designed to study, analyze and interpret user behavioral data to work more efficiently.

Gartner, in a strategic prediction [8], predicts that by 2025 half of the world's population will be influenced by at least one IoB program, whether it be commercial or governmental.

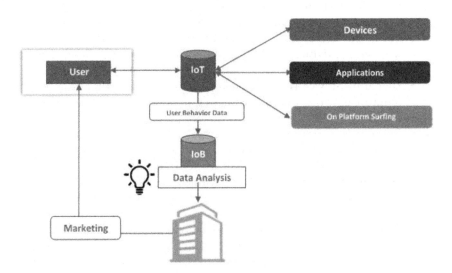

Figure 9.2 IoT and IoB interconnection (reproduced from [7]).

9.3 CYBER SECURITY CONCERNS FOR IOB

The potential of IoB greatly relies on the data collected through a variety of IoT sources. Hence, the security threats present in IoT also percolate to IoB. Apart from security threats in IoT, IoB has its own threats related to safeguarding user data from intruders and hackers. We examine these threats in more detail in next subsections.

9.3.1 Issues of Cyber Security in IoT

IoT is based on wireless sensor network (WSN) architecture. Since the evolution of IoT and its widespread use, researchers have brought up security and privacy issues [9–18]. With recent advancements in sensors and the increasing use of IoT in different applications, these concerns are becoming more prominent. Lopez et al. [9] discussed security threats and protocols for WSNs. The work was further extended for IoT by Roman et al. [10], Hwang [11], Abomhara and Køien [12] and other researchers. Abomhara and Køien listed the main reasons for cyber attacks on IoT as follows (reproduced from [12]):

1. Most IoT devices operate unattended by humans; thus it is easy for an attacker to physically gain access to them.
2. Most IoT components communicate over wireless networks where an attacker could obtain confidential information by eavesdropping.
3. Most IoT components cannot support complex security schemes due to low power and computing resource capabilities.

Kumar and Patel [19] classified the security threats of IoT into three classes: front-end sensors and equipment, network and back end of the IT system, as shown in Figure 9.3. However, with advancements in IoT devices, protocols and applications, one cannot limit threats to these classes, and we need to look at them from a multi-class viewpoint.

The recent advancements in this area are reported by Yang et al. [14], Alrawais et al. [15], Mendez et al. [16], Ahmadi et al. [17], Ogonji et al. [18] and other researchers. In the latest summary published by Trend Micro [20], the main security threats for IoT are:

- **Vulnerabilities:** IoT devices used for most applications have limited computational capabilities, which makes them vulnerable to built-in security weaknesses.
- **Malware:** IoT devices can get infected by malware. IoT botnet malware, cryptocurrency mining malware and ransomware are the most common.
- **Escalated cyber attacks:** Infected devices can be used for DDoS attacks, to infect more machines and to mask malicious activity.

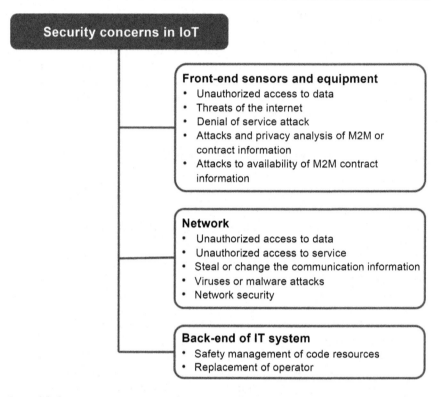

Figure 9.3 Security concerns in IoT (reproduced from [19]).

- **Information theft and unknown exposure**: With the increased use of IoT devices, concern of about unknown exposure is also increasing. This increases the possibilities of technical and/or personal information theft from such devices.
- **Device mismanagement and misconfiguration**: Poor security measures, weak passwords, device mismanagement and so on due to lack of knowledge/capability can escalate security concerns.

In addition to these, other emerging issues that have been reported are [20]:

- **Complex environments**: The increase in the number of IoT devices makes the environment complex. Due to web-interconnected functions, controlling such a complex IoT environment becomes tricky, and any misconfiguration can have adverse effects on the entire system.
- **Prevalence of remote work arrangements**: The COVID-19 pandemic has brought a paradigm shift from work-from-office to work-from-home

culture. Due to this, users are heavily dependent on home networks that are not as secure as those in organizations.

- **5G connectivity**: As we move towards 5G connectivity, a standardized procedure with a focus on security, compatibility and integrity is needed.

9.3.2 Issues of Cyber Security in IoB

Apart from these issues in IoT, the main cyber security concerns in view of IoB are [6, 21–23]:

- **Security**: Behavioral data is highly sophisticated and valuable, as it can reveal or lead to sensitive personal information. In the wrong hands, it can be a disaster for both users and organizations. Also, with the availability of behavioral data, intruders will be able to impersonate individuals to carry out fraud or criminal activities.
- **Privacy**: Buying and selling user behavioral data, mostly without users' consent, is a big privacy issue in IoB.
- **Surveillance**: IoB monitors an individual continuously for location and activities done at that location. This poses a serious surveillance threat for individuals, as it can be used for stalking. The problem is more severe for defense personnel.
- **Regulations**: As regulation policies differ from country to country, IoB devices and systems need to meet regulations across multiple jurisdictions.
- **Value Chain**: IoB systems can use personal and behavioral data to alter the choices that the user makes. This presents a threat to value chains between platforms and humans.
- **Social Impact**: Organizations can use IoB data to manipulate the social and political views of the user.

9.3.3 IoB as a Threat to CIA Triad

In IoB, behavioral facts about users are collected, analyzed and stored. Cyber criminals try to access large IoB databases. Exclusive information about the user can also be compromised if it falls in the hand of unethical users. Hence, IoB poses serious threats to the CIA triad.

9.3.3.1 Confidentiality

Organizations use IoB data to influence customer behavior towards their product or business. Companies even share or sell this data to each other, which itself ethically hampers the confidentiality and privacy of the user.

Also, companies that follow the IoB approach must secure IoB information. Attackers may try to illegally access this confidential data, and if they succeed, they can use it for malicious deeds. Loss of confidentiality is substantially harmful in terms of the financial costs. Behavioral patterns observed in IoB help attackers use targeted phishing attacks to abuse the user's trust and get authentication credentials. Vulnerabilities present in applications that handle IoB could disclose confidential data unknowingly and lead to harm to an individual or organization. For example, a vulnerability of the Strava fitness app reported by *The Guardian* in 2018[24] revels that the app revealed sensitive information about the location and exercise activity of US soldiers, which could be dangerous for military forces.

9.3.3.2 Integrity

In the digital era, most businesses depend on data analytics that find the needs, expectations and experience of customers in big data collected from various sources. For critical decision making, the behavioral database of IoB is helpful to organizations to provide a better and user-friendly experience to customers. Data-driven business depends on the integrity and reliability of the data. In online behavior tracking or user profile building, cookies play important role. Some organizations rely on third-party cookies, which create security concerns about integrity, as these cookies may be transmitted in cleartext. In [25], Tirtea and Castelluccia discussed common types of cookies used on the Internet. Cookies were designed for state management in the interactions between users' browsers and web servers. Currently cookie use has been extended for other purposes, such as advertising management, profiling, tracking and so on. Hence, if proper security is not employed, they pose a serious threat to integrity.

9.3.3.3 Availability

If hackers are able to compromise the authentication of IoB databases, they can change the access control and prevent authorized users from accessing them. From behavioral patterns, hacker can execute phishing attacks to spread malware or botnets in organizational networks. Malware-infected devices can then be used to escalate a DDoS attack on the server. This poses a serious threat to availability for legitimate users.

9.4 REVIEW OF SOLUTIONS

The IoB in general is a combination of IoT, behavioral science and data analytics. According to Lahcen et al. [26], the main reasons for cyber-crimes are (reproduced from [26]):

1. The focus is more on technology than human aspects.
2. Ignoring initial vulnerabilities in design and development of systems and focusing on training.
3. Blaming incidents on a user with or without investigating the system and management failures.

Hence, the solutions for secure IoB operation also need to be twofold. The first manages security aspects while implementing IoB, and the second orients end users, that is, humans, towards secure usage.

9.4.1 Security Measures While Implementing IoB

Different researchers and organizations [5, 6, 20–22] have given insights on how one can securely implement IoB while meeting one's goals. The best practices for secure IoB implementation can be summarized as follows:

- **Sound Security Strategy**: Most cyber attacks can be prevented by implementing sound security strategies. Using firewalls, disabling Wi-Fi protected setup, and enabling the Wi-Fi protected access II security protocol, multi-layered protection and endpoint encryption can greatly enhance security [5, 6, 22].
- **Authentication Protocol**: Use an appropriate privacy-preserving authentication (PPA) protocol and multi-factor authentication to provide access to legitimate users/nodes. Examples of this can be found in [27–29].
- **Analyze Behavior of Nodes/Network**: Use behavior detection methods to sense nodes and networks to prevent attacks from malicious nodes. A few such methods can be found in [30–32].
- **Network Segmentation**: Segmenting the network into independent sub-networks for different applications and employing layered protection can minimize the risk. Readers can refer to [33–35] for more insights.
- **Adaptation to Change**: IoT and IoB are both in the developing phase. Therefore, their security will always have to adapt to ongoing changes and be updated.
- **Cloud-Based Solutions**: The lack of computational capabilities of IoT devices can be countered by using cloud-based solutions. Integrating IoT edge devices with cloud-based solutions can enhance security further.
- **Standardization of Protocols, Unified Privacy and Regulation Policies**: Due to the variety of IoT devices and applications, there is lot of diversity in the protocols used. Also, cyber laws and privacy policies vary from country to country. Hence, to have transparency and explainability in IoB systems, government bodies and system developers across the globe need to work towards standardization of protocols and unifying privacy and regulation policies.

- **Role-Specific Training:** IoB organizations can provide role-specific training to employees and users for secure use and avoid conflicts.
- **Using Novel Polymorphic Security Warnings:** Users tend to ignore warnings that become habitual. Moustafa et al. [36] has suggested the use of novel polymorphic security warnings to grab users' attention regarding security treats.

9.4.2 Orienting Human Behavior Towards Secure Usage

Many times people tend to neglect cyber security protocols or unknowingly carry out activities that place them at risk. Internet addictions like addiction to email, online gaming, social networking and so on fuel the risks of cyber security [37, 38]. Hadlington [37] concluded that aspects of personality, attitude and behavior greatly impact effective information security. He indicated that just providing information to users is not sufficient. Users need to be trained to use it effectively.

Lahcen et al. [26] proposed an interdisciplinary framework for mitigating human error concept. They focused on three areas: behavioral cybersecurity, human factors and modeling and simulation. Lahcen et al. suggested that employees have different credentials or levels of access and responsibilities. Hence, personalized training of cyber awareness is needed for roles and requirements.

A report presented by Coventry et al. [39] listed in detail the reasons for not employing cyber security best practices, which leads to cybercrimes. According to Coventry et al., there are two main reasons for this. The first is a lack of communication within the cyber security user community, and the second is a lack of knowledge and skills. They proposed a Mindspace model to influence people to behave in a way that will keep them safe online where security is a prime concern and that does not rely on the knowledge and behaviors of end-users. According to Coventry et al., it is important to implement security and privacy practices from the start to make the system robust. For effective end-to-end security systems, government, security specialists and application developers need to work in tandem.

Moustafa et al. [36] analyzed the psychological behavior of users and indicated that users possess different cognitive capabilities. These cognitive capabilities are indications of the ability of the user to handle security threats. Individual traits like procrastination, impulsiveness, future thinking and risk taking are also related to cyber security behaviors. This demands the use of cognitive models for predicting attacks. Veksler et al. [40] presented a computational cognitive model which can used to predict the behavior of attackers or computer system users.

Albladi and Weir [41] pointed out that neuroticism plays a vital role in cyber security. A person with higher score of neuroticism will be less oriented towards security aspects. The same is found by Kelley [42], López-Aguilar and Solanas [43] and other researchers.

Summarizing this and the other works reported in the literature, the important points for orienting human behavior towards secure usage are:

- **Security Awareness Training**: Security awareness training is essential to make the user aware of cognitive dissonance and threats in the environment.
- **Password Protection**: Always use a strong password. Change the password at regular intervals. Avoid sharing password information.
- **Maintain Cyber Hygiene**: Scanning devices for viruses/malware, backing up data, using authentic software and avoiding red-flagged websites/emails are examples of good cyber hygiene that minimize vulnerability to attacks.
- **Proactive Tech Refresh**: Regularly check for patches and updates to keep devices up to date to counter security threats.
- **Inattentional Blindness**: Many times users accept security policies blindly. This can cause serious security risks. Understanding security policies before accepting is essential.
- **Avoid Impulsive/Neurotic Behavior**: Impulsive/neurotic behavior is more vulnerable to cyberattacks. Such behavior limits one's vision towards security measures.

9.5 CONCLUSION

The data gathered by IoT devices works as fuel for IoB operations. Hence, when we look at security aspects of IoB, one has to concentrate heavily on the security of IoT. Apart from these threats, one needs to address issues of confidentiality, integrity and availability of IoB operations. There is no single-point instant solution for security concerns concerning IoB. In fact, one needs to employ the best practices available at different stages of IoB deployment to reduce the cyber security threats. Also, implementing security protocols only on the system side is not sufficient. The end user of the system also needs to be oriented for safe use. And, most importantly, to build a robust IoB system, governments and system designers need to work hand in hand towards standardization of protocols and unifying privacy and regulation policies.

REFERENCES

1. N. Godbole and S. Belapure, *Cyber Security: Understanding Cyber Crimes, Computer Forensics and Legal Perspectives*. Wiley, 2011.
2. E. Cole, *Network Security*, 2nd ed. Wiley, 2011.

3. C. P. Pfleeger, S. L. Pfleeger, and J. Margulies, *Security in Computing*, 5th ed. Prentice Hall, 2015. [Online]. Available: https://eopcw.com/assets/stores/ Computer%20Security/ lecturenote 1704978481security-in-computing-5-e.pdf

4. W. Stallings, *Cryptography and Network Security: Principles and Practice*, 7th ed. Pearson, 2017. [Online]. Available: www. cs.vsb.cz/ochodkova/courses/kpb/ cryptography-and-network-security – principles-and-practice-7th-global-edition.pdf

5. "What is cybersecurity?" Last Accessed May 2022. [Online]. Available: www. ibm.com/in-en/topics/cybersecurity

6. "What is cybersecurity?" Last Accessed May 2022. [Online]. Available: www. cisco.com/c/en_in/products/security/ what-is-cybersecurity.html

7. "The future of the digital world: Internet of Things (IoT) with Internet of Behaviors (IoB) extension," Oct 2021, Last Accessed May 2022. [Online]. Available: www. evosysglobal.com/blog/internet-of-things-iot-with-internet-of-behaviors-iob

8. "Gartner press release," Oct 2021, Last Accessed on – May 2022. [Online]. Available: www.gartner.com/en/newsroom/press-releases/ 2020–10–19-gartner-identifies-the-top-strategic-technology-trends-for-2021

9. J. Lopez, R. Roman, and C. Alcaraz, "Analysis of security threats, requirements, technologies and standards in wireless sensor networks," in *Foundations of Security Analysis and Design V: FOSAD 2007/2008/2009 Tutorial Lectures*, A. Aldini, G. Barthe, and R. Gorrieri, Eds. Springer Berlin Heidelberg, 2009, pp. 289–338. [Online]. Available: https://doi.org/10.1007/978-3-642-03829-7 10

10. R. Roman, J. Zhou, and J. Lopez, "On the features and challenges of security and privacy in distributed Internet of Things," *Computer Networks*, vol. 57, no. 10, pp. 2266–2279, 2013. [Online]. Available: www.sciencedirect.com/science/ article/pii/S1389128613000054

11. Y. H. Hwang, "IoT security & privacy: Threats and challenges," in *Proceedings of the 1st ACM Workshop on IoT Privacy, Trust, and Security*, ser. IoTPTS '15. Association for Computing Machinery, 2015, p. 1. [Online]. Available: https: // doi.org/10.1145/2732209.2732216

12. M. Abomhara and G. M. Køien, "Cyber security and the Internet of Things: Vulnerabilities, threats, intruders and attacks," *Cyber Security*, vol. 4, pp. 65–88, 2015. [Online]. Available: https: //doi.org/10.13052/jcsm2245–1439.414

13. J. C. Talwana and H. J. Hua, "Smart world of Internet of Things (IoT) and its security concerns," in *2016 IEEE International Conference on Internet of Things (iThings) and IEEE Green Computing and Communications (GreenCom) and IEEE Cyber, Physical and Social Computing (CPSCom) and IEEE Smart Data (SmartData)*, IEEE, 2016, pp. 240–245.

14. Y. Yang, L. Wu, G. Yin, L. Li, and H. Zhao, "A survey on security and privacy issues in Internet-of-Things," *IEEE Internet of Things Journal*, vol. 4, no. 5, pp. 1250–1258, 2017.

15. A. Alrawais, A. Alhothaily, C. Hu, and X. Cheng, "Fog computing for the Internet of Things: Security and privacy issues," *IEEE Internet Computing*, vol. 21, no. 2, pp. 34–42, 2017.

16. D. M. Mena, I. Papapanagiotou, and B. Yang, "Internet of Things: Survey on security," *Information Security Journal: A Global Perspective*, vol. 27, no. 3, pp. 162–182, 2018. [Online]. Available: https: //doi.org/10.1080/19393555. 2018.1458258

17. P. Ahmadi, K. Islam, T. Maco, and M. Katam, "A survey on Internet of Things security issues and applications," in *2018 International Conference on Computational Science and Computational Intelligence (CSCI)*, IEEE, 2018, pp. 925–934.

18. M. M. Ogonji, G. Okeyo, and J. M. Wafula, "A survey on privacy and security of Internet of Things," *Computer Science Review*, vol. 38, p. 100312, 2020. [Online]. Available: www.sciencedirect.com/science/ article/pii/S1574 013720304123

19. J. S. Kumar and D. R. Patel, "A survey on Internet of Things: Security and privacy issues," *International Journal of Computer Applications*, vol. 90, no. 11, pp. 20–26, 2014. [Online]. Available: https://course.ccs.neu.edu/cs7680su18/ resources/pxc3894454.pdf

20. "IoT security issues, threats, and defenses," July 2021, Last Accessed May 2022. [Online]. Available: www.trendmicro.com/vinfo/us/security/news/ internet-of-things/iot-security-101-threats-issues-and-defenses

21. "What is Internet of Behavior? Need, advantages & future," Feb. 2022, Last Accessed May 2022. [Online]. Available: https://www3. technologyevaluation. com/research/article/Internet-of-behavior.html

22. "Cisco's 2021 security outcomes study." 2021, Last Accessed May 2022. [Online]. Available: https://cisco.com/go/SecurityOutcomes

23. "The Internet of Behaviours and how ready we are," Mar 2021, Last Accessed May 2022. [Online]. Available: https://analyticsindiamag. com/ the-internet-of-behaviours-and-how-ready-we-are/

24. "Fitness tracking app Strava gives away location of secret us army bases," 2018, Last Accessed May 2022. [Online]. Available: www.theguardian.com/world/2018/ jan/28/ fitness-tracking-app-gives-away-location-of-secret-us-army-bases

25. D. I. Rodica Tirtea, Claude Castelluccia, "Bittersweet cookies: Some security and privacy considerations," in *European Union Agency for Network and Information Security – ENISA*, 2011. [Online]. Available: www.enisa.europa.eu/ publications/copy_of_cookies/at_download/fullReport

26. R. A. M. Lahcen, B. Caulkins, R. Mohapatra, and M. Kumar, "Review and insight on the behavioral aspects of cybersecurity," *Cybersecurity*, vol. 3, no. 10, pp. 2523–3246, 2020. [Online]. Available: https://cybersecurity. springeropen. com/articles/10.1186/s42400–020–00050-w#citeas

27. X. Zeng, G. Xu, X. Zheng, Y. Xiang, and W. Zhou, "E-aua: An efficient anonymous user authentication protocol for mobile IoT," *IEEE Internet of Things Journal*, vol. 6, no. 2, pp. 1506–1519, 2019.

28. J. Li, W. Zhang, V. Dabra, K.-K. R. Choo, S. Kumari, and D. Hogrefe, "Aep-ppa: An anonymous, efficient and provably-secure privacy-preserving authentication protocol for mobile services in smart cities," *Journal of Network and Computer Applications*, vol. 134, pp. 52–61, 2019. [Online]. Available: www.sciencedirect. com/science/ article/pii/S1084804519300475

29. Z. Ning, G. Xu, N. Xiong, Y. Yang, C. Shen, E. Panaousis, H. Wang, and K. Liang, "Taw: Cost-effective threshold authentication with weights for Internet of Things," *IEEE Access*, vol. 7, pp. 30 112–30 125, 2019.

30. D. He, C. Chen, S. Chan, J. Bu, and A. V. Vasilakos, "A distributed trust evaluation model and its application scenarios for medical sensor networks," *IEEE Transactions on Information Technology in Biomedicine*, vol. 16, no. 6, pp. 1164–1175, 2012.

31. H. Zhu, S. Du, Z. Gao, M. Dong, and Z. Cao, "A probabilistic misbehavior detection scheme toward efficient trust establishment in delay-tolerant networks," *IEEE Transactions on Parallel and Distributed Systems*, vol. 25, no. 1, pp. 22–32, 2014.

32. T. Ye, Z. Ning, J. Zhang, and M. Xu, "Trusted measurement of behaviors for the Internet of Things," *Alexandria Engineering Journal*, vol. 60, no. 1, pp. 1477–1488, 2021. [Online]. Available: www.sciencedirect.com/science/article/pii/S1110016820305846

33. S. K. Tayyaba, M. A. Shah, O. A. Khan, and A. W. Ahmed, "Software defined network (SDN) based Internet of Things (IoT): A road ahead," in *Proceedings of the International Conference on Future Networks and Distributed Systems*, ser. ICFNDS '17. Association for Computing Machinery, 2017. [Online]. Available: https://doi.org/10.1145/3102304.3102319

34. N. Mhaskar, M. Alabbad, and R. Khedri, "A formal approach to network segmentation," *Computers & Security*, vol. 103, p. 102162, 2021. [Online]. Available: www.sciencedirect.com/science/article/ pii/S0167404820304351

35. A. Wasicek, "The future of 5g smart home network security is micro-seg mentation," *Network Security*, vol. 2020, no. 11, pp. 11–13, 2020. [Online]. Available: www.sciencedirect.com/science/article/ pii/S135348582030129X

36. A. A. Moustafa, A. Bello, and A. Maurushat, "The role of user behaviour in improving cyber security management," *Frontiers in Psychology*, vol. 12, 2021. [Online]. Available: www.frontiersin.org/article/10.3389/fpsyg.2021.561011

37. L. Hadlington, "Human factors in cybersecurity; Examining the link between Internet addiction, impulsivity, attitudes towards cybersecurity, and risky cybersecurity behaviours," *Heliyon*, vol. 3, no. 7, E00346, pp. 1–18, 2017. [Online]. Available: http://dx.doi.org/10.1016/j.heliyon.2017. e00346

38. M. Griffiths, "Internet abuse and Internet addiction in the workplace," *Journal of Workplace Learning*, vol. 22, no. 7, pp. 463–472, 2010. [Online]. Available: http://dx.doi.org/10.1108/13665621011071127

39. L. Coventry, P. Briggs, J. Blythe, and M. Tran, *Using Behavioural Insights to Improve the Public's Use of Cyber Security Best Practices*, Government Office for Science, Tech. Rep., 2014. [Online]. Available: www.gov.uk/government/publications/ cyber-security-using-behavioural-insights-to-keep-people-safe-online

40. V. D. Veksler, N. Buchler, C. G. LaFleur, M. S. Yu, C. Lebiere, and C. Gonzalez, "Cognitive models in cybersecurity: Learning from expert analysts and predicting attacker behavior," *Frontiers in Psychology*, vol. 11, 2020. [Online]. Available: www.frontiersin.org/article/10.3389/fpsyg.2020.01049

41. S. M. Albladi and G. R. S. Weir, "Personality traits and cyber-attack victimisation: Multiple mediation analysis," in *2017 Internet of Things Business Models, Users, and Networks*, IEEE, 2017, pp. 1–6.

42. D. Kelley, "Investigation of attitudes towards security behaviors," *McNair Research Journal SJSU*, vol. 14, no. 10, pp. 125–139, 2018. [Online]. Available: https://doi.org/10.31979/mrj.2018.1410

43. P. López-Aguilar and A. Solanas, "Human susceptibility to phishing attacks based on personality traits: The role of neuroticism," in *2021 IEEE 45th Annual Computers, Software, and Applications Conference (COMPSAC)*, IEEE, 2021, pp. 1363–1368.

Chapter 10

Identification of Nutrients and Microbial Contamination in Fruits and Vegetables – Technology Using Internet of Behavior

K. Sujatha, N.P.G. Bhavani, G. Victo Sudha George, D. Kirubakaran, M. Sujitha, and V. Srividhya

CONTENTS

10.1 INTRODUCTION

Currently, no system exists that is equipped with machine vision technology to measure the nutritional content of fruit using an online detection system. In this chapter, fruits such as mangoes, bananas, and papayas are used as input samples to train artificial intelligence algorithms. The origin of this research work lies in developing algorithms for image processing and hybrid artificial neural networks (ANN). Further, quality assessment in terms of nutritional value will enable customers to procure good-quality fruit. The advantage of this technology is that it does not need any additional device to obtain related parameters from the color of the fruit. In the pilot stage of this research work, images were analyzed for training and testing. From the analysis, testing results confirmed that the required precision and recall level were in the range of 80–89% and 100%, respectively. Features are extracted and used as inputs to train the ANN with a back propagation algorithm

DOI: 10.1201/9781003305170-10

(BPA). The weight vectors of the ANN are tuned to optimal values using a genetic algorithm (GA) and particle swarm optimization (PSO). People need to identify and classify their food according to nutrient composition so that they may have a clear understanding of their diet and make the necessary decisions to improve their health. To make predictions on food nutrient composition, a model is proposed that uses a neural network and algorithm to conduct training and implementation of deep learning mode to make predictions on food nutrient composition (Aafia et al. 2018).

Image processing was at the initial level of practical application, and it has been used widely in analyzing the quality of fruit from images. The reason behind the usage of the image process, which reveals that the texture reflects the change in intensity value, includes information about the color and physical structure of the objects. Prior to harvesting, citrus fruit was first used to count the number of ripe and unripe fruits on a tree through image analysis. Subsequently, this technology was applied to various fruits such as strawberry and papaya (Bato et al. 2000) to sort out the mature fruit, and it achieved accuracy of around 80–100%. This proves the potential of the usage of processing techniques for analysis of fruits after harvesting for trader markets.

In the case of climacteric fruits, a little ethylene is enough to cause ripening with appropriate temperature and humidity however, in the case of non-climacteric fruits, ripened fruits are harvested and do not react to ethylene treatment; such fruits are grapes, watermelon, and critic fruits. As the process continues, segmentation of color images is preferred to gray images due to color images having more information, more capacity and high speed of processing information.

The development of technology also leads to improvisation according to researchers' need, which are categorized as image domain based, physics based, and feature space based. The resulting image domain–based study gives a homogeneous region, and physics-based study will help to find the actual material boundaries; further, feature-based technique algorithms are concerned with presence of massive collective pixels in a feature spectral space.

10.2 REVIEW OF STATUS OF RESEARCH AND DEVELOPMENT

10.2.1 International Status

Currently, there are various options to detect ripened fruits and vegetables. However, a machine vision system uses different methods to analyze images of fruits and vegetables. Previously, computer systems were not robust enough to operate on large and real colors of images; thus, the output was mostly grayscale images. Recently, computer systems have gone through enough development to get large and true color images (Cardello 2003).

To analyze the quality and grading of agricultural products, automatic detection systems have been used in recent years with help of a camera and computer-based technology. Hence, two classifier algorithms, the mean color intensity algorithm and area algorithm, were developed, and their accuracy in maturity detection has been assessed. Another detection technique is used to identify the maturity of mangos by using gas sensors. Figaro gas sensors were used to detect gases Artificial intelligence (AI) is an interdisciplinary field which spans computer science, linguistics, psychology, biology, philosophy, and further application-oriented research. AI is used to estimate ethylene gas during ripening; therefore, along with image processing, AI is also used to detect the color of fruits that are ripe or unripe (Srividhya and Sujatha 2018).

In this way, the major problem of people's different perceptions will be sorted out using the AI process after taking images of different stages of ripeness during the ripening process Many diseases can be avoided by consuming a nutritious diet. These foods are free from high fat content. Consumption of foods rich in fiber is good for health.

Regarding marketing of fruits, consumers are attracted to good-quality fruits and vegetables, and they are also confused during purchase if there is no information about nutrition. Hence, in-depth analysis need to be carried out when making decisions about the variations present (Bech et al. 2019).

Buyers are attracted if new technologies are implemented in marketing strategies, which will draw the attention of the buyers, creating success (Busse and Siebert 2018). Developmental activities based on research support the food industry, and such industries will also gain publicity in a very short time span. This will also create awareness between conventional and novel foods (Cardello 2003).

The work proposed by Parisa Pouladzadeh et al. helps consumers identify calories without information about nutrients for various food items that are consumed. Thus, consumers do not have knowledge about the composition of nutrients present in the foods. Therefore, there is a requirement for technology which will provide the nutritional composition available in foods so that people can be conscious about health (Srividhya and Sujatha 2018).

10.2.2 National Status

The habit of consuming fruits and vegetables will be improved by educating people regarding their nutritional facts and their beneficial effects in preventing disease. For instance, identifying fruits that contain a high quantity of potassium to reduce bone loss, those with sufficient fiber for a healthy digestive system, and those with antioxidants in the form of vitamins and minerals to combat oxidative stress responsible for several ailments.

In this scenario, each person is confused about the nutritional value of the food they consume on daily basis. From the literature currently available, there is a lack of a food intake monitoring system that measures the composition of the food; however, there are systems that monitor the calorific content of food items. Developing an app that can facilitate quantifying biochemically important nutritive molecules will help the common person live a normal life by avoiding malnourishment. To this end, people should select colored fruits and vegetables, since they possess antioxidant properties for combating oxidative stress and thereby protect the body from cardiovascular disease, stroke, and cancer (Srividhya et al. 2016, 2018).

Mango is an important fruit crop across the world, and it is used on important occasions Mango is consumed in various forms, like mango pulp juice, ice cream, pickles, candy, and so on. For all such preparations, mangoes need to reach an appropriate ripening stage The mineral magnesium present in mango fruit is responsible for blood pressure regulation as well as normal functioning of the immune system. Mango is well-known for its vitamin A content, which aids in the treatment of night blindness, as well as mangosteen, which acts as a powerful antioxidant in the protection of eye health. It protects the body from diseases such as asthma, anemia, and atherosclerosis and aids in bone health. One 165-gram cup of sliced, raw mango provides 99 calories, 1.35 g of protein, 0.63 g of fat, 24.7 g of carbohydrate, 22.5 g of sugar, and 2.64 g of fiber.

One globally consumed fruit is banana, the fourth most important food crop in the world after rice, wheat, and maize. Inconsistency in the production and export of bananas among countries is chiefly due to the unpreserved nature of bananas and a lack of information and methodological know-how about how to equalize the fruit quality standard with the international standard. Usually referred to as "plantains," they belong to the family Musaceae.

The botanical name for banana is *Musa*. Ripe banana contains high amounts of potassium and vitamins C and D that prevent muscle spasms and fight against ulcers in different regions of the gastrointestinal tract. It is used for the treatment of burns, wounds, anemia, and arthritis. The other benefits of banana are enhancing weight reduction and strengthening muscles and bones. The nutritional value of banana includes 89 calories, 22.82 g carbohydrates (2.6 g dietary fiber, 12.23 g sugars), 1.09 g protein, 0.33 g fat, 8% potassium, 10% vitamin C, 2% iron, and 8% magnesium.

Tomato is an edible berry with botanical name *Solanum lycopersicum* and belongs to the family *Solanaceae*. The red color is due to the rich antioxidant chemical lycopene, which helps to fight against free radicals produced in the body. Tomatoes have a high content of vitamin C and potassium, which helps to protect the body from several types of cancer. The chromium present in the tomato is a blood sugar–lowering agent (Bhowmik et al. 2012). The nutritional value of tomato includes 18 calories carbohydrates (1.2 g dietary fiber, 2.6 g sugar), 0.9 g protein, 0.2 g fat, 5% potassium, 17% vitamin C, and 3% magnesium. Classifiers and machine learning techniques can be used to extract useful information from datasets/images to solve important problems in computer vision and image processing. A feed forward neural network (FFNN)–based food image recognition algorithm is proposed to enhance the accuracy of current measurements of dietary intake using real-world mobile mechanism.

10.2.3 Importance of the Proposed Work

Fruit quality is classified by texture, shape, and color. These features are generally observed through human vision, predominantly in determining the quality of fruits. Thus, the researcher needs to focus on alternative methods for detecting the quality of fruits effectively. In the first stage, the accuracy of estimating the various nutrients present in the fruit is most important and depends on a preprocessing segmentation algorithm. **Machine** learning– or training-based classifiers require an intensive training phase of the classifier parameter, and hence a higher recognition rate is obtained, such as with support vector machines, hidden Markov models, and ANN. The existing methods have pros and cons. However, there are numerous techniques available for more accurate estimation. However, the nutrition value differs for different fruits, making it edible. Thus, there is a need for an appropriate method to identify nutrients and the induced toxicity of a fruit.

- The prime goal of investigation is to develop a technology that will indicate an appropriate level of nutrients with AI-based smart phone app technology. In order to monitor the quality of fruits such as mango, banana, guava, and others by involving the image processing method followed by preprocessing.
- These errorless and noise-free images are further scrutinized via an artificial intelligence technique to detect the nutritional value and microbial contamination of the fruits and vegetables. To investigate the nutritional value present in the fruits and vegetables, various literature is analyzed, and research gaps in the area are identified (Busse and Siebert 2018).
- The prime work toward the objective is to develop a smart phone app which is capable of estimating nutrients like total carbohydrates, including sugars like glucose, fructose, and sucrose; potassium; magnesium; vitamins like vitamin A and vitamin C; and antioxidants, along with microbial contamination present in the fruit or vegetable using a quality monitoring system using fruit images, which extracts the color, shape, average intensity, and standard American diet from the captured fruit and vegetable images using a camera in a mobile phone and informing the exact status through a mobile phone app.

- The brightness value of the each fruit sample was taken; further instantaneous monitoring was done in order to identify microbial contamination.
- Preprocessing was performed by which the segmentation process carried out and noise and background errors were removed. Further, these images were taken for artificial intelligence techniques, which were used to estimate the nutrients in the fruits and vegetables.
- Mobile applications are being created.
  The work is not location specific, but a mobile signal is important for the consumer to know the status of the fruits and vegetables. The mobile application guides the consumer about the exact status of fruits and vegetables along with total carbohydrates, including sugars like glucose, fructose, and sucrose; potassium; magnesium; vitamins like vitamin A and vitamin C; antioxidants; and microbial contamination.

10.3 METHODOLOGY

During the detailed literature analysis, the following gaps were observed. The existing system is not equipped with the following technology.

- Machine vision technology to detect the type of fruits and vegetables and nutrients like glucose, fructose, sucrose, potassium, magnesium, antioxidants, vitamin A and vitamin C present using image processing algorithms.
- Cross-validate the nutritional value of the fruits and vegetables using the proposed intelligent image processing algorithms in comparison with conventional estimation methods.
- Yielding instantaneous information about microbial contamination.
- Replacing laboratory assessment to identify and monitor the quality of fruits with an intelligent smart phone app.

The following are the objectives of the proposed project:

- To detect nutrients like total carbohydrates, including sugars like glucose, fructose, and sucrose; potassium; magnesium; and vitamins like vitamin A and vitamin C present in fruits and vegetables using image processing algorithms.
- To cross-verify and validate the nutritional value (total carbohydrates, including sugars like glucose, fructose, and sucrose; potassium; magnesium; antioxidants; and vitamins like vitamin A and vitamin C) of fruits and vegetables using the proposed machine vision technology.

- To introduce a smart phone app for instantaneous monitoring and detection of microbial contamination of fruits and vegetables to increase marketability.

The objective is to develop a smart phone app for estimating nutrients and induced toxicity by capturing images of fruit. Features are extracted and the hybrid ANN is trained using images of fruits like mangoes, bananas, and papayas. Ensuring quality, which includes attributes like color and aroma, along with enhanced taste, plays an important role in this project. The database, which consists of images related to varieties of mangoes, bananas, and papayas, is extracted. The images are preprocessed, and the features are extracted. These extracted features include intensity, area, median, and standard deviation. These features are used as inputs to train the hybrid ANN using BPA, whose weights are optimized using a genetic algorithm and particle swarm optimization.

The fruit images are captured using a mobile phone camera, and these images are processed as shown in Figure 10.1. Further, the acquired images are preprocessed, followed by feature extraction and classification, as shown in Figure 10.2.

As a continuation process, dithering and filtering image approximation are performed to reduce the number of colors in an image, which results

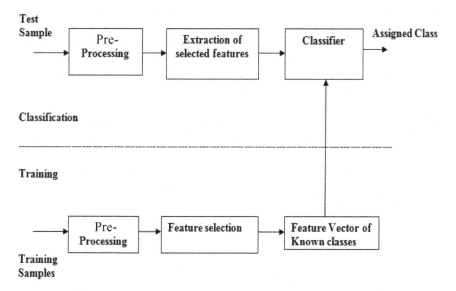

Figure 10.1 Methodology for estimation of nutrients and induced toxicity of fruits using image processing.

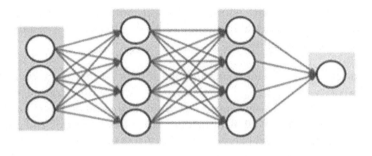

Input layer   Hidden layer 1   Hidden layer 2   Output layer

Figure 10.2 Schematic representation of feed-forward neural network.

in the final image. However, the original image is inferior since some of the colors are lost.

Dithering is performed to increase the color in the output image and also change the colors of the pixels in a neighborhood so that the average color in each neighborhood approximates the original RGB color. RGB-to-gray conversion is a low-level preprocessing, and two main methods are used for it. Unwanted noise is removed by using the average filter. The split and merge algorithms are used in the noise reduction process. Feature extraction measures data and derives the features of the images. The main features used are shape, size, texture, and color. However, different features are extracted from the fruits. This morphological operation, erosion and dilation, is used for the elimination of small objects.

For the classification of fruits, different types of classifiers are used. These features are used to form a training set, and then a classification algorithm is applied to extract a knowledge base, which makes a decision in the given case.

In a computer vision system, there is a wide variety of methods, but we have used a feed-forward neural network for ethylene gas estimation, which is made possible by using a back-propagation algorithm (BPA) for training the FFNN.

The major target is the value of ethylene gas concentration, and the normalized values of the features are used to obtain results from the various intellectual classifiers. Overall, 102 collected images collected (80 for training and 51 for testing) are considered for training and testing purposes with the FFNN using the BPA. Four features are used as input and one as output in the FFNN confirmation.

In the proposed work, several images of various fruits and vegetables were collected for training and testing from the ripening room. The images were preprocessed, and features were extracted. The preprocessing included dithering, filtering, histogram analysis, and morphological closing operation. The extracted features can be used for training a FFNN using BPA. Testing and validation results to be collected will have maximum classification performance. It was understood that classification performance could improve the preprocessing stage of the acquired images. This was proved by our output, as the efficiency percentage increased significantly.

In this segment, another AI method with a genetic algorithm and particle swarm optimization is also implemented to overcome the challenge of a costly and laborious process. Additionally, other AI-based techniques like GA and PSO with BPA are also to be tested, as shown in Figure 10.3.

Physiological and biochemical changes in the natural products are a real concern for understanding metabolic procedures such as natural product aging, relaxing, and general senescence. Even though it is unreasonable to expect to improve the nature of produce after collecting it, it is conceivable to lower the rate of unwanted changes. The person taking care of the framework must intend to guarantee that the organic product comes to the showcase in the condition required by the purchaser or shipper.

The support of physical and chemical properties that give quality to harvested organic products depends predominantly on collection development and mostly upon the capacity to force conditions that limit changes in these characteristics.

Harvest time is essential to acquire a top-notch organic product with great storage potential. For the most part, the gathering of developed, unripe, natural products has been accounted for to improve storability and transportability, while organic products collected at the ripe stage will have a shorter life and their flavor may deteriorate before consummation of the advertising procedure.

The ripening process needs to monitor and analyze the quality of the fruits by conventional methods, and other modified or improved methods were used to gives better predictions. This type of analysis would be an efficient and accessible technique to detect nutrients and induced toxicity of fruit.

The standard values of total carbohydrates, including sugars like glucose, fructose, and sucrose; potassium; magnesium; and vitamins like vitamin A and vitamin C, along with microbial contamination (Table 10.1). These are the reference values that are obtained from the standard nutrition table. By analyzing various samples in laboratory, these parameters are estimated and recorded in the first column in Table 10.1.

Then the values estimated by the hybrid ANN architecture, with features extracted from the fruit images (coded in MATLAB) using a simulation platform, are recorded in the second column. Thereafter, the results from the smart phone app are obtained; fruit and vegetable images captured using a

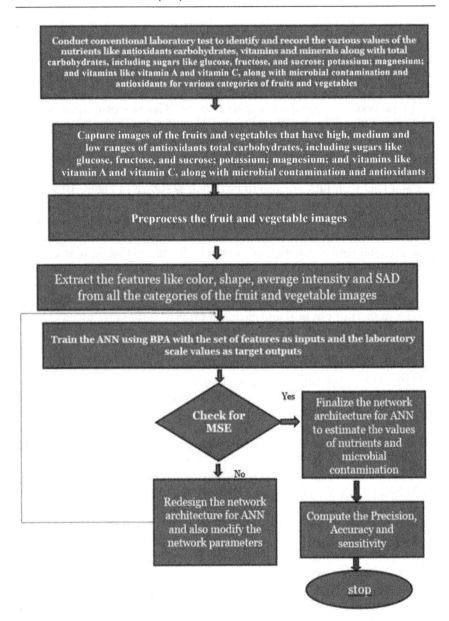

Figure 10.3 Flow chart for training AI algorithms.

mobile phone camera are recorded in the third column of Table 10.1. The deviation for these cases was calculated to ensure the estimated values were within the optimal range. The same table needs to be generated for the testing and validation phase to ensure optimal performance of the smart phone app.

Table 10.1 Comparison Performance Measures

Comparison/ Confirmation	Class 1		Class2		Class 3	
	Recall	Precision	Recall	Precision	Recall	Precision
BPA+GA	1	1	0.894	1	0.85	1
BPA	1	1	0.8358	1	0.8	1

10.4 RESULTS AND DISCUSSION

The conclusive weights are taken once the training of the FFNN with the BPA is finished. Testing the estimated values of all the nutrients and microbial contamination is finished with conclusive weights acquired after feedforward control. The yields of the FFNN prepared with the BPA are shown in Figure 10.4.

A genetic algorithm was used along with the separated highlights to prepare the ANN. The hereditary calculation at each progression to create the cutting edge from the current population is the estimation by GA.

AI is an interdisciplinary field that requires knowledge of software engineering, semantics, brain neuroscience, and reasoning criteria for genuine research. The estimation is shown in Figure 10.5.

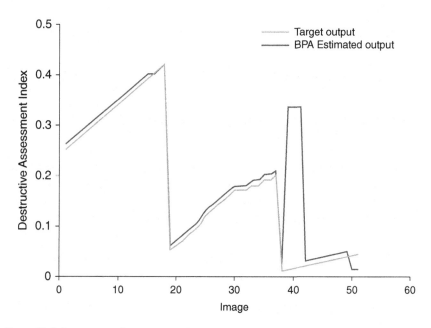

Figure 10.4 Estimation of nutrients and microbial contamination by BPA.

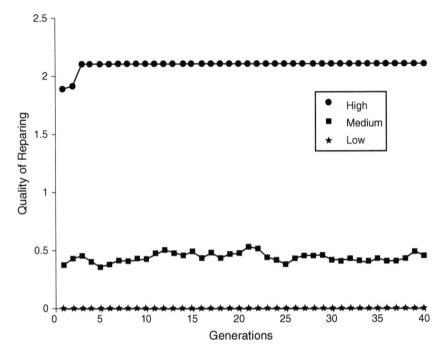

Figure 10.5 Estimation of nutrients and microbial contamination by BPA with GA.

10.5 CONCLUSION

In this work, 102 images were collected (51 for training and 51 for testing) from the ripening room. The images were preprocessed and features extracted. The preprocessing included dithering, filtering, histogram analysis, and morphological closing operation. The extracted features can be used for training of an FFNN using a BPA and a BPA with a GA. Depending on the nutrients and microbial contamination, fruits and vegetables are classified as high, medium, and low quality, with their respective nutrient values and the status of microbial contamination if present. Incidental parameters displayed on the screen of the mobile phone will help buyers purchase the required fruits and vegetables. The success of the mobile phone app will depend on the resolution of the camera present in the phone, along with Internet connectivity.

REFERENCES

Aafia, S., Rouf, A., Kanojia, V. and Ayaz, Q. 2018, Ozone treatment in prolongation of shelf life of temperate and tropical fruits, *International Journal of Pure Applied Bioscience*, vol. 6, no. 2, pp. 298–303.

Hanbury, A. 2003, *Physics based segmentation of colour images in spherical coordinates*, Technical Report-84, Pattern Recognition and Image Processing Group, Institute of Computer Aided Automation, Vienna University of Technology, vol. 9, no. 1832, pp. 1–29.

Bato, P. M., Nagata, M., Cao, Q. X., Hiyoshi, K. and Kitahara, T. 2000, Study on sorting system for strawberry using machine vision: Development of sorting system with direction and judgment functions for strawberry, *Journal of Japanese Society of Agricultural Machinery*, vol. 62, no. 2, pp. 101–110.

Bech, S., Brunoe, T. D., Nielsen, K. and Andersen, A.-L. 2019, Product and process variety management: Case study in the food industry. *Procedia CIRP*, vol. 81, pp. 1065–1070.

Bhowmik, D., Sampath Kumar, K. P., PaSwan, S. and Srivastava, S. 2012, Tomato – a natural medicine and its health benefits, *Journal of Pharmacognosy and Phytochemistry*, vol. 1, no. 1, pp. 33–43.

Busse, M. and Siebert, R. 2018, The role of consumers in food innovation processes, *European Journal of Innovation Management*, vol. 21, no. 1. DOI:10.1108/EJIM-03-2017-0023

Cardello, A. V. 2003, Consumer concerns and expectations about novel food processing technologies: Effects on product liking. *Appetite*, vol. 40, pp. 217–233.

Srividhya, V. and Sujatha, K. 2018, Fruit fly algorithm for estimation of quality ripening of fruits, *International Journal of Pure and Applied Mathematics*, vol. 118, no. 18, pp. 3199–3207.

Srividhya, V. and Sujatha, K. 2018, Role of ethylene in fruits ripening process, International Conference on Energy, Communication, Data Analytics and Soft Computing.

Srividhya, V., Sujatha, K. and Ponmagal, R. S. 2016, Ethylene gas measurement for ripening of fruits using image processing, *Indian Journal of Science and Technology*, vol. 9, no. 31, pp. 1–7.

Sujatha, K., Srividhya, V. and Karthikeyan, V. 2018, Versatile inertial weight based PSO for estimation of quality ripening of fruits, *Journal of Advanced Research in Dynamical and Control Systems*.

Sujatha, V. S., Ponmagal, R. S. and Godhavari, T. 2018, Soft sensor for capacitance tracking in quality assurance of fruit ripening process, in *Materials Today: Proceedings*, Elsevier.

Chapter 11

Plagiarism Detection for Afghan National Languages (Pashto and Dari)

Niaz M. Doostyar and B. Sujatha

CONTENTS

11.1 INTRODUCTION

In the past, there were many problems with detecting academic or scientific theft. People used different methods and techniques to find and prevent plagiarism, and they faced a lot of problems. But such methods didn't work accurately. Plagiarism has become more common among people over time. Plagiarism has been widely used by students in universities because today, information is diverse, comes from a variety of sources, and is easily accessible. The development of the Internet has also undermined the accuracy of the information, and many people are concerned about the quality of information for which plagiarism might have been used (Ali, Abdulla, & Snasel, 2011). Plagiarism is considered a special reportage job in Afghanistan when grading their lives. Here we scrutinize the handling of plagiarism in Afghanistan. Afghan society has faced many misfortunes, and one of those is plagiarism, which is also prevalent here. [sic]

(Sarwanaaz, 2020)

For automatic detection of plagiarism, a variety of techniques and methodologies, primarily in the English language, have been developed. However, there aren't many works in Pashto and Dari. Therefore, the purpose of this work is to create a reliable plagiarism detection system for short paragraphs (Maryam & Mohammad Mahmoodi, 2014).

There is no computer system or software in Afghan society to detect plagiarism academic papers in Pashto or Dari, so this will be the first computer software that will be able to detect plagiarism for the Afghan national languages (Pashto and Dari). This system will have one online database (MongoDB), and whole papers will be stored in the database, so comparisons will be done on all papers included in the database.

11.1.1 Types of Plagiarism

As stated in Melissa and Nicholas (2011), plagiarism is the unauthorized use of another person's thoughts, words, or products without giving due credit or attribution. The following are some ways that plagiarism might be found in academic research articles:

- Passing off someone else's creation as your own.
- Using someone else's creations without attribution or citation.
- Whether or not credit is given, the majority of someone else's contribution is your own.
- Incorrectly crediting other works in your work.

A paper, work, production, or program may contain plagiarism in a variety of ways. Two basic types of plagiarism are shown in Figure 11.1 (El Tahir, Hussam, & Václav, 2011).

11.1.2 Textual Plagiarism

Textual plagiarism is plagiarism in text form. This kind of plagiarism is typically committed by students when writing assignments and by researchers when producing research articles. Researchers have created a set of methods and algorithms to identify this form of plagiarism; however, for the regional languages of Afghanistan, there is no such tool.

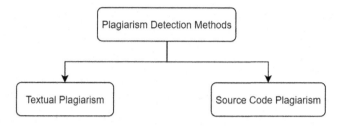

Figure 11.1 Plagiarism detection methods.

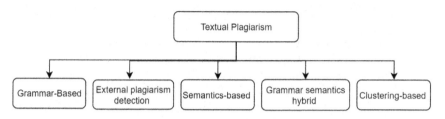

Figure 11.2 Describing the many forms of textual plagiarism.

Therefore (Mayank & Dilip Kumar, 2016). Textual plagiarism comes in a variety of forms, which are detailed in Figure 11.2 and addressed further in the following.

- **Grammar-based method:** Based on the grammatical structure of the text, this technique is used to detect plagiarism. Direct copy-paste works well; however, it is ineffective at accurately identifying updated text.
- **Semantics-based method:** The vector space model is used in this procedure. Because it is difficult to fix the location of copied content in the entire document, it works best on nonpartial documents.
- **Grammar semantics hybrid method:** This efficient strategy can find synonyms or rewrite words. By doing so, it gets beyond the drawbacks of both approaches, which might be grammar based or semantics based.
- **External method:** This technique uses a dataset to look for plagiarism in the text. A dataset is a group of documents from which a group of sentences or a portion of a sentence's content has been reproduced.
- **Clustering-based method:** For a variety of reasons, document clustering is utilized in information retrieval. To boost search time, alternative methods besides document clustering are now available for use in plagiarism detection.

11.1.3 Source Code Plagiarism

The second kind of plagiarism that occurs in the source code is source code plagiarism. Five categories may be used to classify source code plagiarism. Five types are described in Figure 11.3.

- **Strings:** The comparison in this technique will be based on the notion of strings matching; however, this sort of plagiarism can be disguised from detection by renaming the identifiers in the source code.
- **Tokens:** In this approach, the program is first turned into a token with the aid of a lexer or a third-party assistance library. This will make it easier to disregard whitespace, comments in the code, and identifier names.
- **Parse Trees:** This method starts by creating parse trees for both source codes, which are then compared. If the trees are identical, it may be said that both source codes are comparable; if not, it cannot.
- **Program Dependency Graphs (PDGs):** In this approach, the real control flow may be captured with the use of PDGs. These PDGs can determine the equivalence, but they are complicated to use and need a lot of processing, which will slow down the system.
- **Metrics:** This gives the code segments "scores" depending on particular criteria. It is possible to get these scores by counting the number of loops, conditional statements, or variables in the code. It is possible to identify both textual and source code plagiarism using manual or automated detection methods.

11.2 LITERATURE REVIEW

On right-to-left (RTL)–based texts like Pashto, Dari, and Arabic, using free plagiarism detection technologies is ineffective, and the results of these programs are erroneous and untrustworthy because they do not take into account the languages' unique characteristics and structure (Mohamed El

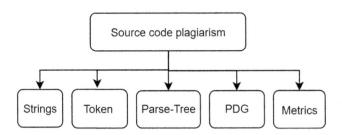

Figure 11.3 Different types of source code plagiarism.

Bachir, 2012). Thus, it is important to employ language-sensitive techniques. Despite recent attempts in this field, there is currently no updated and practical technology available for texts written in the regional Afghan languages (Pashto and Dari).

Miranda, Lucia, and Ruslan (2010) separated the entire project into three parts and introduced a multi-stage new framework that is suited to RTL-based languages to prevent copying with medium accuracy and response time: 1) preprocessing stage: in this phase, preprocessing techniques are employed to separate individual words from a structured text and remove extraneous elements that make it difficult to detect similarities. 2) Similarity comparison stage: in this step, two-word sequences that were created in the stage before are compared using one of the following comparison methodologies: longest common subsequence, 3-gram similarity measurements, 2-gram similarity measures (using Jaccard or Clough & Stevenson used similarity metric). 3) Verdict stage: one of the following verdicts is determined using data generated in earlier stages: since the source texts weren't provided, clean (non-plagiarized) submissions were made using the participants' expertise.

The vector space approach has been developed by Iranian scholars Payman et al. to detect external plagiarism in Persian texts. The researchers created 84 suspect documents and 41 reference papers for their work. The vector space model and cosine similarity between them were used to choose finalist document processing, which is more exact. The 3-gram properties of each document were then shown by the similarity coefficient, where it is likely that similarities will be detected. When looking for documents with similar features, the vector of a document consumes more memory and requires a lot of processing time. This vector's size and the number of features are thus influenced by the paper's length and level of expressiveness (Peyman, Zahra, & Farzin, 2014).

Sh and Braani Dastjerdi 2016) have also provided a proposed combinational technique performance co-pilot (PCP) tool for detecting plagiarism in Persian papers that, despite its poor accuracy, is quick to find plagiarism in a huge corpus of writings. The method, which uses hash-based tree representative fingerprinting to discover phrase similarities of word-based graphs and texts, takes as inputs eight reference articles and one questionable article. The creators determined that employing the PCP using hash-based tree representative fingerprinting is a more appropriate technique in small groups of Persian documents.

A precise approach for identifying plagiarism in brief paragraphs was proposed by Mahmoodi and MahmmodiVarNamkhasti as an additional plagiarism detection tool (2014). It is challenging to detect plagiarism in papers with numerous paragraphs since the inputs of this tool are both a suspect document and a reference document, each of which comprises one paragraph by itself. If either of these papers include more than one paragraph, even if the short paragraphs were accurate to a great degree, it would be hard to detect plagiarism in many of them, and the results would be unreliable and inaccurate.

On the other hand, three more researchers (Rakian, Safi Esfahani, & Rastegari, 2015) used a new fuzzy algorithm to take into account the various levels of a hierarchical text and use the synonyms required in figuring out how similar two sentences in Persian texts are to one another and, as a result, to detect external plagiarism in Persian texts. Here, 1,000 reference papers and 400 suspicious documents were identified, where it was possible to see how phrases were first modified and then changed structurally. Potential commonalities were found using fuzzy algorithms, which were then used to separate the candidate papers relevant to the text and offer recovery keywords. The processing time can be slowed down and memory usage accelerated with more sentence divisions.

11.3 MATERIALS AND METHODS

In this section, we will describe our methods and methodology for preventing Pashto and Dari plagiarism. For implementing this idea, we have composed some methods which will increase accuracy and response time. These are detection, document tree representation, fingerprinting, and text preprocessing are seen in Figure 11.4.

As a result, the text 3-grams produced by various layers of the document tree-based representation served as the foundation for the fingerprints. The bottom-up tree can be used to go to this representation. The volume of the hash formed at the level of the 3-gram words will be less than the final fingerprint of a document produced by the 512-SHA hashing technique and

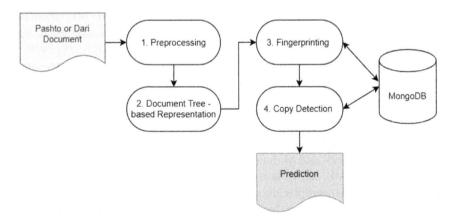

Figure 11.4 Steps for detecting plagiarism for Pashto and Dari documents.

the paragraph-level hash. The error memory usage as shown in Mohamed El Bachir (2012) is enhanced by the compression of a document's fingerprint (Mohamed El Bachir & Manar, 2011). and works that are similar in another language. They generated a significant number of hash word levels in a document's fingerprint because, in their fingerprint notion, hashes at the word level were repeated into their parent. Additionally, the fingerprint concept in the suggested technique differs from the similarity detection strategy used in Mohamed El Bachir (2012) and Mohamed El Bachir and Manar (2011).

11.3.1 Preprocessing

Preprocessing involves cleaning up and eliminating unnecessary text, which improves accuracy and cuts down on the amount of time needed to perform potential similarity detection. Figure 11.5 depicts the stages that make up this metric.

1. **Normalizing:**
   A Pashto and Dari custom normalizer eliminates superfluous spaces and arranges virtual spaces (for example, correcting "ولاړ به سم" to "ولاړ به سم"). In the Pashto language, there are five types of "ی", so this normalizer will not replace any type of "ی" to only one type because it will affect the

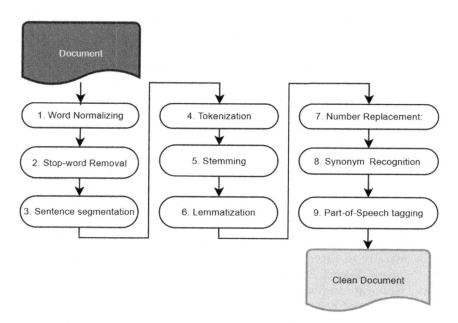

Figure 11.5 Preprocessing stages.

meaning of the word. Because most texts do not follow proper orthography, this preprocessing technique is crucial for Afghan native languages. Additionally, it could make it challenging to spot similarities.

2. **Stop-Word Removal:**
This technique removes common words (articles, prepositions, determiners, and so on) such as "به"، "که"، "چی". These words sometimes have very little effect on meaning but sometimes play a somewhat important role in the text. Two kinds of deep and shallow stop-word removal tables were tested to find the true impact of this technique.

3. **Sentence segmentation:**
Divide the document's text into sentences to enable line-by-line processing for the serial tests (Miranda, Lucia, & Ruslan, 2010).

4. **Tokenization:**
Sentence boundaries with tokens (words, punctuation, etc.) (Miranda, Lucia, & Ruslan, 2010).

5. **Stemming:**
Stemming is the removal and replacement of word suffixes to get to the term's most basic root form. To disguise their plagiarism, some people will occasionally modify a word's form.
Take these two sentences:
"دا پروسیسر کولی شي سیگنال پروسس کړي"
And
"دا دول پروسیسر د سیگنال د پروسس کولو خواک لري"
If the words in this example are not transformed into stems, the similarity checker results will be incorrect.

6. **Lemmatization:**
To expand the comparative study, convert words into their dictionary-based versions (Miranda, Lucia, & Ruslan, 2010). Lemmatization can occasionally be confused with stemming. There is, however, a crucial distinction. Stemming only works with single words without taking context into account; hence it is unable to discriminate between words with multiple meanings (Zdenek & Chris, 2011).

7. **Number Replacement:**
This process substitutes a false character for any number (for instance, "#"). This is necessary because a dishonest individual may simply adjust the numbers in some scientific studies to manipulate the results.

8. **Synonym Recognition:**
Synonym recognition is motivated by human behavior, where people may try to cover up plagiarism by changing words to suitable synonyms (Zdenek & Chris, 2011).
Synonym identification is critical in Afghan national languages since every word has several synonyms. Synonyms are the foreign equivalents of terms such as:
In the Pashto language: "الوګان" can be replaced with "پتاتی" to trick a plagiarism detector.

In the Dari language: "کیبورد" can be replaced with "صفحه کلید" to trick a plagiarism detector.

9. **Part-of-Speech Tagging:**
   For spotting instances when words have been replaced, but the style in terms of grammatical categories stays the same, give each word a grammatical tag such as "noun" (اسم), "verb" (فعل), etc. (Miranda, Lucia, & Ruslan, 2010).

11.3.2 Fingerprinting

To identify a text, a document tree-based representation is used. The suggested strategy is to identify the document's fingerprint at the word level in the text, divide it into 3-grams, apply the hash function to them to obtain hashes, and then construct the document's fingerprint in the 3-gram words. The created hashes in the 3-grams are split into the following 3-grams as well, where the hash function would be used in the next phase to create a fingerprint of the document in sentences. The hashes created in sentences are then again broken down into 3-grams and subjected to the hash function to obtain the document's final fingerprint (at the paragraph level). The hashed 3-grams at each level would be generated by the final fingerprint of a document made using a tree representation and the hash function, which has better volume and efficiency than the method described in El Bachir (2012) and El Bachir and Manar (2011).

Figure 11.6 illustrates this with the tree-based document as the stem, all refined text paragraphs as the second level, and paragraph sentences as the third level.

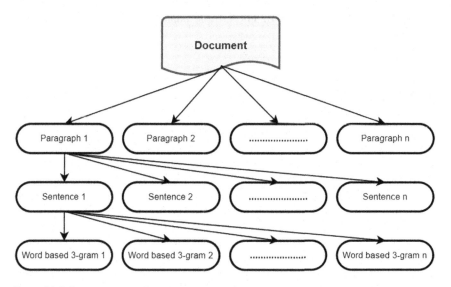

Figure 11.6 Document tree-based representation.

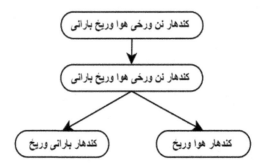

Figure 11.7 Representation of a document tree as an example.

Sentences are then broken down into word-based 3-grams and trans-formed into numbers using a suitable custom hash function. The detecting operation is processed more quickly at this point.

Figure 11.7 illustrates the single sentence paragraph as a tree:

Example: "ده باراني او وریخ هوا ورځی نن د کندهار د"
Text of the document: د کندهار د نن ورځی هوا وریځ او باراني ده
Preprocessing: کندهار نن ورځی هوا وریخ باراني
Paragraph level:
Sentence level:
Word based 3-gram level:

It is important to utilize a hash function that minimizes collisions brought on by mapping different chunks to the same hash (Martin et al., 2010; Sh & Braani Dastjerdi, 2016). The unique hash function is utilized in our implementation.

11.3.3 Detection

The document tree-based representation's main objective is to speed up simi-larity checks and prevent unnecessary comparisons.

In the recommended technique, a fingerprint in each level of the suspect document fingerprint and the corresponding level of the reference document fingerprint form the foundation for a related detection method. For instance, each of the three 3-grams that manufactured this hash (each of the three hashes that manufactured this hash) at the sentence levels is checked sepa-rately to see if a hash value of a fingerprint (at the paragraph level) in the suspect document exists in the hash fingerprint collection (at the paragraph level) of the reference document. The pseudo-code in Figure 11.8 describes how a top-down traversal is used to survey a tree and how the fingerprints of two texts are assessed at the document level. The star-tagged portions of the code that may typically be eliminated from the method are inserted

Detection Algorithm
1. **Input:** Fingerprinting of Doc suspect, Fingerprinting of Doc source,
2. **Output:** Similarity
3. **Begin**
4.   **For** each hash_ paragraph _suspect
5.   **If** (suspect_ paragraph in source_ paragraph)
6.   **For** each hash_ sentence _suspect
7.   **If** (suspect_ sentence in source_ sentence)
8.   **For** each hash_ words _suspect
9.   **If** (suspect_ words in source_ words)
10.   Similarity = True
11.   **Else**
12.   Similarity = False
13.   **Else**
14.   Similarity = False
15.   **Else**
16.   Similarity = False
17. **End**

Figure 11.8 Detection algorithm.

to ensure the outcome because there is no injective hash function and they provide identical hashes for various words.

1. The reference documents and suspect documents' fingerprints are used as the algorithm's inputs.
2. If there is any similarity or dissimilarity in any of the stages, the "Similarity" variable, which determines the algorithm outcome, will either be "True" or "False."
3. The similarity finding process starts.
4. The next few steps will be repeated for each of the document's existing paragraph-level hashes.
5. If the subsequent paragraph-level hashes of the suspicious document are the subsets of the reference document's paragraph-level hashes, evaluate the comparison process at the sentence level. The comparison procedure continues at the level of the current word for each hash in the sentence level of the suspicious text.
6. The comparison process moves on to the word level of the suspect documents' hashes if they are subsets of the reference document's hashes at the sentence level.
7. Every hash in the suspicious document is compared at the word level and the 3-gram level.
8. If the suspicious document's 3-gram level hashes are subsets of the reference document's 3-gram level hashes,
9. The probable similarity is found.
10, 11. Otherwise, the comparison procedure moves on to the suspicious document's sentence-level hashes.

12, 13. Line 9 states that the comparison procedure moves on to the suspicious document's paragraph-level hashes if the sentence-level hashes of the suspicious document are not the subsets of the reference document's sentence-level hashes.

14, 15. Line 7 states that the comparison procedure terminates if the paragraph-level hashes of the suspect document are not a subset of the paragraph-level hashes of the reference document.

16. The similarity finding operation is complete.

11.4 RESULTS AND DISCUSSION

The implementation is operated using the ASP.net MVC programming framework with MongoDB for better performance, where the features, functions, and classes are employed, and the entire system is created using object-oriented programming for a better software engineering experience.

The testing procedure is carried out twice: once using the duplicate content checker tool, which compares similar texts and is located in the language-free categories, and once using similarity parameters and the native algorithm in "Winnowing" (Sh & Braani Dastjerdi, 2016; similar-text-checker, 2022).

11.4.1 Datasets

There is no dataset for the local languages spoken in Afghanistan, making it impossible to test the effectiveness of the suggested technique using a standard textual dataset. Therefore, we have collected some academic papers written in Pashto and Dari, seven sets of texts consisting of one suspicious and one reference text.

The specification of these texts is given in Table 11.1

Table 11.1 Document Sets Created Randomly

Doc Number	Number of Words	Type of Construction
1	120	Rand
2	116	Doc 1
3	532	Rand
4	903	Rand + Doc 3
34	576	Doc 3 + Doc 4
5	828	Rand
6	499	Rand + Doc 3 + Doc 5
7	5391	Doc 1 + Doc 3 + Doc 4 + Rand
8	3002	Doc 7

11.4.2 Considered Parameters

In addition to the Jaccard similarity coefficients (1) to (4), recall, precision, and F-measure scales are the three crucial metrics of the effectiveness of plagiarism detection algorithms, as follow (Sh & Braani Dastjerdi, 2016):

1. $\text{Recall} = \dfrac{TP}{TP + FN}$

2. $\text{Precision} = \dfrac{TP}{TP + FP}$

3. $\text{F-measure} = \dfrac{TP}{TP + \dfrac{1}{2}(FP + FN)}$

4. $\text{Jaccard similarity coefficient} = \dfrac{TP}{TP + FP + TN}$

where *TP* is the number of instances that are correctly identified as copies, *FN* is the number of instances that are incorrectly identified as originals, and *FP* is the number of instances that are incorrectly identified as copies (Sh & Braani Dastjerdi, 2016).

11.4.3 Testing Results

Think about Table 11.2. This suggested approach is tested using seven randomly chosen document-generated datasets, which are summarized in Table 11.1 with eight tests.

To demonstrate the enhanced accuracy in similarity identification in Afghan national language phrases, the "Winnowing" algorithm and proposed approach are used to analyze the similarity rate of each pair in the tested text, and thus the needed parameters are delivered.

Table 11.2 Document Set for Suspicious and Reference Documents

Document Set	Suspicious Document	Reference Document	Used in
1	Doc2	Doc1	Test 1,2
2	Doc34	Doc3	Test 3
3	Doc34	Doc4	Test 4
4	Doc6	Doc3	Test 5
5	Doc6	Doc5	Test 6
6	Doc5	Doc6	Test 7
7	Doc8	Doc7	Test 8

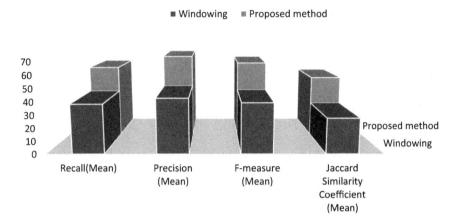

Figure 11.9 Similarity chart for proposed and windowing algorithms.

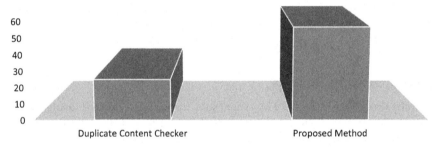

Figure 11.10 Similarity (mean) between proposed and duplicate content checkers.

Figure 11.9 shows that by using this suggested method, which considers the meaning of each word as well as the replacement of inappropriate pluralization and synonyms, the average values for recall, precision, and F-measure are improved by between 24.45%, 25.75%, and 22.87%, respectively. Additionally, the average improvement in accuracy for plagiarism detection as measured by these metrics is 25.23%. The similarity coefficient between the two texts has improved by 25.19% and now includes more safety factors. Given that the proposed technique makes use of both word stems and tree-based representation of documents, the effectiveness of all the hashes generated during the fingerprinting phase of each document, which can raise accuracy in a related detection process, is boosted.

This similarity scale is 31.65% more trustworthy than the similarity derived with language-free techniques. Figure 11.10 shows the similarity (mean) between the proposed and duplicate content checkers.

Language-free methods are insufficient for identifying similarities and differences in Pashto and Dari texts because they do not take into account word appearances or the unique traits of the Afghan National languages in the text. Instead, compared to the language-free technique, our proposed strategy enables the achievement of more accurate findings.

Additionally, word ordering is impossible because of the nature of fingerprinting technology, text restructures, and text alterations.

11.5 CONCLUSION

There are lots of free and paid tools which are used to detect plagiarism in academic research or documents, but for English and many languages, their accuracy is high, and for Afghan local languages, do not work properly, and the accuracy rate is low. We have developed a software system to solve this problem. It can detect plagiarism in both Pashto and Dari languages. This software could benefit researchers and students by encouraging them to be more aware of academic integrity and to develop their skills in academic writing.

In this chapter, we demonstrated the impact of NLP techniques and preprocedures on Afghan national language plagiarism detection to create a more accurate system.

The semantics of the text's current words and the document's tree-based representation, as well as the fingerprinting method based on the word-based 3-grams technique, are used to improve the similarity detection accuracy of copied phrases in texts written in the Afghan national languages.

Considering word meanings, correct pluralization, and synonym replacement, the findings show that the proposed strategy increased the texts' similarity coefficient by 25.19%.

The result of this work is now implemented using ASP.net MVC with MongoDB and some of the. NET libraries like spire Spire.Doc.

REFERENCES

Ali, A. M., Abdulla, H. M., & Snascl, V. (2011). Survey of plagiarism detection methods. *IEEE (Institute of Electrical and Electronics Engineers)*, 39–42. doi:10.1109/AMS.2011.19

Asim M. El Tahir, A., Hussam, A., & Václav, S. (2011). Overview and comparison of plagiarism detection tools. *Semantic Scholar*, 161–172.

Martin, P., Alberto, B.-C., Benno, S., & Paolo, R. (2010). Cross-language plagiarism detection. *Springer Science*, 45–62. doi:10.1007/s10579-009-9114-z

Maryam, M., & Mohammad Mahmoodi, V. (2014). Design a Persian automated plagiarism detector. *International Journal of Engineering Trends and Technology (IJETT)*, 465–467.

Mayank, A., & Dilip Kumar, S. (2016). A state of art on source code plagiarism detection. In *2016 2nd International Conference on Next Generation Computing Technologies (NGCT)* (pp. 236–241). Dehradun: IEEE. doi:10.1109/NGCT.2016.7877421

Melissa S, A., & Nicholas H, S. (2011). The problem of plagiarism. *Urol Oncol*, Jan–Feb;29(1). doi:10.1016/j.urolonc.2010.09.013

Miranda, C., Lucia, S., & Ruslan, M. (2010). *Using Natural Language Processing for Automatic Detection of Plagiarism*. Research Gate.

Mohamed El Bachir, M. (2012). Detection of plagiarism in Arabic documents. *International Journal of Information Technology and Computer Science (IJITCS)*, 80–89. doi:10.5815/ijitcs.2012.10.10

Mohamed El Bachir, M., & Manar, B. (2011). APlag: A plagiarism checker for Arabic texts. In *The 6th International Conference on Computer Science & Education (ICCSE 2011)* (pp. 1379–1383). Singapore: Research Gate. doi:10.1109/ICCSE.2011.6028888

Peyman, M., Zahra, S., & Farzin, Y. (2014). Automatic external Persian plagiarism detection using vector space model. In *2014 4th International eConference on Computer and Knowledge Engineering (ICCKE)* (pp. 697–702). doi:10.1109/ICCKE.2014.6993398

Rakian, S., Safi Esfahani, F., & Rastegari, H. (2015). A Persian fuzzy plagiarism detection approach. *Journal of Information Systems and Telecommunication (JIST)*, 182–190.

Sarwanaaz, S. (2020). Plagiarism in Afghan context. International Journal for Innovative Research in Multidisciplinary Field, 52–54.

Sh, R., & Braani Dastjerdi, A. (2016). Plagiarism checker for Persian (PCP) texts using hash-based tree representation fingerprinting. *Journal of AI and Data Mining*, 125–133. doi:10.5829/idosi.JAIDM.2016.04.02.01

similar-text-checker. (2022, April 10). Retrieved from seomastering: www.seomastering.com/similar-text-checker.php

Zdenek, C., & Chris, F. (2011). The influence of text pre-processing on plagiarism detection. In *Proceedings of the International Conference RANLP-2009* (pp. 55–59). Borovets: Association for Computational Linguistics.

Chapter 12

COVID-19 Vaccine Acceptance and Hesitancy in India Scenario

Viren Modi, Karan Ajit Shah, Spriha Shekhar,
Aayush Gupta, and Shilpa Sonawani

CONTENTS

12.1 INTRODUCTION

Vaccination is undoubtedly one of humankind's most successful practices in the field of medicine and health. It has led to the eradication and control of diseases that were once considered deadly and were fatally debilitate to millions of patients. Before the onset of mass vaccination drives, people susceptible to disease-causing viruses and bacteria became severely ill or even died from infectious diseases like smallpox, polio, diphtheria, measles, and pertussis. Also, with the outbreak of COVID-19, vaccines have become a household name for prevention of this deadly virus. COVID-19 vaccines like Oxford–AstraZeneca, Pfizer–BioNTech, Moderna, Covaxin, and Sputnik [1] have become synonymous with prevention of and safety from the novel coronavirus. However, the World Health Organization stated in 2019 that vaccine hesitancy is one of the top ten global health threats. Vaccine hesitancy is defined [2] as a delay in acceptance, reluctance to accept, or refusal of vaccines despite the availability of vaccination services. Most countries worldwide have encountered vaccine hesitancy, which has been seriously hindering the successful implementation of vaccination campaigns [2]. Vaccine hesitancy is complex and is influenced by multiple factors. Some of these factors associated with COVID-19 vaccine hesitancy include, but are not limited to lack of confidence in the vaccine itself, lack of adequate information about the vaccine, misinformation from social media, conspiracy theories, and fear of side effects.

Widespread acceptance of COVID-19 vaccines is crucial in order to achieve sufficient immunization against the coronavirus that has taken more than 6,000,000 lives across the world. There are a plethora of studies that have investigated COVID-19 vaccination attitudes in lower-income countries like India, and it has been evident that vaccine hesitancy, among other factors, has led to the number of vaccinations being quite low. Moreover, large-scale vaccination has begun quite recently, and various variants have made achieving sufficient vaccinations a tedious task. It has become necessary for students like us to throw light on these facts. India started COVID-19 vaccination January 16, 2021 [3]. We analyze COVID-19 vaccine acceptance and hesitancy in India to ensure that COVID-19 vaccines and relevant information reach even the remotest of places in India, be it rural or urban, by observing the results and outcomes of our research. Our aim is to generate results that are as accurate as possible, and we hope to help the Indian government in the process of making informed decisions for the vaccine-hesitant groups of India.

Generally speaking, vaccine-hesitant individuals are a heterogeneous group in the middle of this continuum. Vaccine-hesitant individuals may refuse certain vaccines but at the same time be agreeable to others [4]. These groups of individuals may delay vaccines or accept vaccines according to the recommended schedule but be unsure in doing so.

Despite the growing number of articles published in recent years that refer to vaccine hesitancy, there are discrepancies among publications about what exactly falls under the umbrella of "vaccine hesitancy." The expression can be used to refer to a "gap in knowledge" or to "reflection and deliberation about the benefits of specific vaccines." It is hard to have a clear picture of vaccine hesitancy at the ground level, that is, within the population, because hesitancy is not directly related to vaccine uptake, as vaccine-hesitant individuals may accept all recommended vaccines in a timely manner but still have significant doubts in doing so. In addition, hesitancy can vary according to the vaccine involved; for example, one can be hesitant regarding the flu vaccine but accept with confidence the vaccines for all other diseases. This trend has been going on for decades, with newer vaccines usually engendering more hesitancy. Thus, caution is needed when trying to draw a general picture of vaccine-hesitant individuals' characteristics.

12.2 RELATED WORK

One of the foremost things to notice in all the papers we have referred to is the lack of research done on India for this topic. Most papers focus on countries like the United States, Canada, and China [5–7] to form their outcomes and surveys and often overlook lower middle middle–income countries like India. Therefore, it is notable that research in India is a less-traveled path, and it indeed opens doorways for us to expand our work and evaluation. Hence, the lack of vast research done on the Indian subcontinent seems to be a huge research gap, and we aim to fill it in our project.

The papers we have referred to contain datasets and other information that have been accumulated from various sources such as surveys or their government's datasets, but there are very few to no papers that have used the publicly available data from CoWin [8] and Twitter. A combination of data sourced from the Indian government's CoWin platform and the micro-blogging website Twitter can prove helpful for us to analyze the trends of vaccination, the reasons for hesitancy, and other useful points. Therefore, our project aimed to fill this research gap by using a combination of collected data from CoWin and Twitter. Region-wise vaccination study based on parameters like population has not been widely done and remains a literature gap to date. Our project intended to make sure to conduct a region-wise examination of the vaccine data available to us through CoWin and Twitter, and we made the best use of this regional data.

The precautionary dose or booster shot is a relatively new term in the field of medicine and COVID-19; therefore, it isn't a stretch to state that a lot of papers have missed out on coverage of these precautionary doses or booster shots that are offered around the world, especially India. Hence it is a research gap today, and we fetched booster shot/precautionary dose data from these platforms and evaluated it to generate meaningful results [9].

The research timeline plays an important role, with the constant development of new variants. Most of the research work done in late 2019 or early 2020 does not have data on COVID-19 variants like Delta and Omicron. Since the mutation of the virus is a constant and ever-changing thing, it is impossible for the research papers we mention to stay updated with the entire list of variants of the novel coronavirus. Therefore, there is a research gap present in the papers we have sourced from the years 2020 or even 2021, and our project aimed to be up to date with the newest developments in variants of COVID-19 in 2022 (Figure 12.1).

12.3 MATERIALS AND METHODOLOGY

12.3.1 System Architecture

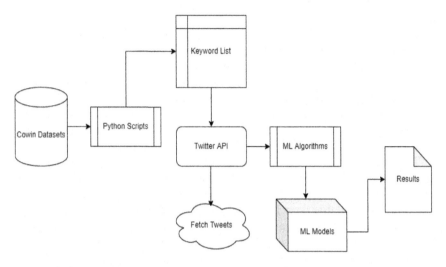

Figure 12.1 System architecture.

12.3.2 Computational Tools/Libraries

Covid Vaccine Intelligence Work (CoWIN) is the government of India's web portal for COVID-19 vaccination registration, owned and operated by India's Ministry of Health and Family Welfare. It was introduced by the central government of India to simplify the vaccination process. CoWIN, a digital platform [8], was created to monitor COVID-19 vaccination and vaccine delivery in real time.

The CoWIN portal acts as one of the primary sources of data for our analysis. The portal provides services like vaccine registration, certificate download, and certificate verification. One can also download real-time vaccination statistics from the portal in JSON or CSV format from the CoWin dashboard [10]. The data and statistics we can source from the dashboard include state-wise vaccination counts, namely the first (partial vaccination), second (totally vaccinated), and precautionary doses, and other information like age-wise categorization and vaccine registration information.

Colaboratory, or "Colab" for short, is a product from Google Research. Colab allows anybody to write and execute arbitrary Python code through a browser and is especially well suited to machine learning, data analysis, and education. We used Google Colab [1] notebooks to analyze the collected data and performed data processing with the help of Python libraries such as pandas and matplotlib.

12.3.3 Sentiment Analysis

In this section, we describe the methodology of our work to perform sentiment analysis on Twitter data related to COVID-19 vaccination.

12.3.4 Twitter Data Collection

We used the Twitter API to collect around 714 million original tweets using the Python library Tweepy. We filtered the tweets by keywords associated with different COVID-19 vaccines and keywords mentioning a safe, healthy lifestyle after vaccination [11].

The tweets were collected over a five-month period beginning on December 5, 2022, and ending on May 5, 2022. We discarded retweets during this time period with the Twitter API filter. We also only collected tweets in English, and we used NLTK for further data analysis. Twitter's API provides access to 1% of the public tweets by random sampling in near real time. Although questions might arise regarding biased or imbalanced data for collecting just a 1% sample from all tweets, it has been shown that sentiments found from samples of tweets obtained via the API and the full tweet dataset reflect the same sentiment percentage with very little deviation (<1.8%). In compliance with the Twitter content redistribution policy, we only made the tweet IDs publicly available corresponding to the collected tweet text used in this work.

12.3.5 Dataset Generation

In order to understand public sentiment better and correlate information we accumulated from the previous steps, we turned to the microblogging site Twitter. Tweets from the Twitter API hence acted as the second data source for our analysis. Using the Twitter API, we scraped tweets related to COVID-19 vaccinations by using keywords related to the topic, that is, COVID-19 vaccination. These keywords act as a filter while scraping tweets from the platform [12]. We had tried to figure out locations with minimal vaccination in India through the datasets from CoWin, and we utilized this information to further improve our research. The tweets we fetched were from locations in India which had comparatively lower vaccination counts per the data analyzed from the CoWIN portal. Next, we performed sentiment analysis on the scraped tweets using libraries such as TextBlob [13]. Sentiment analysis (or opinion mining) is a natural language processing (NLP) technique used to determine whether data is positive, negative, or neutral. Sentiment analysis studies the subjective information in an expression, that is, the opinions, appraisals, emotions, or attitudes towards a topic, person, or entity. Expressions can be classified as positive, negative, or neutral [14]. TextBlob is a Python (2 and 3) library for processing textual data. It provides a simple API for diving into common natural language processing tasks such as part-of-speech tagging, noun phrase extraction, sentiment analysis, classification, translation, and more. Therefore, the tweets were basically categorized into three types: positive tweets, negative tweets, and neutral tweets. The categorization of tweets was done on two parameters: polarity and subjectivity. Polarity can range from a value of +1 to −1, while subjectivity ranges from a value of 0 to 1. A negative polarity indicates a negative sentiment in the tweet, while a positive polarity indicates a positive sentiment. The higher the subjectivity value, the stronger the feeling/emotion in the tweet.

The technique of determining whether a piece of writing is positive, negative, or neutral is known as sentiment analysis, sometimes known as opinion mining or emotion AI. Finding out how individuals feel about a given topic is a popular application for this technology. For a number of purposes, sentiment analysis is commonly used in reviews and social media. To summarize the procedure briefly, we first break the input down into individual sentences or words [15]. We then label each token with its part-of-speech component (i.e., noun, verb, determiners, sentence subject, etc.). From −1 to 1, we then assign an emotion score and optional scores such as subjectivity. As shown in Figure 12.2, the dataset generated consists of the tweet information along with the sentiment analysis parameters.

12.3.6 Tweet Filtration Using Support Vector Machine Algorithm

The dataset that we used for training the machine learning models included words that are related to vaccines (tagged as 1) and not related to vaccines (tagged as 0). These words were acquired from the keywords that we got for each tweet using twitter API. We tried machine learning (ML) models like XGBoost, support vector machine (SVM), and CatBoost, and SVM proved the most accurate. This model was then used on the dataset consisting of tweets to filter out the tweets related to vaccines.

Support vector machine is one of the most popular supervised learning algorithms and is used for classification as well as regression problems. However it is primarily used for classification problems in machine learning. XGBoost stands for extreme gradient boosting, which was proposed by researchers at the University of Washington. It is a library written in C++ which optimizes the training for gradient boosting. CatBoost is a high-performance open-source library for gradient boosting on decision trees [16]. It provides a gradient boosting framework, which, among other features,

Location	User	Tweet	Tweeted_at	Polarity	Subjectivity	Sentiment	Tags
Ahmedabad, Gujarat	Ahmedabad mirror	Less than 1 in 100 come forward to take #boost . . .	2022-05-03 02:45:02	−0.055556	0.355556	Negative	[less, # booster # shot, age group, covid, sho . . .
Ahmedabad, India	The NisargSoni	The western pharma lobby & their domestic . . .	2022-05-06 09:18:52	0.000000	0.050000	Neutral	[western pharma lobby, domestic agents, make in . . .
Akhand Bharat	I_Bob The Builder	This is an amazing feat.\n1 00 crore plus hav . . .	2022-05-06 08:00:58	0.425000	0.616667	Positive	[amazing feat, second . . . https]
Ambala	Chandigarh Story	Heavy rush at a vaccination centre at Sukhna L . . .	2022-05-02 06:29:31	−0.200000	0.500000	Negative	[vaccination centre, sukhna,# Chandigarh #su . . .
Bangalore	skchaudharytech	Covovax Vaccine Now Available For 12–17 Age Gr . . .	2022-05-02 16:55:52	0.200000	0.387500	Positive	[covovax vaccine, age, centres, covovax, cost
. . .	. . .	. . .	. . .	. . .	. . .	. . .	. . .
Noida (UP) India	KailashHealth	Kailash Hospital, Sector 71, Noida organized V . . .	2022—05-02 12:26:56	0.000000	0.000000	Neutral	[kailash, sector, noida, vaccination, may, 11 t . . .
Noida, India	HLFPPT	Meeting with DSWO, Balangir Odisha by Mommentu . . .	2022-05-06 07:08:33	0.000000	0.000000	Neutral	[meeting, dswo, balangir odisha, mommentu rou . . .
Odisha	Sambad_English	No individual can be forced to get Covid-19 va . . .	2022-05-02 06:06:09	−0.150000	0.300000	Negative	[covid-19, supreme court#, covid19, vaccine]
Pakistan	Askar_Bank	Get Vaccinated, Save Lives!\ nIn#AskariBank #CO . . .	2022-05-07 07:03:00	0.000000	0.000000	Neutral	[vaccinated, save, askaribank, covid19, vaccin . . .
Patna	neelmani1305	If possible please share link of #Games on #AN . . .	2022-05-04 16:25:02	0.000000	1.000000	Neutral	[share link, anc, immunization, family planning . . .

Figure 12.2 Dataset generated using Twitter data.

Table 12.1 Performance Evaluation of ML Techniques

	SVM	XGBoost	CatBoost
Accuracy (%)	83	50	75
F1-positive, F1-negative	(0.923, 0.909)	(0.625, 0.25)	(0.8, 0.667)
Hamming Loss	0.0834	0.5	0.25
Confusion Matrix	[[5, 1], [0, 6]]	[[1, 6], [0, 5]]	[[3, 3], [0, 6]]

attempts to solve for categorical features using a permutation-driven alternative compared to the classical algorithm. Table 12.1 shows the comparison of metrics for the machine learning models used.

12.4 RESULTS AND DISCUSSION

Through our extensive research on COVID-19 vaccine hesitancy and acceptance in India, we came across numerous articles, journals, and websites that had done previous work in this area or were currently working on it. It is evident that vaccine hesitancy is a grave problem given the consequences of it on society. These past few years have taught us how important it is to be immunized from contagious diseases like COVID-19, and if someone is hesitant to get a vaccine shot, then we must go into the depth of the problem to seek out all the possible reasons this could have happened [17]. Therefore, with the help of data gathered from CoWin and Twitter, along with the several papers we referred to during this project, we are able to the results here.

The reasons for accepting or hesitating take the COVID-19 vaccine remain sensitive. With new variants emerging and becoming more entangled and the advent of new vaccines entering the market, it is difficult to maintain a balance between communicating what is known and acknowledging the remaining uncertainties [18]. Researchers and pharmaceutical companies need to respond as much as possible and make research data on vaccines against COVID-19 readily available to the general public and government agencies [19]. The government needs to remain transparent about the availability of COVID-19 compliance programs and vaccines and how important decisions are being made. Some possible reasons behind vaccine hesitancy we came across during our exhaustive research are ethnicity, working status, personal belief, religiosity, politics, gender, education, age, COVID-19 infection, and income [20].

Moreover, it was found that people living in suburban or rural areas are more likely to be anti-vaccine, and political diversion indicates a divided opinion about potential COVID-19 vaccines [7]. The most commonly stated reason for vaccine refusal is concern about safety (side effects) [6]. The numeric outcomes of our work can best be understood with the help of visual aids; hence we have provided data visualizations and their explanations in a concise form for better understanding.

12.4.1 Data Visualizations

In order to provide an accessible way to see and understand the trends, outliers, and patterns in the data we accumulated during the course of work, we have added a few visual elements like charts, graphs, maps, and data visualization tools.

In Figures 12.3, 12.4, and 12.5, we can see word clouds, which are also known as tag clouds. These are visual representations of text data. We have used this information visualization to show the density, frequency, and occurrence of keywords extracted from the tweets we gathered. We have visualized these keywords in a word cloud form to represent the sentiments of citizens of India about COVID-19 vaccines through tweets. The tags are usually single words, and the importance of each tag is shown with font size or color. In Figure 12.3, we have used green to signify the keywords extracted from tweets marked with a "Positive" sentiment during sentiment analysis. In Figure 12.4, we have used yellow similarly, to represent the keywords

Figure 12.3 Positive tags word cloud.

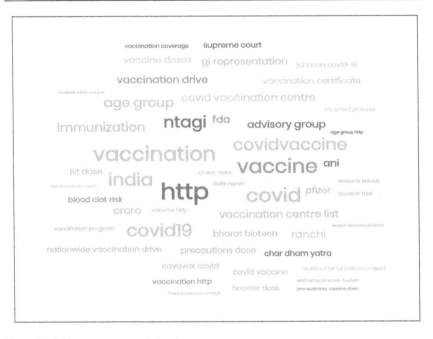

Figure 12.4 Neutral tags word cloud.

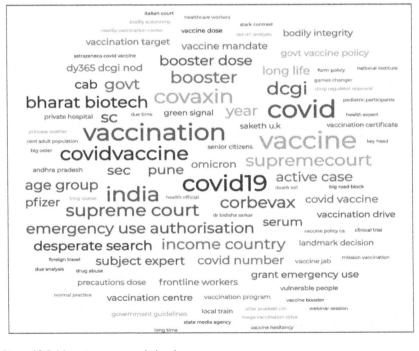

Figure 12.5 Negative tags word cloud.

from "Neutral" tweets. Finally, we have shown the keywords of "Negative" tweets with red. To summarize these word clouds, we can say that the positive response (Figure 12.3) is mainly focused on the availability of the vaccines; administration of shots free of cost; new approvals and mandates; rollouts; and the immunization provided by various COVID-19 vaccines like Sputnik, Covaxin, Covishield, and Pfizer. On the other hand, the negative sentiment (Figure 12.5) focuses on factors such as emergency use, pediatric participants, active cases, death tolls, variants of COVID like Omicron, senior citizens, bodily autonomy, and the remoteness of vaccination camps.

Figure 12.6 is a Choropleth map, which is a type of statistical thematic map that uses intensity of color to correspond to an aggregate summary

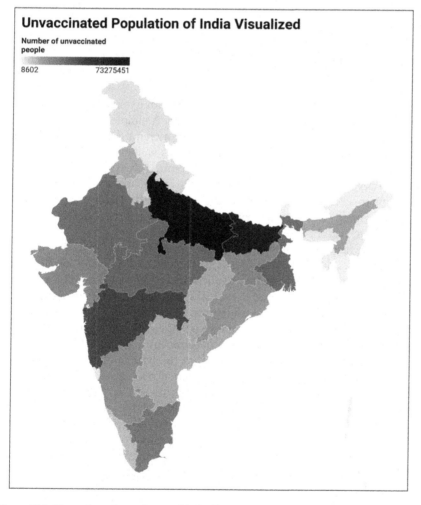

Figure 12.6 Unvaccinated population of India [21].

of a geographic characteristic within spatial enumeration units. Here we have used the unvaccinated population density depicted through the political map of India (2007). Choropleth maps display divided geographical areas or regions that are colored, shaded, or patterned in relation to a data variable, in this case, the unvaccinated population, that is, the total population state wise minus the partially vaccinated population [22]. This has provided us with a way to visualize values over a geographical area, which clearly shows the variation or patterns across the displayed locations of Indian states and union Territories (UTs).

Power Business Intelligence (BI) is a set of software services, apps, and connectors that work together to transform disparate data sources into logical, visually engaging, and interactive insights. The data can be in the form of an Excel spreadsheet or a collection of hybrid data warehouses that are both cloud based and on premises. We used Power BI to visualize the various insights we gathered from our research. In order to depict the unvaccinated population of the Indian states and union territories, we opted for a line graph which uses lines to connect individual data points [23]. This line graph displays quantitative values that are the number of unvaccinated people in each state/UT.

Figure 12.8 is a double line graph, which is an extension of a simple line graph and is also known as Cartesian Graph. A simple line graph like Figure 12.7 is used to represent the growth of a trend. On the other hand, a double line graph is used for representation as well as comparison between the growth of two trends. Here we have plotted the trend of polarity and subjectivity of the extracted tweets over the course of time to track people's reaction to events with regard to the respective polarity and subjectivity spike/downfall. We can also visually sense a repetitive pattern from the graph, which can be interpreted in various ways.

A bubble map (also known as a proportional symbol map) is a sort of map chart that uses the visual variable of size to depict differences in the magnitude of a discrete, rapidly changing phenomenon such as population counts, accidents, and so on. We used Power BI's bubble map chart to visualize the two key aspects of our project, the unvaccinated population density and the partially vaccinated population density of India [24]. The data accumulated from CoWin about the ongoing vaccinations in India helped us to come up with numbers that could be visualized on the bubble map. In Figure 12.9, the chart describes the bulk of unvaccinated people in all the states and union territories of India. The data visualization can be read and interpreted through the size and opacity of the red bubbles on the respective states/UTs. Figure 12.10, on the other hand, illustrates partially vaccinated people in all the states and union territories in a similar fashion to Figure 12.9.

Figures 12.11 and 12.12 are pictorial representations of the statistics we gathered about vaccination through the CoWin dashboard. The former is

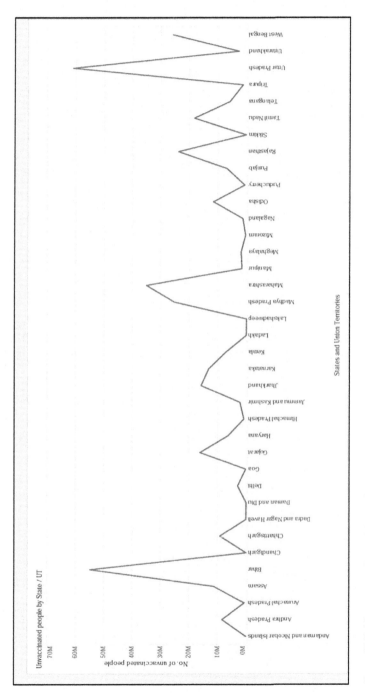

Figure 12.7 Unvaccinated population of India (by state/UT).

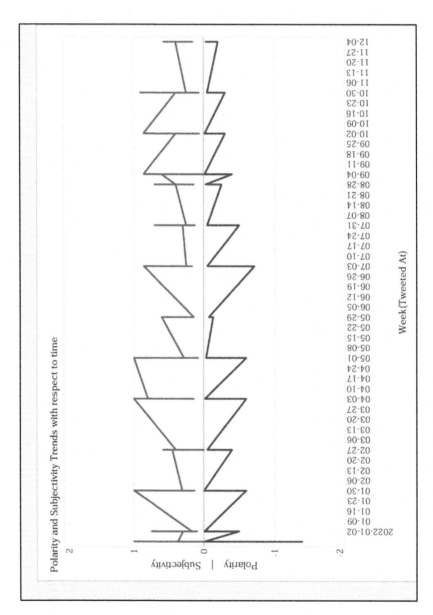

Figure 12.8 Weekly polarity and subjectivity trend.

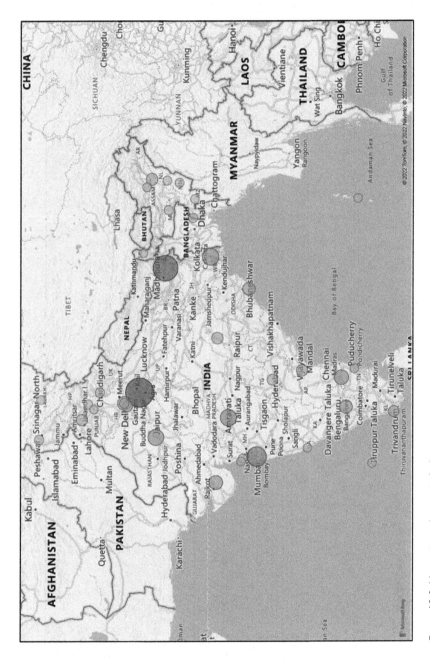

Figure 12.9 Unvaccinated areas in India.

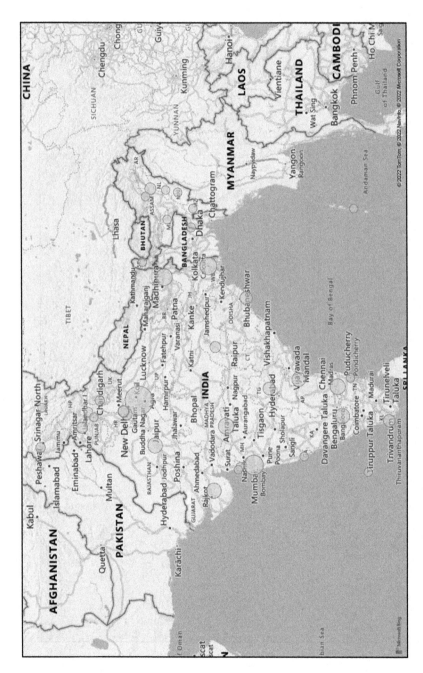

Figure 12.10 Partially vaccinated areas in India.

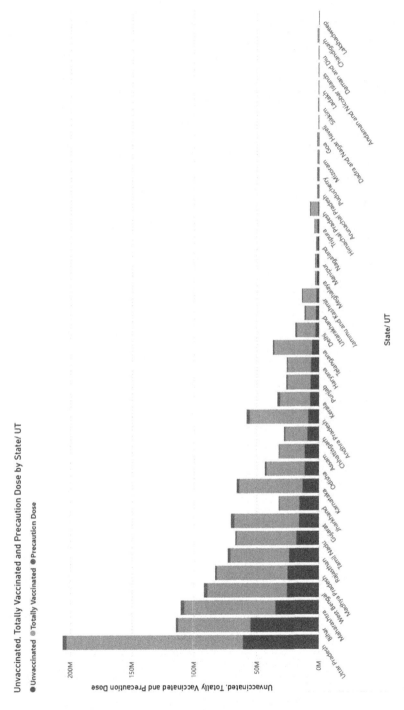

Figure 12.11 State-wise vaccination statistics (bar graph).

Figure 12.12 State-wise vaccination statistics (line graph).

a bar graph, and the latter is a comparative line graph. A bar chart or bar graph presents categorical data with rectangular bars with heights or lengths proportional to the values that they represent. A vertical bar chart is sometimes called a column chart. Figure 12.11 is a stacked bar chart where one can see the number of unvaccinated people, totally vaccinated people (both doses), and people who took a precaution dose together to get a sense of the vaccination situation in India. Figure 12.12 shows the same data but in line graph form, where it is easier to spot the differences and trends in the previously mentioned statistics of India's vaccination drive.

Figure 12.13 is a pie chart showing the percentage of vaccinated people divided by age group. In other words, the size of each slice of the pie is proportional to the size of that category in the group as a whole. The chart shows that the age group 18–45 has taken the maximum number of vaccine doses in India, whereas the age group 45–60 comes in second, with more than 407 million vaccinations, amounting to 21.5% of total vaccinations. Indians above 60 amount to approximately 13% of the total vaccinations and are followed by the younger citizens for whom vaccinations have just begun, explaining the lower contribution to the total, with just 2.1% from the 12–14 group and 5.4% from the 15–17-year-olds.

Figure 12.14 is a correlation heatmap developed using the Seaborn library in Python. Seaborn is a Python data visualization library based on matplotlib. It provides a high-level interface for drawing attractive and informative statistical graphics. By definition, a correlation heatmap is a graphical representation of a correlation matrix representing the correlation between different variables [25]. Here, the variables used are the polarity and subjectivity of the tweet. The value of correlation can take any value from –1 to 1. Values closer to 0 mean there is no linear trend between the two variables. Values closer to +1 mean the correlation is more positively correlated; that is, as one increases, so does the other, and the closer the value to +1, the stronger this relationship. A correlation closer to –1 is similar, but instead of both increasing, one variable will decrease as the other increases. The diagonals are all dark colored because those squares correlate each variable to itself (a perfect correlation). Per the correlation heatmap, we can determine that there is a weak negative correlation between the polarity and subjectivity.

Other Seaborn visualizations include a pair plot and scatter plot of the polarity and subjectivity values, as shown in Figures 12.15 and 12.16, respectively. The pair plot depicts pairwise relationships in the dataset. The scatter plot represents the relationship between two variables, polarity and subjectivity. It shows the weak negative correlation between the polarity and subjectivity values, as determined by the correlation heatmap earlier.

Figures 12.17 and 12.18 depict the histograms of polarity and subjectivity values, respectively. Both histograms were developed using the Seaborn library in Python. By definition, a histogram is a classic visualization tool

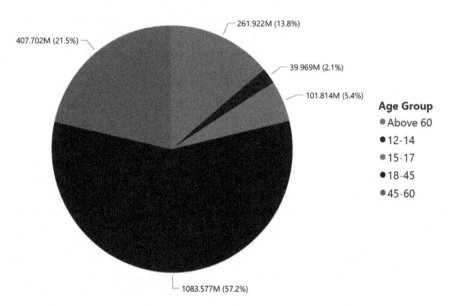

Figure 12.13 Age-wise vaccination statistics.

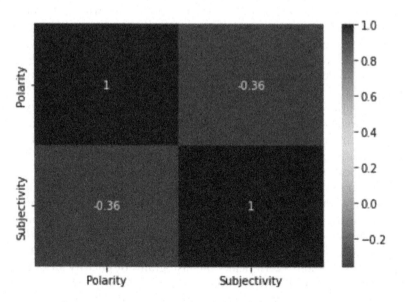

Figure 12.14 Correlation heatmap using Seaborn.

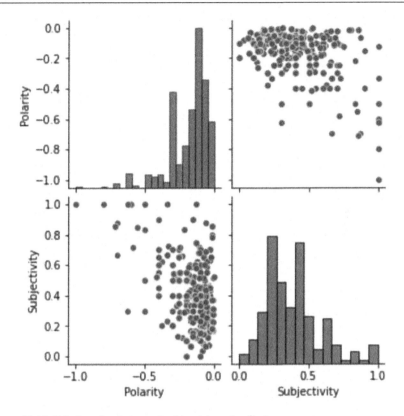

Figure 12.15 Pairplot of polarity and subjectivity using Seaborn.

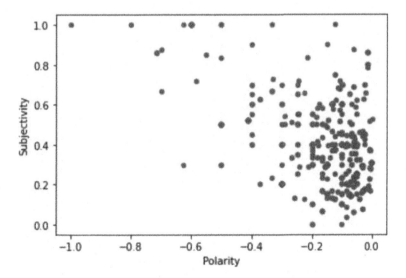

Figure 12.16 Polarity vs. subjectivity scatter plot using Seaborn.

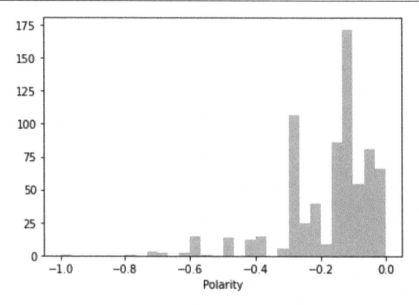

Figure 12.17 Polarity histogram using Seaborn.

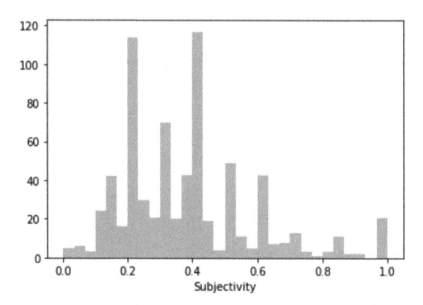

Figure 12.18 Subjectivity histogram using Seaborn.

Table 12.2 State-Wise Reasons for Vaccine Hesitancy

Location	Reasons
Bareilly	Fluctuating blood pressure among patients; certain people believe vaccinations kill
Bihar	Worried about long-term side effects
Bengaluru	Misinformation on social media; side-effects such as skin reactions, itches, scars on body
Chandigarh	Ban on vaccination for children in Punjab due to shortage of Corbevax supply
Dehradun	Slowing down of production of Covaxin
Guwahati	Personality tests at age 18 showed people in the vaccine-resistant group were vulnerable to frequent extreme emotions of fear and anger [26]
New Delhi	Certain patients say the vaccine caused tinnitus; slow start to booster program; people believe vaccinations and their policies are weak; long queues for infant vaccinations
Madurai	Patients developed frequent dizziness after taking the booster dose
Mumbai	Certain people believe that using vaccines on children is unethical because they are not affected by COVID-19 or die from it.lesser provisions for poor young people with fading immunity for booster doses; high vaccination prices and service charges; The gap for the precaution dose is reduced from 9 months to 6 months, which has a scientific basis; charges for the booster dose are high, with over 20 crore doses lying at centers.
Pune	Side effects
Kolkata	Fear of booster side effects and high vaccination prices
Noida	Late approval (DCGI granted emergency use authorization to Corbevax for children aged 5 to 12 years)
Srinagar	The Supreme Court of India says no person can be forced to get vaccinated against COVID-19
Hyderabad	No approval for Covaxin for ages 6–12 for a long time; vial size of 20 for Corbevax vaccine is a big road block in speeding up vaccination for kids; Adverse Event Following Immunization (AEFI) Panel confirms 9 deaths due to vaccine-induced reaction; 45 unexplainable sudden deaths after vaccine
Gurgaon	Poor management of vaccination centers
Tamil Nadu	Girl lost vision after receiving vaccine
Varanasi	Vaccination registration scams

that represents the distribution of one or more variables by counting the number of observations that fall within discrete bins. Per the visualizations, a majority of the negative tweets show a subjectivity value of 0.2 and 0.4 and a polarity value close to −0.2.

The various reasons people gave in their tweets were studied with immense care and precision during our project, and we have arranged these reasons region-wise to showcase why certain locations might have low vaccination counts.

As shown in Table 12.2, we have identified and analyzed the reasons for vaccine hesitancy in 17 major areas in India.

12.5 CONCLUSION

In our ongoing study of COVID-19 vaccine acceptance and hesitancy in the India, we analyzed the vaccination data and statistics from the government of India's CoWin platform and the public's sentiment on vaccination from a dataset we generated from tweets from Twitter's public API. After reviewing the CoWin data, we were able to classify different regions with varying vaccination ratios and simultaneously collect tweets from those particular areas to understand their reasons for vaccine hesitancy. Although the majority of the tweets were deemed neutral (~50%) and positive (25–30%), there was still a considerable amount of tweets showing negative sentiment (15–20%). While it is a relief that negative sentiments do not exceed positive sentiments in any of the cases, our aim was to understand the reason for the disparity so we could help the government make informed decisions in the process of getting the entire population vaccinated.

This study can help health and government institutions plan better and conduct more informed vaccination campaigns in the areas that currently lack proper attention. The constraints we came across during this exploration are present in the form of the dataset size and time period during which it was collected. Also, the public opinions of some of the less populous states or union territories could not be reflected due to the presence of inadequate data. It would be useful for future research prospects to have information gathered over a larger longer time span to find how sentiments change in the course of a longer frame of time, especially if and when the pandemic comes to an end. By combining social media data and that collected more traditionally through surveys, we hope to acquire deeper insights into the public opinions in the future on potential COVID-19 vaccines and thus inform more effective vaccine dissemination policies and strategies.

REFERENCES

1. Status of COVID-19 vaccines within WHO EUL/PQ evaluation process. World Health Organization (WHO). https://extranet.who.int/pqweb/key-resources/documents/status-covid-19-vaccines-within-who-eulpq-evaluation-process
2. Mose, A., Haile, K. and Timerga, A., n.d. Covid-19 vaccine hesitancy among medical and health science students attending WOLKITE University in Ethiopia. *PLoS One*. Retrieved May 29, 2022, from https://doi.org/10.1371/journal.pone.0263081

3. Immunization | UNICEF | www.unicef.org/immunization
4. Dubé, E., Laberge, C., Guay, M., Bramadat, P., Roy, R. and Bettinger, J., 2013. Vaccine hesitancy: An overview. *Human Vaccines & Immunotherapeutics*, 9(8), pp. 1763–1773. doi:10.4161/hv.24657
5. Murphy, J., Vallières, F., Bentall, R., Shevlin, M., McBride, O., Hartman, T., McKay, R., Bennett, K., Mason, L., Gibson-Miller, J., Levita, L., Martinez, A., Stocks, T., Karatzias, T. and Hyland, P., 2021. Psychological characteristics associated with COVID-19 vaccine hesitancy and resistance in Ireland and the United Kingdom. *Nature Communications*, 12(1).
6. Solís Arce, J., Warren, S., Meriggi, N., Scacco, A., McMurry, N., Voors, M., Syunyaev, G., Malik, A., Aboutajdine, S., Adeojo, O., Anigo, D., Armand, A., Asad, S., Atyera, M., Augsburg, B., Awasthi, M., Ayesiga, G., Bancalari, A., Björkman Nyqvist, M., Borisova, E., Bosancianu, C., Cabra García, M., Cheema, A., Collins, E., Cuccaro, F., Farooqi, A., Fatima, T., Fracchia, M., Galindo Soria, M., Guariso, A., Hasanain, A., Jaramillo, S., Kallon, S., Kamwesigye, A., Kharel, A., Kreps, S., Levine, M., Littman, R., Malik, M., Manirabaruta, G., Mfura, J., Momoh, F., Mucauque, A., Mussa, I., Nsabimana, J., Obara, I., Otálora, M., Ouédraogo, B., Pare, T., Platas, M., Polanco, L., Qureshi, J., Raheem, M., Ramakrishna, V., Rendrá, I., Shah, T., Shaked, S., Shapiro, J., Svensson, J., Tariq, A., Tchibozo, A., Tiwana, H., Trivedi, B., Vernot, C., Vicente, P., Weissinger, L., Zafar, B., Zhang, B., Karlan, D., Callen, M., Teachout, M., Humphreys, M., Mobarak, A. and Omer, S., 2021. COVID-19 vaccine acceptance and hesitancy in low- and middle-income countries. *Nature Medicine*, 27(8), pp. 1385–1394.
7. Lyu, H. et al., 2021. Social media study of public opinions on potential COVID-19 vaccines: Informing dissent, disparities, and dissemination. *Intelligent Medicine*. doi:10.1016/j.imed.2021.08.001
8. CoWIN Dashboard | https://dashboard.cowin.gov.in/
9. Praveen, S., Ittamalla, R. and Deepak, G., 2021. Analyzing the attitude of Indian citizens towards COVID-19 vaccine – A text analytics study. *Diabetes & Metabolic Syndrome: Clinical Research & Reviews*, 15(2), pp. 595–599.
10. Unvaccinated Population of India Visualized (dwcdn.net). https://datawrapper.dwcdn.net/QLUcw/1/
11. Schlak, A. E., Aiken, L. H., Chittams, J., Poghosyan, L. and McHugh, M., 2021, January 12. *Leveraging the work environment to minimize the negative impact of nurse burnout on patient outcomes*. MDPI. Retrieved May 30, 2022, from www.mdpi.com/1660-4601/18/2/610
12. Danabal, K., Magesh, S., Saravanan, S. and Gopichandran, V., 2021. Attitude towards COVID 19 vaccines and vaccine hesitancy in urban and rural communities in Tamil Nadu, India – a community based survey. *BMC Health Services Research*, 21(1).
13. https://monkeylearn.com/sentiment-analysis/
14. https://pypi.org/project/textblob/
15. Chandani, S., Jani, D., Sahu, P., Kataria, U., Suryawanshi, S., Khubchandani, J., Thorat, S., Chitlange, S. and Sharma, D., 2021. COVID-19 vaccination hesitancy in India: State of the nation and priorities for research. *Brain, Behavior, & Immunity–Health*, 18, p. 100375.

16. Lucia, V., Kelekar, A. and Afonso, N., 2020. COVID-19 vaccine hesitancy among medical students. *Journal of Public Health*, 43(3), pp. 445–449.
17. https://research.google.com/colaboratory/faq.html
18. Abdool Karim, S. S. and de Oliveria, T. N., 2021. New SARS-CoV-2 variants – clinical, public health, and vaccine implications. *England Journal of Medicine*, 384, pp. 1866–1868.
19. Machingaidze, S. and Wiysonge, C. S., 2021. Understanding COVID-19 vaccine hesitancy. *Nature Medicine*, 27, pp. 1338–1339. https://doi.org/10.1038/s41591-021-01459-7
20. Troiano, G. and Nardi, A., 2021. Vaccine hesitancy in the era of COVID-19. *Public Health*, 194.
21. India to begin Covid vaccination drive from January 16, *India News, The Indian Express*. https://indianexpress.com/article/india/covid-vaccination-drive-date-india-7139700/
22. Umakanthan, S., Patil, S., Subramaniam, N. and Sharma, R., 2021. COVID-19 vaccine hesitancy and resistance in India explored through a population-based longitudinal survey. *Vaccines*, 9(10), p. 1064.
23. Rodrigues, F., Block, S. and Sood, S., 2022. What determines vaccine hesitancy: Recommendations from childhood vaccine hesitancy to address COVID-19 vaccine hesitancy. *Vaccines*, 10(1), p. 80.
24. Melton, C. A., Olusanya, O. A. and Ammar, N. Arash Shaban-Nejad: Public sentiment analysis and topic modeling regarding COVID-19 vaccines on the Reddit social media platform: A call to action for strengthening vaccine confidence. *Journal of Infection and Public Health*, 14(10).
25. Dror, A., Eisenbach, N., Taiber, S., Morozov, N., Mizrachi, M., Zigron, A., Srouji, S. and Sela, E., 2020. Vaccine hesitancy: The next challenge in the fight against COVID-19. *European Journal of Epidemiology*, 35(8), pp. 775–779.
26. New study links negative childhood experiences to vaccine resistance in adulthood (psypost.org). www.psypost.org/2022/04/new-study-links-negative-childhood-experiences-to-vaccine-resistance-in-adulthood-63031

Chapter 13

Applications of Internet of Behavior

M. Mahalakshmi, B. Venkateshwar Rao,
A. Rahul Raj, and Anusha Vasamsetti

CONTENTS

13.1 INTRODUCTION

The Internet of Things (IoT), cloud computing, and artificial intelligence (AI) have all made it easier to track and influence user behavior through IoT behavior changes. By 2023, it is expected that 40% of the world's population would be tracked digitally in order to affect human behavior. Göte Nyman, a psychologist, was the first to propose the concept of the Internet of Behavior (IoB). In 2012, he stated that if human behavioral patterns are assigned to devices (e.g., IoT devices) with specific addresses, there will be an opportunity to benefit from the knowledge gained from analyzing the history of patterns in a variety of fields, including business, society, health, politics, and many others. As a result, concentrating on behavior will allow us to better understand how to influence and treat the individual.

It is observed that the number of devices used in the network of Internet of Things has doubled over half a decade. Internet of Things is normally an interconnection of physical objects that collects and mutually exchanges information and data through the Internet. These objects autonomously process and link with equipments; thereby data in the cloud grew more and more completely through IoT. The accumulation of usage data containing valuable information about consumer behaviors, interests, and preferences led to generating the terminology of Internet of Behavior. In order to get more clarity about IoB, one should know how to properly utilize the user data collected to fetch the companies. In practice, most companies depend on the Internet to provide service to the costumers and coordinate supply schedules. Thus, companies ensure that by development of web-based systems or introducing Intranet support, Internet-based systems will minimize costs and thereby increase productivity. The Internet is a way of attaining the values of the business by breaking down impediments of both time and distance based on measures of supply and demand.

Information convention is one of the major concerns among the organization, which makes them use the Internet daily. Accessing required data is a major barrier for organizations to using the Internet [1]. Information gathered for tasks has become a fundamental feature of Internet of Behavior [2]. The key points of processing information rely on the relation between the required information and organizational tasks. Further, the information gathered by application software will be helpful to analyze customers' behavior. This also enlightens and encourages customers to fix with their behavior related to consumer notices [3, 4].

IoB is derived from marketing and psychology based on people's web interactions. Hence, psychology and behavioral analysis provide new insights from the data gathered by the Internet of Things. IoB has become a significant tool in upcoming markets for both businesses and organizations across the globe. It provides a good understanding between customers and companies for developing business. Earlier, studies of focus groups would normally be used to verify the trends of consumer behavior towards a new released product or service. Based on the responses provided by the customers, towards a product or service can be determined. Göte Nyman, a professor of psychology, proposed a scheme of collecting data on consumer use and their behavior during the use of Internet of Things. Many of them considered this the start of a new era of Internet of Behavior.

An analytic process that can track and collect to examine the bulk volume of data created by us through online activities is an automated ecosystem for assessing consumer data in relation to corporate objectives [5, 6]. IoT transforms data into information, whereas IoB may transform knowledge into genuine wisdom, as shown by the pyramidal representation in Figure 13.1.

Internet of Behavior is considered a convergence of three fields: technology, data analytics, and behavioral science. Further, behavioral science is divided into four areas: emotions, decisions, augmentation, and companionship.

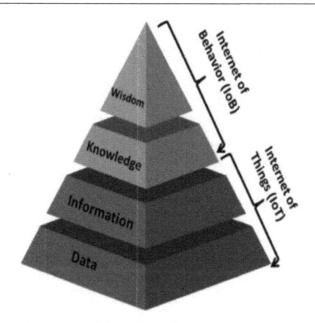

Figure 13.1 Internet of Things and Internet of Behavior pyramid.

13.2 MATERIALS AND METHODS

IoT is not limited to just optimizing and automating processors. It is a customized method of working and developing industries, which includes digital marketing. The technological impact of IoT and IoB cannot be ignored today. They influence a lot of consumer behavior and draw their attention through marketing platforms. Introducing an IoB approach to digital marketing strategies will benefit industries by satisfying a great number of customers. Following are a few methods to boost market behavior through the concept of IoB.

1. **Big data:** The basic functionality of the Internet of Things is to collect information by connecting to multiple points. This data is then analyzed to explore the requirements and needs of a customer to a satisfactory level. It also helps to develop communication between companies and consumers to achieve better profit.
2. **Research-oriented marketing opportunities:** Internet of Things-based data collection and processing is a complicated task that may not be accessible to most companies, such as Google and Facebook, that look to be more comprehensive. In some cases, the topic discussed with friends about certain products may resemble an advertisement when

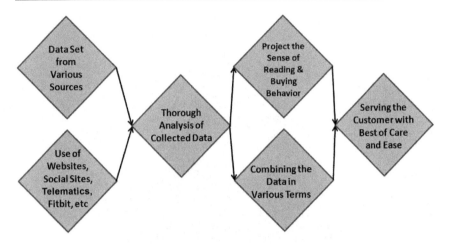

Figure 13.2 Successive working steps for realizing IoB customer service.

viewed on the Internet. IoB recognizes actual consumer behavior that allows individuals' desires to be fulfilled [7].

3. **Information based on consumer lifestyle:** In order to meet the requirements of the consumer, several steps were opted by IoB to know the process of workflow that makes consumers happier just by exchanging the data, as shown in Figure 13.2. The first step is to collect data from all relevant sources, such as websites, social media, telematics, and Fitbit. Then terms are critically analyzed, estimated, and combined to make meaningful inferences. By considering the relevant services of IoB, data graphs are plotted from the information collected based on consumer behavior [8, 9].

13.3 RESULTS AND DISCUSSION

When new technologies are introduced, people's lifestyles can be changed. This creates more excitement and creative thinking to develop technical advancements. It has become easier to include various new solutions with the support of Internet of Behavior and to analyze consumer opinions with data collected. This has facilitated product research, experimental research, observation research, and simulation results for industry [10–13]. This system gives a better interrelationship that leads to the production of bulk sources of information. However, companies collect customer data directly, even they are interested in collecting the data from non-consumers with the help of connected devices shared within the connections.

Benefits of IoB

Analyze customer buying habits across platforms	Study previously unobtainable data about how customers interact with devices and products	Gain deeper insights into where a customer is in the buying journey	Provide real-time point-of-sale notifications and target ads	Quickly resolve issues to close sales and keep customers happy

This is meant to help companies analyze past experiences in terms of their performance so that they can judge the future behavior. In practice, the information collected from the Internet of Things creates a base for companies for their development, sales efforts, and marketing.

In recent days, it is observed that there has been exponential growth in the application of IoB. This modern approach has developed a close relation between companies and consumer behavior. Companies can choose innovative methods of sharing information and storage. So as to develop and sell goods, IoB points out that it must acknowledge and be able to use the data properly [14–18]. IoB can help one understand, merge, and activate data from various sources, like consumer or citizen data, which can be processed by private and government departments [19–23].

The following are some of the application of IoB.

1. **Scrutinize consumer activities:** This activity is related to consumer behavior in all aspects. It enhances the development of companies; these in turn satisfy the needs of consumers day to day.
2. **Consumer policy:** Cybercriminals are interested in the data collected by the Internet of Things. Policies created by consumers can create sophisticated paths for operating Facebook, Google, online marketing, and so on.
3. **Observation:** The behavioral impact on industries through apps that can monitor various health records like diet maintenance, heart rate, BP, and sugar levels on smart phones This helps consumers be cautious about their health issues.

4. **Association with all behavioral ventures:** Internet usage provides awareness in our daily life pertaining to jobs and other activities. This also ensures data and money transfer is provided with proper security.
5. **Analyzing past and future activities:** This feature allows both consumers and companies for a better understanding to serve each other. This optimizes industry relations to find better opportunities to market in digital mode.

As stated earlier, IoB enables evaluation and analysis of consumer practices of purchasing behavior. Today, the principles of IoB have improved a lot regarding its features because of maintaining a proper communication channel between companies and consumers that can satisfy both clients and users.

IoB has been in used in various areas, including the following:

1. Location tracking and consumer behavior
2. Physical status and facial detection
3. Health care and patient recovery
4. Social credit score system
5. Chronic disease tracking
6. Travel booking
7. Entertainment
8. Transportation

13.3.1 Location Tracking and Consumer Behavior

- Do you often get an immediate request from the restaurant you just left to leave a review on Google or Yelp? This is the same logic Uber uses to understand its customers' experiences and create better strategies to serve them.
- Most location-based services use cell phone GPS technology or other techniques such as near-field communication (NFC) and Bluetooth to track the user's location and send appropriate notifications or emails. This also helps gather information in real time rather than after a lag, which helps businesses make changes to their offerings quickly.

13.3.2 Physical Status and Facial Detection

- A few coffee shops have recently implemented a sophisticated bot that scans the customer's face, gender, and mood in order to recommend a suitable coffee based on their mood and desire for refreshment. For instance, coffee chain Barista started using IoB for this purpose.

- The same technology can be used in clothing stores to scan our physical appearance and color preferences in order to recommend a suitable dress without us having to put it on. It shows us a duplicate of ourselves wearing that clothing.
- Amazon was the first to use product recommendations, which analyze customer behavior to make recommendations. Facial recognition achieves the same thing, but it does it by looking at the consumer's current state.

13.3.3 Health Care and Patient Recovery

- As we all know, health apps are common these days, and they monitor our pulse, blood sugar levels, blood pressure, and what to eat and not eat, as well as how many steps we need walk to burn a particular number of calories, and so on.
- In addition, a health app can also alert a patient about their present health status, suggest rest, and help change their dietary habits or medication consumption as needed. This vital information has the potential to save lives by assisting doctors in diagnosing diseases and initiating the appropriate treatment sooner.
- BMC Software in the United States, for example, has created a health app that measures food, sleep habits, heart rate, blood sugar levels, stress levels, and oxygen levels. The software can detect problems with the user's health and recommend behavioral changes that would lead to a better outcome.

Figure 13.3 Health tracker.

Figure 13.4 China's social credit system.

13.3.4 Social Credit Score System

- In a few countries, people have a credit system. If a citizen crosses a government-drawn line, they will receive a credit deduction, so we can say that the entire population of the country is under control.
- For example, in China, it is based on face recognition, where each entry receives a social credit score, with high scores being rewarded and bad scores being punished. As a result, people are provided with government services based on their score.

13.3.5 Chronic Disease Tracking

- Chronic and non-communicable diseases (NCDs) have increased at an unprecedented rate in the last 10 to 12 years. Non-communicable illnesses claim the lives of about 41 million people each year, resulting in high medical costs. IoB is a viable strategy for establishing real-time remote health monitoring systems for BCD patients, especially diabetics and heart disease patients. Artificial pancreas technology has advanced significantly thanks to IoB-enabled devices. By detecting anomalies in the patient's body and alerting them to contact a doctor as soon as feasible, vital sign monitoring helps to prevent hospitalization. IoB devices, according to a 2015 survey, lowered 30-day hospitalization rates by 50%.

13.3.6 Travel Booking

- By examining consumers' social-demographic features and previous online behavior, travel companies may generate personalized and relevant offers and recommendations. For instance, Booking.com lets customers book hotels, resorts, and staycation accommodations at a chosen destination; the software continuously learns and examines data to deliver customized hotel location choices in order to improve the in-app browsing experience.

13.3.7 Entertainment

- Users want the best recommendations when it comes to watching shows, movies, and other forms of entertainment. YouTube recommendations are a popular technique that uses user behavior, particularly viewing history and actions, to improve the app or website experience. Using deep neural networks, the algorithm analyzes the collected data and attempts to recommend films and shows that a user could be interested in watching. Furthermore, practically all social media platforms employ the same method for delivering feeds depending on watching habits, time spent in one account, or interest in subscribing to specific channels.

13.3.8 Transportation

- IoB can also help with services in the transportation sector. Driver or passenger seat? After a long history of conflicts with drivers and high turnover rates, according to Uber Try to solve these problems and resolve the dispute by influencing the behavior of the driver through gamification. Uber has tricks like loss avoidance, perception, intrinsic, etc. Motivation to reward or fear losing a driver Win. Ford is also expanding its reach by participating. Forces the development of self-driving cars using Argo AI to adapt to road infrastructure design and behave and drive differently. This technology has been tested in Miami, Washington, and other cities.

13.4 CONCLUSION

In recent years, IoB has played a vital role in the global market with the aid of consumer behavior. Initially, information is gathered based on Internet of Things irrespective of a particular task. The data collected through this process is analyzed to estimate the consumer's interest and behavior regarding a particular activity. Such innovative thinking brings profit to industries for their growth and simultaneously satisfies customers. The process of gathering consumer data is a continuous journey that needs updates to develop a better understanding between users and companies. This updated information enhances business and can suggest various techniques to attract consumers and reach company goals. By following up, IoB continuously increases income from the market and objects connected to it. These are linked with the Internet to gather and transfer information through wireless networks without involving human beings. IoB analyzes the information gathered based on the knowledge and skills of the consumers through the Internet of Things. The behavior of consumers can interconnect individuals by synthesizing their psychological behavior. It is estimated that by 2025, IoB will predominate, and more than half of the world's population will be engaged with at least one program of IoB.

REFERENCES

1. C. Soh, Q. Y. Mah, F. J. Gan, D. Chew, E. Reid, The use of the Internet for business: The experience of early adopters in Singapore, *Internet Res.* 7 (3) (1997) 217–228.
2. C. W. Choo, Towards an information model of organizations, *Can. J. Inf. Sci.* 16 (3) (1991) 32–62.
3. D. N. Smith, K. Sivakumar, Flow and Internet shopping behavior: A conceptual model and research propositions, *J. Bus. Res.* 57 (10) (2004 Oct 1) 1199–1208.
4. A. Tsitsika, M. Janikian, T. M. Schoenmakers, E. C. Tzavela, K. Olafsson, S. Wójcik, G. F. Macarie, C. Tzavara, EU NET ADB Consortium, C. Richardson, Internet addictive behavior in adolescence: A cross-sectional study in seven European countries, *Cyberpsychol. Behav. Soc. Netw.* 17 (8) (2014 Aug 1) 528–535.
5. Z. Pan, W. Yan, G. Jing, J. Zheng, Exploring structured inequality in Internet use behavior, *Asian J. Commun.* 21 (2) (2011 Apr 1) 116–132.
6. V. Lala, V. Arnold, S. G. Sutton, L. Guan, The impact of relative information quality of e-commerce assurance seals on Internet purchasing behavior, *Int. J. Account. Inf. Syst.* 3 (4) (2002 Dec 1) 237–253.
7. L. Lancieri, N. Durand, Internet user behavior: Compared study of the access traces and application to the discovery of communities, *IEEE Trans. Syst. Man Cybern. Syst. Hum.* 36 (1) (2005 Dec 19) 208–219.
8. M. Javaid, A. Haleem, R. P. Singh, R. Suman, Pedagogy and innovative care tenets in COVID-19 pandemic: an enhancive way through Dentistry 4.0, *Sens. Int.* (2021 Jul 24) 100118.
9. A. M. Oberlander, M. Roglinger, M. Rosemann, A. Kees, Conceptualizing business-to-thing interactions – A socio-material perspective on the Internet of Things, *Eur. J. Inf. Syst.* 27 (4) (2018 Jul 4) 486–502.
10. M. Javaid, A. Haleem, S. Rab, R. P. Singh, R. Suman, Sensors for daily life: A review, *Sens. Int.* (2021 Jul 24) 100121.
11. M. Bagheri, S. H. Movahed, The effect of the Internet of Things (IoT) on education business model, In 2016 12th International Conference on Signal-Image Technology & Internet-Based Systems (SITIS), IEEE, 2016 Nov 28, pp. 435–441.
12. C. N. Verdouw, A. J. Beulens, J. G. Van Der Vorst, Virtualisation of floricultural supply chains: A review from an Internet of Things perspective, *Comput. Electron. Agric.* 99 (2013 Nov 1) 160–175.

13. M. A. Al-Garage, A. Mohamed, A. K. Al-Ali, X. Du, I. Ali, M. Guizani, A survey of machine and deep learning methods for Internet of Things (IoT) security, *IEEE Commun. Surv. Tutor.* 22 (3) (2020 Apr 20) 1646–1685.

14. M. Ammar, A. Haleem, M. Javaid, R. Walia, S. Bahl, Improving material quality management and manufacturing organisations system through Industry 4.0 technologies, *Mat. Today: Proc.* 45 (4), doi:10.1016/j.matpr.2021.01.585.

15. D. Gil, A. Ferrández, H. Mora-Mora, J. Peral, Internet of Things: A review of surveys based on context-aware intelligent services, *Sensors* 16 (7) (2016 Jul) 1069.

16. M. Jia, A. Komeily, Y. Wang, R. S. Srinivasan, Adopting Internet of Things for the development of smart buildings: A review of enabling technologies and applications, *Autom. ConStruct.* 101 (2019 May 1) 111–126.

17. D. Boos, H. Guenter, G. Grote, K. Kinder, Controllable accountabilities: the Internet of Things and its challenges for organisations, *Behav. Inf. Technol.* 32 (5) (2013 May 1) 449–467.

18. F. Gu, B. Ma, J. Guo, P.A. Summers, P. Hall, Internet of Things and big data as potential solutions to the problems in waste electrical and electronic equipment management: An exploratory study, *Waste Manag.* 68 (2017 Oct 1) 434–448.

19. I. U. Din, M. Guizani, S. Hassan, B. S. Kim, M. K. Khan, M. Atiquzzaman, S. H. Ahmed, The Internet of Things: A review of enabled technologies and future challenges, *IEEE Access* 7 (2018 Dec 20) 7606–7640.

20. A. Rejeb, J.G. Keogh, H. Treiblmaier, Leveraging the Internet of Things and blockchain technology in supply chain management, *Future Internet* 11 (7) (2019 Jul) 161.

21. P. Brous, M. Janssen, P. Herder, The dual effects of the Internet of Things (IoT): A systematic review of the benefits and risks of IoT adoption by organisations, *Int. J. Inf. Manag.* 51 (2020 Apr 1) 101952.

22. R. El-Haddadeh, V. Weerakkody, M. Osmani, D. Thakker, K. K. Kapoor, Examining citizens' perceived value of Internet of Things technologies in facilitating public sector services engagement, *Govern. Inf. Q.* 36 (2) (2019 Apr 1) 310–320.

23. J. Qi, P. Yang, A. Waraich, Z. Deng, Y. Zhao, Y. Yang, Examining sensor-based physical activity recognition and monitoring for healthcare using Internet of Things: A systematic review, *J. Biomed. Inf.* 87 (2018 Nov 1) 138–153.

Chapter 14

Smart Facilities and 5G-Supported Systems in Social IoB

J. Banumathi and S.K.B. Sangeetha

CONTENTS

14.1 INTRODUCTION

With the tremendous growth of smart phones in today's world and technology advancing every day, there has been a significant development in the capabilities of smart phones, and their potential has been increasing exponentially. Today, a typical smart phone comes with a variety of embedded sensors (such as GPS, cameras, and microphones) and communication interfaces (e.g. Cellular, WiFi, Bluetooth, etc.). As a result, a smart phone provides a remarkable source of sensory data that is ready for use in numerous crucial applications [1]. Figure 14.1 illustrates an example of a mobile service architecture with cloud assistance.

Today, online interaction between users across the globe on social media platforms like Instagram and Facebook has increased. These platforms make the process of sharing information easy and reliable. As stated in [1], social

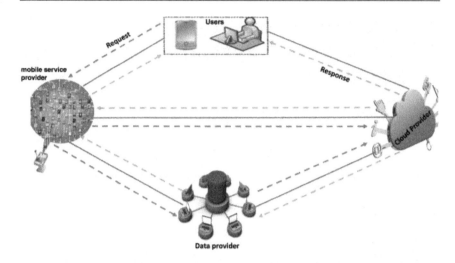

Figure 14.1 Cloud-assisted mobile service architecture [1].

networks not only offer appealing platforms for interpersonal communication, they also present unheard-of opportunities for social data analysis or broad perspectives on what people are saying. This because social networking sites comprise a flood of opinions, viewpoints, and conversations from millions of users on a spectrum that is not conceivable using conventional networks like the world wide web and circuit-switched telecommunication networks. With 5G, the new global standard network, communication is now more dependable and fast thanks to its high speed and security. By the time 5G is completely adopted, there will be tens or hundreds of billions of devices that need to employ 5G technology, both for personal use and for numerous new applications, as described in [2].

The major application that will help in this exponential growth of connecting devices and improving communication is the Internet of Devices. Today, several devices are connected in Internet of Behavior (IoB), and with 5G supplying high speed and increasing reliability, there will be a growth in industries as well. With vast information and communication available on the Internet, a great amount of data will be generated by monitoring devices or personnel. This ultra-large network covers a wide range of services and applications that need 5G for efficiency and low latency.

In this chapter, we will cover the major applications of 5G-enabled devices and smart spaces in social IoB such as in smart phone usage and context awareness. We will explore how 5G has increased smart phone usage in the 21st century and how using usage data, the sensors in the phone, will identify location information and adapt accordingly, hence providing relevant data to the user [3]. But this large network is not easy to handle, and some issues arise every time there is a change in this vast system, so we will focus on some general issues and find effective solutions to them. Therefore, we can summarize this chapter as a comprehensive background of 5G standards, and their IoB-specific applications are considered while highlighting energy consumption and context awareness.

14.2 5G INCREASING SMART PHONE USAGE AND BRINGING CONTEXT AWARENESS

Today, every one of us is using a smart phone, and with advancing technology, our smart phone usage has increased exponentially. As smart phones are expanding their potential and increasing their capabilities, they are becoming more powerful every day. With 5G as the new mobile telecommunication network, data transfer will not only become fast, it will engage users more with smart phones. With increased smart phone usage, there will be more devices connected over the Internet, exchanging more data, and, hence, context awareness will be activated by smart phones. Your smart phone will collect and recognize the surrounding data and accordingly adapt itself to it. Therefore, in this section, we will deeply understand how 5G will increase smart phone usage in this century and how usage data will be used by the smart phone as context and to build awareness regarding its surroundings [3].

Smart phones are regarded as the next iteration of multipurpose cell phones, capable of greater wireless communication and data processing. Cellular network coverage has reached 96.8% of the world's population, and in industrialized nations, this percentage is even as high as 100% of the populace [4].

We are already tied up to our smart phones. The more we use the phone, the more data we provide to it to analyze and make context-aware rules. Before we understand the relation between smart phone usage and context awareness, we need to have a better understanding of smart phone usage. It may look like a very simple term, but the things it can do with present technology are countless. Smart phone usage was very limited in the very beginning when smart phones were just launched because, back then, we had slower networks, but over time, usage has increased, and now they have become so advanced that we just need to type a word Google, and the next thing we know, we can view more than 100 pages with articles related to that one word. This is a result of smart phone usage. Smart phone usage has two parts: the first part is the amusement and information we get through it, and the second part is that the time and information we put in using it are recorded to analyze and sort data, customizing it for users according to their behaviors and surroundings. With a faster network like 5G, there will be significant growth in the future of smart phone usage and hence faster analyzing and processing of collected data. There will be almost no buffering while watching a video on YouTube, and there will be unlimited information while you are browsing the Internet for content or ideas. Many studies have shown that there will be significant growth in the usage of social media applications, and in the future, with advanced privacy options, people will feel more secure to share information with their family and friends.

Increased smart phone usage along with a faster network means an increased number of devices and users connected in IoB space, making data exchange more secure, reliable, and fast. 5G is going to change the shape of IoB through smart phones in the 21st century, as they are the most integral part of IoB. They are the future of IoB. Hence, 5G is going to help in the rapid growth of smart phone usage and connect more people and more devices in IoB.

Internet of Behavior is all about connected devices and making data exchange easy. But where does this data go in these devices and how are they used? When there is data exchange between two users or when a user uses something in IoB such as doing a Google search for something in his/ her smart phone, the data collected is monitored and analyzed by the data sensors embedded in our standard smart phones, which suggest relevant data. Ever wondered how Google suggests you add relevant words to your choice or something related to a product you searched for once? Well, in simple words, we can call this personalized/customized ads that have been generated using the surrounding and behavioral data of the user. This is a part of a bigger topic called context awareness, which can be defined as the ability of a system to collect data about its surroundings at any given time and adapt behaviors subsequently. Context-aware computing uses software and hardware to automatically collect and analyze data to guide responses.

Web browsers, cameras, microphones, GPS receivers, and other sensors are all viable information sources for context-aware computing. These and other sources of information can be used to gather data for a context-aware system, which can then act in accordance with pre-established rules or by using artificial intelligence. Such a system might potentially use context-based assumptions to inform its replies. Context awareness can direct services for user applications and provide improved experiences, such as augmented reality, distribution of information that is pertinent to the user's context, and contextual marketing messaging [5]. Smart phones can gather raw contextual data about users' surroundings and the behaviors that correspond to those environments thanks to their enhanced features. As a result, the data gathered is a great resource for learning about user behavior in various settings and gathering pertinent data. Two sections of a context-aware rule are formulated using the IF-THEN logical structure [6]. Users' surrounding contextual information is represented in the first component, such as their temporal, spatial, social, or other pertinent contextual information, and their related behavioral activities or usage are represented in the second part [7].

Context-aware rules using smart phone data are challenging to fully comprehend for a variety of reasons, from applications to interpreting raw data. Numerous studies [8–10] have been conducted on opening context-aware rules from smart phone data for various reasons. To effectively learn such principles and create intelligent context-aware algorithms, we will need to conduct a deeper examination of individual smart phone users' contextual data usage behaviors. In many context-aware test cases for smart phones, advanced data analysis based on machine learning approaches can be employed to build effective and efficient decision-making skills [7]. These smart phone data analysis issues can be resolved by using a variety of machine learning and data mining approaches, such as contextual data clustering, feature optimization, and selection, among others. These techniques are more accurate for evaluating huge amounts of contextual data. These sophisticated analytical methods will uncover data and see obscure patterns and undiscovered connections among the contexts and finally provide rules that are aware of their context.

For instance, a thorough examination of time-series data and the related data clustering based on comparable behavioral patterns may enable more effective time-based context-aware rules than conventional methods [11, 12]. Therefore, when taking into account multi-dimensional contexts, intelligent data-driven decisions employing machine learning techniques can benefit from superior decision-making power than compared to traditional approaches. So we'll talk about different methods here and try to fully comprehend context awareness.

- **Satellite navigation system as context-aware system:** Here the current location is the original contextual parameter that is used to automatically adjust the visualization (e.g. map, arrows, directions . . .) to the user's current location. However, with the advancement in smart phones, there could be a change and use of more parameters; for example, with the current GPS position, contextual parameters may include the time and the traffic situation on the calculated route or the user's preferred places [13].
- **Automatic light as context-aware system:** Automatic light systems can also be simple context-aware systems. The contextual parameters considered are the current light conditions and if there is any motion in the environment. The adaptation mechanism is very simple. If the situation recognizes is that it is dark and that there is movement, the light will be switched on, while the light will switch off as soon as the movement stops.
- Therefore, as stated in [14], sensors provide data about activities and events in the real world. Perception algorithms will make sense of these motives and analyze the situations in context. Based on the observed context, actions of the system will be triggered [15].

- Context awareness is a very important feature of any standard smart phone today, and with 5G, it is expected that the data collected through smart phone usage and hence contextual analysis will become smoother and faster. The faster the network, the sooner the data will be collected; hence, the smart phone will adapt to the situation faster. Embedded sensors embedded don't have a direct relation to a fast tele-communication network like 5G, but they do have a direct relation to smart phone usage, so we can expect significant development in context-aware features in smart phones in the future and hence a better and stronger connected network in IoB, as the sooner the data is transferred, faster the connections will be developed, and a large network will be created connecting almost everything and everyone [16].

14.3 5G IN IOB SMART SPACES

Internet of Behavior is a system in which several devices are connected over the Internet, collecting and sharing data. With advanced technology and a faster network in the 21st century, this network is expected to become faster and more reliable. It is feasible to transform everything into something bigger and a component of the IoB thanks to incredibly cheap computer chips and wireless networks [17]. By integrating all of these technologies and equipping them with sensors, we can give them a level of digital intelligence that allows them to convey real-time data without the need for human intervention. The world around us is becoming smarter and more responsive thanks to Internet of Behavior, which combines the digital and physical worlds [18].

With the creation of smart environments like smart cities, smart homes, smart transportation, and smart monitoring services, many services are predicted to experience improvements in terms of speed and dependability. Numerous Internet-connected gadgets, including computer devices and sensors, must be organized in these smart environments. These smart cities aim to provide several services to their residents in fields like transportation, healthcare, and business. Many devices are connected for the collection of data and hence analysis [19].

Consequently, a super-network is required to handle and regulate the enormous amounts of data gathered and transmitted to these devices. The Internet of Things phenomenon has significant potential to be helped by 5G [20]. In this section, we cover the capabilities of 5G in IoB smart spaces and how it is going to revolutionize this large system of connected devices and smooth the process of data exchange.

14.3.1 Smart Cities Enabled by 5G and IoB

- In the future, 5G will connect the world through the Internet in a system we are all familiar with called the Internet of Things. This combines smart cities, smart homes, and IoB into a single yet large comprehensible infrastructure. In this section, we'll learn about a four-layer model that uses distributed artificial intelligence, 5G, the Internet of Things, and the cloud of things to connect and these components and let them interact [21]. This method has various benefits, including integrating artificial intelligence into our smart homes and interconnecting smart cities.

- The technical field of smart homes has been active for decades. It deals with enhancing the living environment using technology in order to help residents and raise their standard of living [22]. The most significant advancements have been in the field of home automation, which focuses on giving systems remote and timer control while also enhancing security and comfort [23].
- Smart cities are designed to offer a sustainable and economical urban environment. The task of creating such a setting is difficult [24].
- Information and communication technologies (ICT) are a fundamental requirement for smart cities in order to manage their novel difficulties. A strong, sustainable, and highly leveraged network that offers connectivity, intelligence, security, and effective energy management must be incorporated into these technologies [21]. Artificial intelligence, Internet of Things, and 5G are the primary contributing technologies that are covered in this chapter [25].

  5G: The challenge with 5G is no longer transfer capacity measured as bits/second rather the focus will be on efficient delivery in terms of services and experiences [21]. These services will include a combination of information based on user location and interests, which we earlier termed context awareness, and 5G will enhance this experience by delivering information faster, making the system more reliable. Therefore, 5G will help us achieve the biggest goal that every user has been promised – connecting everyone in a human-centric system that meets user needs.

  Internet of Behavior: The Internet of Behavior is bringing about the biggest reform in the world of technology and the Internet. Combining the Internet with technologies like wireless communications and context awareness transforms everyday objects into smart, intelligent, and context-aware IoBs. Common objects, with the help of IoB, will implement Internet-addressable AI. Thus, these IoBs will offer context awareness and communication features, and they will share some level of pseudo-intelligence depending on their processing capability and power consumption limitation [26].

  Artificial intelligence (AI) in smart homes: Artificial intelligence is a vast subject to understand, and its applications spread to even a wider extent, such as scientific research tools, medical diagnosis, and robot control. Today many services we use or that are provided by different companies are based on AI such as face recognition, speech recognition, and industrial robots. Smart environments mainly support the feature of context awareness, which, after analyzing usage data with the help of AI, helps ease your simple household chores like cooking and cleaning. These systems have sensors embedded in them. These systems will be able to learn activities using the sensors from users' behaviors and environment, such as when the user moves around and performs actions within the smart home. When these actions are learned, the system must be able to detect the "learning situation" with a high degree of probability, and it must be able to perform the learned actions autonomously [21]. It is advanced artificial intelligence (AAI) systems which control and process the data and behaviors of the user, using 5G to access the Internet and hence help in the development of smart cities with smart homes all connected in IoB.

- **What can we expect from 5G and IoB for smart spaces?**
  The 5G network guarantees faster speeds and a more reliable Internet connection to all devices. The exponential increase in the capacity to carry more data faster makes a significant change in IoB projects and services, for example, advancing smart cities. 5G has the potential to change the world and connect the whole world in the IoB system. As noted in [27], providers and consumers globally will wager approximately $1 trillion between 2018 and 2025 on 5G becoming the de facto modern communications standard everywhere. This wager is unquestionably secure for a slew of reasons, many of which are related to the changes that 5G ushers in for the Internet of Things.

  Therefore, we'll go over six ways that 5G will fundamentally alter the Internet of Things.

- **Change in bandwidth**
  The digital transition will be felt more widely than with any prior network change once 5G is fully operational. The speed of 5G networks will be 100 times that of current networks. Megabytes to gigabits per second will represent a dramatic shift in bandwidth, reducing the load on batteries and equipment. Additionally, it will boost the capability of embedded devices and sensors.

  According to [28], network coverage is now frequently tailored to people using smart phones while on the go, and 5G is ready to connect everything by fusing new technologies in novel ways. The coverage advantages that 5G brings will increase the power of the network to reach an exponentially greater number of users, devices, sensors, and connected cars by utilizing beamforming techniques, mid-band spectrums (between 1 and 6 GHz), and smaller cells.

- **Easier setup process**
  With the increase in speed with 5G, not only will the current generation protocols improve, but network installation and device setup will also become easier and faster. Consider 5G a next-generation WiFi.

5G connectivity will let each device connect wirelessly and directly to your Internet service provider [27]. 5G enables devices to use less power by maintaining connectivity because of its advanced infrastructure.

It is expected that all devices in the future will have faster direct connectivity and that IoB device installation will become better.

- **Helps in the growth of smart cities**
Cities have always been our hubs of socialization and economic and technological development. Cities with 5G will help the concept of smart cities come of age. These smart cities will use sensors, big data, and wireless communication to not only increase efficiency in connecting people but will also improve the user experience by using technology to manage traffic. Moreover, it will also provide great business opportunities to many people around the globe. With better, capable networks, there will be a rise in several technologies that will help businesses grow and hence cause a rise in the economy.

By investing in this innovation, cities all across the world can start obtaining much higher economic competitiveness and inclusivity [7].

- **Better business and agricultural management**
All our sectors are connected in the system of IoB; hence, a faster network like 5G will not only create more business but will also help in the rapid growth of these businesses by expanding them across the globe faster, connecting people and bringing employment. With new business models every day, 5G will help implement these models, creating a better world for everyone. In other words, 5G will do away with universally applicable plans for business clients who have a variety of devices to connect to the Internet [27].

However, 5G will benefit both the corporate and agriculture sectors. In a relatively short period of time, the Internet of Behavior and artificial intelligence have appeared to blossom into fully developed products [27].

IoB supplies interconnected agricultural equipment and monitoring devices with vast amounts of valuable data. This data analysis will be made simple by 5G, and we will be able to determine how to spend our resources most effectively.

14.3.2 Enhanced Resource Administration

- Many businesses are interested in implementing IoB for resource management. They will find sensors not only very beneficial but also reasonably priced. They can almost always add these sensors, which entirely connect their supply chains and are incredibly simple, quick, and reliable with 5G. Data will be moved between business partners and within organizations considerably more easily.

14.3.3 Connecting Ignored

- Although 5G and its products can be used by those who live in cities, there are many areas around the world that lack access to infrastructure and services, particularly healthcare providers. With the capabilities of 5G, telemedicine will become a far more practical tool in hospitals and private offices [27].
- For patients and their doctors, 5G might provide vital functionality with no-setup connectivity and high-speed Internet. Other telemedicine services will also benefit from this improvement in quality. The number of emergency department visits will decline as a result of telemedicine, and all towns would practically be connected via a single 5G network.

14.3.4 Energy Consumption Using 5G

With so many devices getting connected to each other every day over such a wide network, a major setback that comes along is energy consumption. When many devices are connected and operate at the same time, then they consume a lot of power, which then has a negative impact on our environment. When we are focusing on building a smart city using 5G, our motive is to make our environment smart by not harming it; hence, the idea of low power consumption using IoB technology is a great field of research. It will not be easy to find an effective solution, as it is such a wide research area. There have been several systems proposed to consume less power, but a green IoB system is assumed to be the most efficient one. It uses technologies like green tags and green sensing networks, as suggested in [29]. There are numerous green technologies that should be included, such as green RFID tags and green sensing networks. Here, we will discuss radio frequency identification (RFID) tags, as they are expected to be a great technology in monitoring and understanding energy consumption in 5G and hence saving it.

Radio frequency identification uses a small electronic device that includes several tags that can store information regarding the objects to which they are linked [29]. The tag is made up of an integrated circuit and an antenna with a protective material that holds the pieces together and protects them from environmental conditions.

With little to no human interference, RFID employs radio waves to identify items and enter the data acquired directly into computer systems. The radio waves are transformed into a useable form of data with the aid of a reader. The information gathered from the tags is subsequently transmitted to a host computer system via a communications link, where it can be saved in a database and later evaluated [30].

Today, RFID is crucial to the development of IoB. Retail, transportation, healthcare, payments, and security are all significantly impacted by RFID.

A single RFID tag's ability to integrate different applications has gained widespread acceptance, as was mentioned in [31], thanks to the widespread use of RFID. A secure RFID application enables users to securely and effectively use the multi-application RFID tag. Some reasons RFID is growing all over the world are its reliability and secure system, which help keep users anonymous. With 5G, RFID is expected to have a certain impact in the making and growth of smart cities, connecting several systems in this scheme and hence making a global network, with great performance, extreme reliability, and a strong security system. Data collection and hence insertion into systems becomes faster with 5G and secure with RFID, and then user connections throughout the IoB network are not a big deal.

In the future, this technology is expected to make a notable change in energy conservation and will be used worldwide. This serves the purpose of energy conservation in IoB well, and you will be able to connect as many as devices as possible with little energy consumption.

14.4 GENERAL ISSUES AND DISADVANTAGES

The fifth generation of mobile technology is bringing about major change in the communication network, delivering high speeds and reliability. However, we know nothing is 100% perfect in this universe; hence, 5G technology, in spite of being studied and conceptualized to solve all communication problems, has the following shortcomings:

1. **Physical obstructions can affect connectivity:** The 5G frequency wave range is not great, as they are only able to travel a short distance. Moreover, if there are any physical obstructions such as walls or trees, they can block, interrupt, or occupy these high-frequency signals. To deal with this problem, telecommunication industries are expanding the current cell towers to increase broadcast distance.
2. **High cost:** 5G, being a powerful network, requires good infrastructure, but making changes in the existing cellular infrastructure can have a very high cost. Since the initial rollout costs are so high and include the costs of additional needs such as maintenance to provide high-speed connectivity to customers, there is a big rise in the price tags of network packs. Cellular operators are still trying to figure out solutions to minimize the cost.
3. **Rural areas still cannot access:** In the last year, 5G has expanded throughout metropolitan cities and urban areas, but people in rural areas still can't access and enjoy the benefits of this high-speed connection. 5G carriers are focusing on cities with high populations but also trying to make way to rural areas, but they have still failed to do this for various infrastructural and economical reasons. It seems that for

the next few years, rural areas won't be able to benefit from 5G and its wonders.

4. **Battery drain in devices:** Devices that are connected to 5G have batteries that are not able to last for a long time. As you see, phones that were launched last year seem to have a poor battery life, but this is mainly because 5G connectivity puts stress on the phone's operation, and even though it has great potential, supporting high-speed Internet is hard for it. Battery technology needs to improve to support enhanced connectivity. Besides drained batteries, users are also complaining about the surfaces of phones becoming hot.

5. **Difference in upload and download speeds:** The download speeds of 5G technology are high. However, the upload speed is not as great as the download speed.

6. **Diminishing of aesthetics:** The construction of cellphone towers, or even expansion of the existing cellphone towers, is not welcomed by many cities because they seem to diminish the look and feel of an area. The 5G network is going to need increased infrastructure, which won't necessarily be accepted by residents of the area.

14.5 PROMISING INDUSTRIES FOR 5G AND IOB

With 5G emerging as such a strong and powerful network, there will surely be a great change in IoB and with improved and strong connectivity among devices and smart cities. There is going to be a rise in the number of industries. The promising industrial applications for 5G and IoB are shown in Figure 14.2. It is expected that there will be five main industries rising and growing in this fifth-generation world. Those five industries are as follows:

1. **Self-driving cars:** The increased number and capabilities of sensors due to high-speed connectivity allow smart cars to collect data, including time-critical data, and these self-driven cars will be able to generate a large amount of data and perform various unexpected functions like recording temperature, weather, and GPS. Moreover, the requirement of a high amount of battery and dependence on real-time communication becomes reliable using modern technology. Even dealing with complex algorithms becomes easy [32].

2. **Healthcare:** There will be an improvement in the medical field as well, such as proper healthcare facilities reaching remote areas that right now are unable to access the benefits of 5G and IoB [33].

3. **Logistics:** The 5G network will enable complex IoB tracking devices to completely change logistical activities. Highway speeds can improve the efficiency of genuine data collecting. For instance, a consumer would have access to specific information like the location of the fish

she just purchased, the temperature at which it was transported, and the date it was delivered to the shop [34].

4. **Smart cities:** As discussed earlier, along with the expansion of various facilities, there will be an increase in the number of smart cities. These cities will enjoy various benefits because of the sensors in their infrastructure. Along with handling high speed and a great amount of data, 5G allows various intelligent systems to operate and maintains constant communication between devices, bringing people and cities closer.

5. **Retail:** The use of 5G in IoB will improve customer interaction (retail) through mobile devices. Customers and owners will be able to interact with an enhanced network more quickly thanks to better connectivity and the addition of more devices to the network. By allowing effective omnichannel retail operations, retailers will be able to enhance the shopping experience [35].

One article [36] claims that the combination of 5G and IoB would also aid in the creation of digital twins for every item on the market, bringing it online. If billions of hardware-connected devices are anticipated, then the likelihood that common consumer goods with digital twins will be a part of the new Internet of Behavior is significantly higher. Administering so many goods is difficult with the present network infrastructure, but 5G makes it possible. By establishing connections between customers and network members, advancing technology, and enabling owners to grow their businesses, smart packaging and digital labels will revolutionize the retail sector.

14.6 FUTURE OF 5G COMMUNICATIONS

4G, although it is a high-speed network, is unable to handle the high data load from an increased number of sensors. Increased connection of devices online is limited because of 4G in IoB. But with 5G and its high speed, low latency, and flexibility, devices will be connected easily in IoB, and data transfer will be smooth. It also reduces energy consumption and is pocketbook friendly. In this last section, we will look at the various possibilities of 5G in business, and how the future of IoB is going to evolve with 5G.

14.6.1 Possibilities

- The necessity for a fast network with increased capacity to meet all connection requirements, as well as the 5G spectrum's expansion of wavelengths via which information will be carried, make 5G essential for the Internet of Things.
- The augmented reality/virtual reality (AR/VR) world benefits from 5G as well [37]. The relevance of AR/VR in opening doors for technological

growth in business, academia, and other disciplines is improved by 5G's ultra-low latency.

- Business IoB: 5G-enabled IoB is anticipated to accelerate technical advancement around the world, and job development is anticipated to result from the digitization of the manufacturing, transportation, and agricultural sectors.
- The development of smart industrial equipment and machinery is encouraged by 5G. IoB might undertake almost instant traffic assessments with the help of 5G, improving security and public safety [38].

14.7 CONCLUSIONS

Now you have an idea of how 5G, as the leading telecommunication network, is bringing about significant change in the world of IoB, not only on increasing the speed of data transfer, but also, providing a good security system to encrypt the data and identify the user, protecting them from any sort of threat. It is expected that with 5G, there will be exponential growth in the development of smart cities, and the world will become one huge network. 5G increases the possibility of the emergence of various stable industries, and this will help increase the connection of several smart cities, people, and devices throughout the world. 5G is just not a network with high speed; it also helps in improving the connectivity which is the basis of IoB. The possibilities that come with 5G were never possible with 4G. 5G is a luxury that every urban city is able to enjoy. It has increased job possibilities and industries, and employment rates have increased. Even with a tough situation like COVID-19, people were able to start their own businesses and connect to their customers because of the fast network 5G provided. Hence, 5G is the revolution we were looking for in our lives, and now we have on at our doorsteps. There are several disadvantages, too, but it is expected that, with the advancement of technology, each and every person, area, and city will be able to enjoy the perks of 5G in IoB.

REFERENCES

1. Al-Turjman, F. "5G-enabled devices and smart-spaces in social-IoB: An overview." *Future Generation Computer Systems* (2017). doi:10.1016/j.future.2017.11.035
2. Akhil, G., & Jha, R. K. "A survey of 5G network: Architecture and emerging technologies." *IEEE Access* 3 (2015): 1206–1232.
3. Dhaya, R., Kanthavel, R., & Ahilan, A. "Developing an energy-efficient ubiquitous agriculture mobile sensor network-based threshold built-in MAC routing protocol (TBMP)." *Soft Computing* 25.18 (2021): 12333–12342.

4. Han, B., Wong, S., Mannweiler, C., Crippa, M. R., & Schotten, H. D. Context-awareness enhances 5G multi-access edge computing reliability. *IEEE Access*: 1–1 (2019). doi:10.1109/access.2019.2898316

5. Dhaya, R., Kanthavel, R., & Venusamy, K. Dynamic secure and automated infrastructure for private cloud data center. *Annals of Operations Research* (2021): 1–21.

6. Dhaya, R., Ahanger, T. A., Asha, G. R., Ahmed, E. A., Tripathi, V., Kanthavel, R., & Atiglah, H. K. "Cloud-based IoE enabled an urban flooding surveillance system." *Computational Intelligence and Neuroscience* (2022): 1–11.

7. International telecommunication union. Measuring the information society. Technical report; 2015. www.itu.int/en/itu-d/statistics/documents/publications/misr2015/misr2015-w5.pdf.

8. Sarker, I. H. "Behavminer: Mining user behaviors from mobile phone data for personalized services." In: *Proceedings of the 2018 IEEE International Conference on Pervasive Computing and Communications (PerCom 2018)*, Athens, Greece: IEEE; 2018.

9. Dhaya, R., & Kanthavel, R. "Energy efficient resource allocation algorithm for agriculture IoT." *Wireless Personal Communications* (2022): 1–23.

10. Radhakrishnan, K., Ramakrishnan, D., Khalaf, O. I., Uddin, M., Chen, C. L., & Wu, C. M. "A novel deep learning-based cooperative communication channel model for wireless underground sensor networks." *Sensors* 22.12 (2022): 4475.

11. Sarker, I. H. "Context-aware rule learning from smartphone data: Survey, challenges, and future directions." *Journal of Big Data* 6.95 (2019).

12. Satyaraj, R. et al. "Analysis on prediction of COVID-19 with machine learning algorithms." *International Journal of Uncertainty, Fuzziness and Knowledge-Based Systems* 30.Supp 1 (2022): 67–82.

13. Dhaya, R., Indhuja, P., Sinduja, S., & Swetha, M. "Finest power efficient steering algorithm for wireless sensor networks for surveillance," 2015 IEEE 9th International Conference on Intelligent Systems and Control (ISCO), 2015, pp. 1–6. doi:10.1109/ISCO. 2015. 7282308.

14. Mehrotra, A., et al. "Prefminer: Mining user's preferences for intelligent mobile notification management." In: *UbiComp*, Seattle, WA, USA: ACM; 2016.

15. Kanthavel, R., & Dhaya, R. "Wireless underground sensor networks channel using energy efficient clustered communication." *Intelligent Automation and Soft Computing* 31.1 (2022): 649–659.

16. Banumathi, J., Sangeetha, S. K. B., & Dhaya, R. "Robust cooperative spectrum sensing techniques for a practical framework employing cognitive radios in 5G networks." *Artificial Intelligent Techniques for Wireless Communication and Networking* (2022): 121–138.

17. Sangeetha, S. K. B., Dhaya, R., & Kanthavel, R. "Improving performance of cooperative communication in heterogeneous Manet environment." *Cluster Computing* 22.5 (2019): 12389–12395.

18. Srinivasan, V. E. A. "Mobileminer: Mining your frequent patterns on your phone." In: *UbiComp*, Seattle, WA, USA: ACM; 2014, pp. 389–400.

19. Dhaya, R., & Kanthavel, R. "Cloud-based multiple importance sampling algorithm with AI based CNN classifier for secure infrastructure." *Automated Software Engineering* 28.2 (2021): 1–28.

20. Zhu, H. E. A. "Mining mobile user preferences for personalized context-aware recommendation." *ACM Transactions on Intelligent Systems and Technology* 5.4 (2014): 58.
21. Margaret Rouse https://whatis.techtarget.com/definition/context-awareness
22. Albrecht Schmidt www.interaction-design.org/literature/book/ the-encyclopedia-of-human-computer-interaction-2nd-ed/context-aware-computing-context-awareness-context-aware-user-interfaces-and-implicit-interaction
23. www.charterglobal.com/5-promising-industries-for-the-future-of-5g-and-IoB/
24. www.abr.com/what-is-rfid-how-does-rfid-work/
25. https://smartcardamerica.com/2020/04/14/the-world-is-changing-faster-with-the-5g-IoB-rfid-and-on-the-way-to-6g/
26. Steve Ranger www.zdnet.com/article/what-is-the-Internet-of-things-everything-you-need-to-know-about-the-IoB-right-now/
27. Dhaya, R., & Kanthavel, R. "Dynamic automated infrastructure for efficient cloud data centre." *CMC-Computers Materials & Continua* 71.1 (2022): 1625–1639.
28. Sarker, I. H., Colman A., Kabir, M. A., & Han, J. "Individualized time-series segmentation for mining mobile phone user behavior." *Computer Journal* 61 (2017): 349–368.
29. Sangeetha, S. K. B., & Dhaya, R. "Deep learning era for future 6G wireless communications – theory, applications, and challenges." *Artificial Intelligent Techniques for Wireless Communication and Networking* (2022): 105–119.
30. Poncha, L. J., Abdelhamid, S., Alturjman, S., Ever, E., & Al-Turjman, F. (2018). "5G in a convergent Internet of Behaviours era: An overview." 2018 IEEE International Conference on Communications Workshops (ICC Workshops), 2018. doi:10.1109/iccw.2018.8403748
31. Dhaya, R., Kanthavel, R., Algarni, F., Jayarajan, P., & Mahor, A. "Reinforcement learning concepts ministering smart city applications using IoT." In: *Internet of Things in Smart Technologies for Sustainable Urban Development*, Cham: Springer; 2020, pp. 19–41.
32. Liu, J., & Tong, W. "Dynamic services model based on context resources in the Internet of Things." Wireless Communications Networking and Mobile Computing (WiCOM), 2010 6th International Conference on, 2010.
33. Albreem, M. A. M., El-Saleh, A. A., Isa, M., Salah, W., Jusoh, M., Azizan, M., & Ali, A. "Green Internet of Behaviours (IoB): An overview." 2017 IEEE 4th International Conference on Smart Instrumentation, Measurement and Application (ICSIMA), 2017. doi:10.1109/icsima.2017.8312021
34. Chris Wiegand www.ibm.com/blogs/Internet-of-things/IoB-what-to-expect-from-5g-network/
35. Dhaya, R., Kanthavel, R., & Mahalakshmi, M. "Enriched recognition and monitoring algorithm for private cloud data centre." *Soft Computing* (2021): 1–11.
36. Balasubramanian, K., & Cellatoglu, A. "Improvements in home automation strategies for designing apparatus for efficient smart home." *Consumer Electronics, IEEE Transactions* 54.4 (2008): 1681–1687.

37. Kayla Matthews www.IoBforall.com/6-ways-5g-will-change-the-IoB-solutions-space
38. Skouby, K. E., & Lynggaard, P. "Smart home and smart city solutions enabled by 5G, IoB, AAI and CoT services." 2014 International Conference on Contemporary Computing and Informatics (IC3I), 2014. doi:10.1109/ic3i.2014.7019822

Index

130, 139, 188, 192, 209, 210, 212, 216, 221, 225, 228
social networking, 73, 144, 150, 226
Sputnik, 187, 197
staff, 6, 7, 10, 107, 112
statistics, 2, 35, 73, 190, 198, 203, 204, 205, 206, 210, 239
surveillance, 9, 10, 75, 84, 147, 239
suspicious, 9, 176, 181, 182
Swiggy, 17
switches, 87, 89, 91, 94, 95
SWOT, 20

T

temperatures, 21
topology, 87, 93, 94, 95, 96
traffic ratio, 96, 97
treatment, 7, 20, 158, 160, 169, 219
trustworthy, 80, 184

U

Uber, 5, 21, 76, 107, 108, 218, 221
ultra-low latency, 238
unified, 149
unique, 68, 104, 119, 121, 126, 164, 174, 180, 185
user experience, 2, 6, 18, 28, 62, 65, 110, 233
user information, 18, 38
user interface, 5
utilization, 10, 13, 41, 42, 78, 86, 91, 94, 97, 100

V

vaccination, 187, 209
viewers, 5, 35
virtual controller, 87, 88, 89, 90, 93, 98
virtualization, 86, 88, 90, 98
virtual link, 86, 87, 88, 89, 90, 91, 92, 93, 94, 96, 98
virtual link capacity, 86, 88, 92, 98
virtual routing, 86, 88, 92, 95, 98
virtual software-defined network, 87, 94
visibility, 9
visual recognition, 17
voice-enabled gadgets, 36

W

wearable, 16, 26, 28, 34, 37, 42, 111
wearable technology, 7, 22
wearing masks, 72
website, 38, 64, 68, 71, 73, 105, 107, 113, 120, 125, 126, 129, 151
Whatsapp, 68
wisdom, 9, 71, 74, 214

Y

YouTube, 16, 77, 127, 221, 228

Z

zettabytes, 62
Zomato, 17

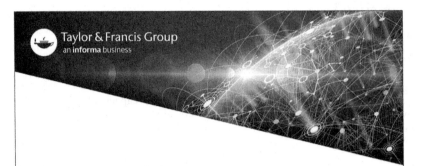

Printed in the United States
by Baker & Taylor Publisher Services